DUQUESNE STUDIES

Philosophical Series

15

THE
PHENOMENOLOGICAL
PHILOSOPHY OF
MERLEAU-PONTY

DUQUESNE STUDIES

Philosophical Series

15

THE PHENOMENOLOGICAL PHILOSOPHY OF MERLEAU-PONTY

by

REMY C. KWANT, O.S.A., PH.D.

DUQUESNE UNIVERSITY PRESS, Pittsburgh, Pa.
Editions E. Nauwelaerts, Louvain
1963

DUQUESNE STUDIES

Philosophical Series

Andrew G. van Melsen, D.Sc., D.Ed., and Henry J. Koren, C.S.Sp., S.T.D., editors.

Volume One—*Andrew G. van Melsen*, From Atomos to Atom. Pp. XII and 240. Price: paper $3.50, cloth $4.25. Published also in Dutch, German, Spanish and Italian.

Volume Two—*Andrew G. van Melsen*, The Philosophy of Nature. Pp. XII and 265. Third edition, fourth impression. Price: paper $3.75, cloth $4.50. Published also in Italian and Dutch. Polish edition in preparation.

Volume Three—*P. Henry van Laer*, Philosophico-Scientific Problems. Out of print.

Volume Four—*Cajetan's*, The Analogy of Names and the Concept of Being. Pp. X and 93. Second edition. Price: $2.25, cloth.

Volume Five—*Louis de Raeymaeker and others*, Truth and Freedom. Pp. VII and 132. Second impression. Price: $3.00, cloth. Published also in French.

Volume Six—*P. Henry van Laer*, The Philosophy of Science. Part One: Science in General. Pp. XVII and 164. Price: cloth $3.75.

Volume Seven—*Stephan Strasser*, The Soul in Metaphysical and Empirical Psychology. Pp. X and 275. Second impression. Price: cloth $6.00. Published also in German, Dutch and French.

Volume Eight — *Albert Dondeyne*, Contemporary European Thought and Christian Faith. Pp. XI and 211. Price: paper $5.00, cloth $5.75. Published also in French.

Volume Nine—*Maxwell J. Charlesworth*, Philosophy and Linguistic Analysis. Pp. XIII and 234. Second impression. Price: paper $4.75, cloth $5.50.

Volume Ten—*Remy C. Kwant*, Philosophy of Labor. Pp. XI and 163. Price: paper $4.50, cloth $5.25.

Library of Congress Catalog Card Number 63—10693

Printed in the United States of America by

The Ad Press, Ltd., New York, N. Y.

Volume Eleven—*Remy C. Kwant,* ENCOUNTER. Pp. VIII and 85. Price: cloth $3.25. Published also in Dutch.

Volume Twelve—*William A. Luijpen,* EXISTENTIAL PHENOMEN-OLOGY. Pp. XIII and 355. Second impression. Price: paper $6.00, cloth $6.75. Published also in Dutch.

Volume Thirteen—*Andrew G. van Melsen,* SCIENCE AND TECH-NOLOGY. Pp. X and 373. Price: paper $6.20, cloth $6.95. Published also in Dutch.

Volume Fourteen—*P. Henry van Laer,* PHILOSOPHY OF SCIENCE. Part Two: A STUDY OF THE DIVISION AND NATURE OF VARIOUS GROUPS OF SCIENCES. Pp. XIII and 342. Price: paper $5.75, cloth, $6.50.

Volume Fifteen—*Remy C. Kwant,* THE PHENOMENOLOGICAL PHILOSOPHY OF MERLEAU-PONTY. Pp. VIII and 257. Price: paper $4.50, cloth $5.25.

IN PREPARATION:

John Peters—METAPHYSICS
M. G. Plattel—SOCIAL PHILOSOPHY
Joseph A. Kockelmans—PHENOMENOLOGY AND PHYSICAL SCIENCE

OTHER SERIES OF DUQUESNE STUDIES:

Philological Series (three volumes to date)

Psychological Series (one volume to date)

Spiritan Series (six volumes to date)

Theological Series (one volume to date)

PERIODICALS PUBLISHED BY DUQUESNE UNIVERSITY PRESS:

Annuale Mediaevale. $4.00 per year.

Duquesne Hispanic Review. $3.00 per year.

Duquesne Review. A Journal of the Social Sciences. $2.25 per year.

Duquesne Science Counselor. $3.00 per year (foreign $3.25).

Review of Existential Psychology and Psychiatry. $5.00 per year.

TABLE OF CONTENTS

PREFACE

The American edition of this book has been personally supervised by the author. For greater facility of reading subtitles have been inserted throughout the work. A bibliography of Merleau-Ponty and indexes of names and subject matter have been added.

The announcement that Maurice Merleau-Ponty's main works, *La phénoménologie de la perception* and *La structure du comportement,* are to be published soon in English translations, came too late to be taken into account in this study.

Our thanks are due to the Reverend John R. Kanda, C.S.Sp., Ph.D., for his kind assistance in the translation of this book.

DUQUESNE UNIVERSITY   HENRY J. KOREN, C.S.Sp.
October 8, 1962

INTRODUCTION

Importance of Merleau-Ponty's Work. Maurice Merleau-Ponty was born in 1908 at Rocheford-sur-Mer, France. After finishing his studies he became instructor in philosophy at a secondary school in Saint Quentin, then professor at the University of Lyons, transferring to the Sorbonne later on, before he finally accepted an appointment to teach philosophy at the *Collège de France.* He died a sudden death in 1961.

After World War II he stood very much in the public eye because he was one of the founders of *Les temps modernes,* a magazine to which Sartre, Jeanson, Simone de Beauvoir and Merleau-Ponty contributed philosophical articles. At first he was somewhat overshadowed by Sartre and considered to belong to Sartre's group of leftist existentialists with strong Marxist leanings. Merleau-Ponty never drew so much attention from the public at large as Sartre, which may be explained by the fact that he did not express his philosophical thoughts in the literary forms of novels or plays.

Although there are still people who continue to see a close connection between Sartre and Merleau-Ponty, the truth is that Merleau-Ponty has always taken a philosophical standpoint of his own which differs considerably from that of Sartre. It is only gradually, however, that the distinct character of Merleau-Ponty's philosophy has drawn attention.

The high esteem in which his thought was held manifested itself in his appointment to the Sorbonne and even more so in that to the *Collège de France,* which undoubtedly is the greatest distinction a philosopher can obtain in France. Outside France there are two European university centers that have shown a lively interest in his work—namely, the Higher Institute of Philosophy of Louvain and the University of Utrecht.

If we want to name a few persons from Louvain who have particularly interested themselves in Merleau-Ponty, the first name to suggest itself is undoubtedly that of Professor Alphonse de Waehlens. Aside from drawing attention to this philosopher in his courses and discussions, he has published an important book about him, *Une philosophie de l'ambiguïté: l'existentialisme de Maurice Merleau-*

Ponty, Louvain, 1951. Another person who deserves to be named in this context is Professor Albert Dondeyne, whose work manifests a profound knowledge of this French philosopher. His book, *Contemporary European Thought and Christian Faith,* Pittsburgh, 1958, is to a large extent a dialog with Merleau-Ponty. In Utrecht the most important person to be named is Professor Frederick Buytendijk, who saw the importance of phenomenology for psychology and has made many contributions to the creation of a phenomenological psychology. Because of the international reputation of his works, his influence has contributed greatly to the importance of Merleau-Ponty. Buytendijk's successor Professor Johan Linschoten, likewise is profoundly influenced by Merleau-Ponty in his lectures and publications. The same may be said of Professor M. J. Langeveld, who utilizes the philosopher's ideas in his pedagogical studies.

In the English-speaking world Merleau-Ponty is much less known. Although a translation of his main works will appear soon, no more than a few articles have been devoted to him. Yet there is a growing interest in phenomenology, especially among certain groups of psychologists, such as those belonging to the Association of Existential Psychology and Psychiatry. For this reason the publication of this work in English may help to stimulate and guide this interest in one of the most profound thinkers of our time.

Merleau-Ponty's Philosophical Books. In the following pages we will enumerate the philosophical works of this thinker and make a few remarks about their contents.

In 1942 he published *La structure du comportement*[1] (Presses universitaires de France), which appeared in 1949 in a new edition with a preface by Alphonse de Waehlens. In this work Merleau-Ponty studies the behavior of plants, animals and man. He tries as much as possible to follow the scientistic, i.e., causal, explanation of behavior but only to show that this method is wholly unsatisfactory. The causal explanation does not satisfy because the behaving organism is not one of the elements of the causal process but a center of meaning. Consequently, the stimuli are not merely causes but have a meaning for, and because of this organism. At the end of this work Merleau-Ponty concludes therefore that behavior has to be approached through a different method. Thus this book may be

---

[1]An English edition of this work will be published by The Beacon Press.

considered a preparation for the author's main work, which we will consider now.[2]

Merleau-Ponty's main work, entitled, *Phénoménologie de la perception,* was published in 1945 by Gallimard, Paris. The title of this book is somewhat misleading. Considering the current conception of phenomenology, many would expect here a description of perception as it manifests itself in conscious life. The book, however, does not live up to this expectation. True, Merleau-Ponty admits that perception is our primordial contact with the world and that, therefore, the world is first given to us through perception. But perception is not simply a conscious event at which the reflective gaze of our consciousness can look. In many respects perception is pre-conscious and pre-personal. In perception it is the body which plays the preponderant role and this body Merleau-Ponty calls the "body-subject." He wants to penetrate into our bodily being as the most profound and primordial level of our existence as giver of meaning. For this reason the book could have been entitled, "the philosophy of the body subject."

The main lines of Merleau-Ponty's philosophical synthesis are contained in this work. None of his later works comes even close to it in philosophical significance. Accordingly, it is through this book that he has established his reputation as a philosopher.

The Preface[3] (*Avant-Propos*) of this work contains in a very condensed form Merleau-Ponty's view of phenomenology and its various procedures, such as the eidetic and phenomenological reductions. This preface, however, does not describe an accepted method but presents a creative interpretation of a philosophical movement. Its pages are among the very best that have been written about phenomenology.

In the rather long introduction following the preface Merleau-Ponty shows that the phenomenon, that which appears to us, is at once a meaningful whole. The introduction, therefore, is a refutation of the elemental theory, according to which the concrete is built from so-called psychical elements, united through association and complemented by memory and judgment. For Merleau-Ponty the realities appearing to us are already a structure, a form, a Gestalt.

---

[2]For an excellent explanation of the relationship between *La structure du comportement* and *Phénoménologie de la perception* see de Waehlens, *Une philosophie de l'ambiguité,* pp. 10-13.

[3]Translated into English by John F. Bannan, *Crosscurrents,* vol. VI (1956), pp. 59-70.

Together they constitute the "phenomenal field," which is at the same time the "transcendental field," i.e., the "phenomenal field" cannot be reduced to anything else but is the ultimate foundation of our philosophical thought.

The first part of the book then considers bodily being as the giver of meaning. For the phenomenal structures are not realities independent of us but are unbreakably connected with our existence as the giver of meaning. Our existence, however, is in the first instance bodily being and therefore Merleau-Ponty speaks here about bodily being as the giver of meaning. He shows how our body, e.g., as moving, as sexual and as speaking, gives meaning to the world.

The second part is devoted to the perceived world. He begins by showing that so-called sensation is already a form of perception and then considers how we are aware of space. Next, he tries to show how we perceive things and the world. He ends this part by speaking about our knowledge of other human beings. The last-named point is, in our opinion, one of the weakest chapters of his book.[4]

The two parts, which are dedicated mainly to our preconscious existence, are followed by a third, devoted to our conscious existence. It is not so much concerned with an internal analysis of this existence as with showing that our conscious existence is rooted in preconscious existence.

Accordingly, the main theme of Merleau-Ponty's chief work is our preconscious existence, meaning-giving bodily being. Man's bodily being is constantly emphasized as the heart of our existence, as the root of all human phenomena.

In 1947 Gallimard published Merleau-Ponty's book, *Humanisme et terreur, essai sur le problème communiste*. In this work the author studies the problem of Communism and asks himself whether Marxist terrorism is a sign that Marxism possesses an inhuman character. Although he does not simply approve of this terrorism, he endeavors to understand it and to show that it is often a necessary phase on the road to humanity. The book is a plea for a "third road," for Merleau-Ponty refuses to adhere to bourgeois Capitalism and, on the other hand, is unable to accept Communism as it reveals itself here and now.

---

[4]Cf. Reinout Bakker, "Der andere Mensch in der Phänomenologie Merleau-Pontys," *Evangelische Ethik*, Heft 1, 1960, pp. 10-26.

In 1948 Nagel, Paris, published Merleau-Ponty's book, *Sens et non-sens,* a collection of most divergent articles which had already been published separately in various magazines. The collection shows the wide range of Merleau-Ponty's philosophical perspective. He presents a refined analysis of Cézanne's art of painting and makes valuable remarks about the art of writing novels in connection with a novel by Simone de Beauvoir. He tries to explain the reactions against Sartre's philosophy and proposes a captivating consideration of the connection between modern psychology and the development of the film. The collection contains striking studies of Hegel and Marx, of the post-war situation in France and of the attitude of Catholicism toward global affairs. The chapter, *"Le métaphysique dans l'homme,"* is a remarkable summary of Merleau-Ponty's fundamental perspective. For anyone who wants to become acquainted with the author and does not have the time or the opportunity to read his more extensive works *Sens et non-sens* is the book to read. The various articles of which it is composed can be read separately, but all of them are permeated with the leading ideas of Merleau-Ponty's thought.

Eloge de la philosophie, published in 1953 by Gallimard, contains the text of Merleau-Ponty's inaugural address delivered at the *Collège de France.* After devoting attention to his predecessors at the same institution, the author outlines his own philosophical attitude in an imposing description of Socrates. The philosopher knows that absolute knowledge is not possible and that, because of his awareness of this impossibility, his mind is open for genuine truth. The author then confronts his philosophical attitude with two forms of absolute knowledge, i.e., with Christianity and Marxism.

In 1955 the same firm published Merleau-Ponty's *Les aventures de la dialectique.* The book is devoted to dialectic reason as it manifests itself in history and as it is—or should be—understood in the philosophy of history. He begins by considering Max Weber's philosophy of history and then speaks of Lucacs' interpretation of Marxism. Attention is paid also to the reaction of orthodox Marxism against the views of Lucacs. A substantial part of the book, however, is dedicated to a sharp analysis of Sartre's philosophy. Merleau-Ponty shows here how Sartre destroys dialectic reason through his absolute concepts. As is well known, this analysis signalled the open break of Merleau-Ponty with Sartre.

Finally, in 1960 Gallimard published *Signes,* a collection of writings previously published elsewhere, preceded by a rather long introduction. In this introduction Merleau-Ponty devotes attention, *inter alia,* to the relationship of philosophy and praxis and describes this relationship in a way that differs somewhat from the way he had previously described it. The chapter, *"Le philosophe et la sociologie,"* considers the relationship of philosophy and the sciences. A very striking chapter is *"L'homme et l'adversité,"* in which Merleau-Ponty speaks of the progress of philosophical thought in the first half of our century. His own work is presented there as a reconsideration of contemporary philosophical knowledge.

We will not devote any attention here to Merleau-Ponty's numerous articles, for the simple reason that practically all of them have been incorporated in the above-mentioned books.

As should be evident from the preceding pages, Merleau-Ponty's main work, *Phénoménologie de la perception,* surpasses all others greatly in importance. Nevertheless, this work certainly was not final or definitive—if this term may be used in connection with Merleau-Ponty—, it demands a continuation, but this continuation has never been published.

The Character of this Book. In previous years we have written nearly a dozen articles about the philosophy of Merleau-Ponty. When the request was made that these articles be organized in the form of a book, it appeared impossible to do so. The reason was that they were meant to illustrate various aspects of Merleau-Ponty, such as his idea of meaning, his attitude toward realism and his philosophy of history, in the perspective of his fundamental way of thinking. As a result, the fundamental perspective had constantly to be repeated in each of these articles and, on the other hand, the subject matters of the different articles taken together did not offer an integral picture of the philosophy in question. For this reason we have preferred to write an entirely new book.

The character of this book should be viewed in the light of its origin. The author's earlier studies of Merleau-Ponty followed the text of this philosopher very closely. Through these detailed text studies he gradually obtained a comprehensive view of Merleau-Ponty's philosophical thought and became able to express and evaluate it without literally adhering to the philosopher's words. The book is critical also because it constantly raises the question whether and to what extent Merleau-Ponty's perspective is acceptable. It is not impossible that some readers would have preferred a less critical approach and a closer following of the text. On the other hand, however, the way in which the book has been written has its advantages, for the fundamental lines of Merleau-Ponty's philosophical synthesis present themselves with greater clarity and, in addition, our critical evaluation gives more emphasis to the import and scope of the philosopher's standpoint.

The fact that this book criticizes Merleau-Ponty's philosophy does not at all mean that its author wants to minimize his importance. He has the greatest respect for this philosopher and realizes that in his own philosophical thinking he is profoundly influenced by Merleau-Ponty, even where he deviates from him. We consider Merleau-Ponty one of the great thinkers of our time. One who wants to make a philosophical study of our world can hardly avoid a confrontation with Merleau-Ponty's thought. His philosophy is "true to life."[5] His eyes are wide open to the fundamental facts of our period and he is full of the spirit of our era. His philosophy most strikingly mirrors both the light and the shadows of our time.

It is the author's hope that those for whom Merleau-Ponty's original works are not accessible will find in this book an introduction to the wealth of thought and the stimulating ideas of this philosopher.

Merleau-Ponty's Way of Thinking. We may terminate this introduction by adding a few remarks about this philosopher's way of thinking. According to Merleau-Ponty, philosophy is the enemy of the system[5a]. This statement warns us not to seek any system in his work. By a system he means a whole of statements which claims once and for all to determine the fundamental lines of reality or of a part of reality. A system is characterized by rigid demarcations between "yes" and "no." It leaves no room or hardly any for flexible and dynamic concepts.

Many of the concepts used by Merleau-Ponty are new or at least have a new shade of meaning. He is in possession of an original vision of reality and such a vision seeks new concepts or endows old ones with a new meaning. It is characteristic of new concepts that they are used before they are reflected upon and described. Anyone who reads Merleau-Ponty attentively will note the groping character

---

[5]Cf. Remy C. Kwant, "Levensechte wijsbegeerte. Naar aanleiding van de dood van Maurice Merleau-Ponty," *Gawein, Tijdschrift voor Psychologie*, vol. 10, no. 2, Dec. 1961, pp. 71-81.

[5a]"La métaphysique est le contraire du système." *Sens et non-sens*, p. 189.

of his thought. Ideas which in a given passage begin to delineate themselves are given further shades of meaning in the next, not because the author wants to acquaint the reader gradually with a thought that is already fully elaborated in his mind but because he himself is still seeking greater clarity. This search is not the kind that is sometimes used as a literary form of writing, for in such a case the writer knows beforehand exactly what he wants to say, although he mentally places himself on the standpoint of the reader and thus introduces him to the truth. Merleau-Ponty's seeking and groping is not a question of descending to the level of the reader but characterizes a thinker who himself, while writing, is still searching for the truth.[6] Some of his ideas are, as it were, born during his writing. This character of Merleau-Ponty's work must be respected and, therefore, we must abstain from ascribing to him definitive and sharply circumscribed concepts.

The above-mentioned characteristic of Merleau-Ponty occasionally becomes a source of reproaches. The complaint is made that his concepts are vague and that it is difficult to determine exactly what he wants to say. Especially the proponents of so-called "hygienic" thinking, who do not permit a philosopher to use a concept until he has circumscribed it clearly and sharply, feel themselves on unfamiliar ground when they encounter Merleau-Ponty's way of thinking. They are inclined to say that his work is literature but not real philosophy. According to Merleau-Ponty, however, this alleged vice is precisely a virtue. For the philosopher may not seek to dwell in a world in which all boundaries of things are sharply traced, in which the meaning of reality is clearly defined. This is the case, e.g., in the realm of technology and in the world of the sciences. However, it is man himself who by means of a certain attitude determines the lines assumed by these realms of making and thinking. He delineates them from a realm of existence that precedes them. But this realm of existence is a chiaroscuro and has no room for Cartesian clear and distinct ideas. In this realm of existence everything is interwoven with everything, and everything refers to everything, so that sharp demarcation lines would do violence to this interconnection. True, we may and even must try to form concepts of this primordial realm of

---

[6]"Il y a lieu de craindre que notre temps, lui aussi, rejette le philosophe en lui-même et qu'une fois de plus la philosophie n'y soit que *nuées*. Car philosopher, c'est chercher, c'est impliquer qu'il y a des choses à voir et à dire. Or, aujourd'hui on ne cherche guere. On 'revient' à l'une ou à l'autre des traditions." *Eloge de la Philosophie*, p. 57.

existence, but should keep in mind that on this level the concept will have to be permeated with the flexibility, the "ambiguity,"[7] the density and the chiaroscuro of the realm of existence. In other words, according to Merleau-Ponty, the reproach addressed to him means that his thinking is in accordance with the realm he is trying to clarify. If he tried to speak differently, he would go against the very character of the realm which he investigates.[8]

Merleau-Ponty's philosophical vision is not a view resulting in complete mastery of the realm studied. He does not blame this deficiency on a provisional imperfection of his philosophical thought, but attributes it to the character of the realm of existence that has to be penetrated philosophically. For this reason his philosophy continues to have the character of a living search, and this living search reveals itself in the typical features of his philosophical concepts. His ideas are not, and cannot be, described with sufficient sharpness and definitiveness to become part of a system. As soon as concepts are suitable for incorporation into a veritable system, they are, strictly speaking, no longer philosophical concepts.

All this, however, should not be interpreted as if there were no coherence or synthesis in Merleau-Ponty's philosophical utterances. He cannot simply deny in one passage what he affirms in another, and his philosophical ideas obviously have to fit in with one another. However, they do not cohere as parts of a finished system but as interconnected expressions of a careful groping and seeking. A remark he made in connection with Catholic theology and orthodox Marxism may serve to illustrate his meaning. Calling Catholic theologians and orthodox Marxists "those who know," Merleau-Ponty asks how he who does not know, and knows that absolute knowledge is impossible, can converse with those who claim to know.[9] The distinction shows that his philosophy is a knowing permeated with not-knowing. Knowing is never finished according to Merleau-Ponty, because there is no end to the knowable. Knowledge retains an

---

[7]For Merleau-Ponty "ambiguity" has not so much the sense of equivocation as that of rejection of the clean-cut distinction between the different aspects which constitute one and the same reality.

[8]It is hardly possible to conceive a greater opposition than that which exists between Merleau-Ponty's thinking and analytic philosophy. The exactness of philosophical language demanded by the linguistic analysts is in principle unacceptable for Merleau-Ponty.

[9]"De nouveau, entre les chrétiens et les autres, comme entre les marxistes et les autres, la conversation devient difficile. Comment y aurait-il véritable échange entre celui qui sait et celui qui ne sait pas?" *Signes*, p. 308.

"ambiguous" character because the knowable is "ambiguous." Knowledge cannot form any sharply defined concepts because in the knowable everything is interwoven with everything.

It was important to make these few remarks before we undertake to describe the fundamental lines of Merleau-Ponty's philosophical thought. For now we know how these basic lines must be understood. They are lines drawn by a thinker who has not quite finished with his thought and with the realm of his thinking and who, moreover, knows that in principle it is impossible ever to reach the finish. Later we will see how Merleau-Ponty gives a philosophical foundation to this attitude and why philosophy, if it wants to remain faithful to its realm of thought, must always continue to retain this groping character, why, in other words, this character is not an imperfection that can be overcome. Speaking about Sartre, Merleau-Ponty does not hesitate to use strong language and to refer to his "accursed lucidity."[10] The clarity which he finds in Sartre is something which he rejects in principle. Accordingly, in our explanation of Merleau-Ponty's philosophy we have to be on guard against trying to provide a clarity which he finds himself forced to reject.

In the following pages we will devote our attention first to Merleau-Ponty's fundamental discovery of the "body-subject." We will then follow him in his efforts to understand man from this perspective. We will see that being-man has to be understood as an historical coming-to-be of meaning, situated in the fundamental sphere of contingence. For this reason we will successively devote attention to meaning, history and contingence. At the same time it will become clear to us why Merleau-Ponty thinks that he has to reject the absolute.

---

[10]"Sa précoce lucidité," *Signes*, p. 32; "Sa maudite lucidité," *op. cit.*, p. 33.

CHAPTER ONE

MERLEAU-PONTY'S FUNDAMENTAL DISCOVERY:
THE BODY-SUBJECT

1. INTRODUCTORY CONSIDERATIONS

The Victory over Cartesian Dualism. It is somewhat dangerous to apply the term "fundamental discovery" to a certain view of a thinker who is as close to our era as Merleau-Ponty. Nevertheless, we consider it justified to say that his theory of the "body-subject" is the focal point of Merleau-Ponty's philosophical reflection. Various facts may be put forward to confirm this assertion. First of all, he himself repeatedly represents his philosophy as a radical victory over Cartesianism, which is characterized by Descartes' sharp dichotomy between the thinking mind and the mechanical body.[1] For this reason we suspect that the affirmation of the "body-subject" as the ambiguous unity—not union—of bodily being and subjectivity is the most fundamental affirmation of Merleau-Ponty's philosophy. Secondly, the conclusions which he draws from extensive analyses in his *Phénoménologie de la perception* are nearly always concerned with the subjective character of the human body.[2] Finally, Merleau-Ponty himself explicitly confirmed the central character of the "body-subject" in his philosophy in an address entitled, *L'homme et l'adversité*.[3]

This address arose from an invitation to summarize the result of half a century of philosophical thought in an international congress.[4] He began by making the remark that the proposed task was, strictly speaking, impossible because philosophy does not produce intellectual

---

[1]"Si au contraire nous voulions définir sans préjugé le sens philosophique de la psychologie de la Forme, il faudrait dire qu'en révélant la 'structure' ou la 'forme' comme un ingrédiant irréductible de l'être, elle remet en question l'alternative classique de l' 'existence comme chose' et l' 'existence comme conscience', elle établit comme un mélange de l'objectif et du subjectif." *Sens et non-sens*, pp. 171 f. Cf. also the final paragraph of *La structure du comportement* on p. 241. These two passages contain, as it were, the program or scheme followed in most chapters of *La phénoménologie de la perception*, for it is in a dialog with empiricism and intellectualism that Merleau-Ponty develops his own thinking.

[2]See, e.g., pp. 61-63, 76-77, 86, 105, 113, 171-172.

[3]Later published in *Signes*, pp. 284-308.

[4]Delivered on September 10, 1951 at the *Rencontres internationales* of Geneva.

11

achievements of a definitive nature.[5] However, he continued, we ourselves are involved in the growth of light occurring in the common
life of philosophical inquiry, for this light casts its rays also on ourselves and forms a "sediment" in our own way of thinking.[6] He then
tried to indicate this "sediment" in a few points and presented his
own philosophical view as the result of the growth of light in the
common inquiry. While one may be inclined to consider it presump-
tuous for anyone to offer his own ideas in such a fashion, Merleau-
Ponty could hardly have done anything else. He was supposed to
take as his theme how the common efforts of many have led to a
growth of light. What else could anyone do in such circumstances
than describe this growth in terms of his own philosophy?

For this reason Merleau-Ponty presented the international congress in question with a summary of his own philosophy. The first
and most extensively treated point in it is precisely the victory over
the opposition of body and spirit,[7] over dualism or, positively expressed, the recognition of the body as a reality which is the unity of
these two aspects.[8] After this first point two others follow, namely,
the unity of thinking and speaking and the essential bond of fact and
value. Both of these, however, are applications or rather concretiza-
tions of the unity of body and spirit.[9] Accordingly, when Merleau-

---

[5]"Comment oserait-on dénombrer des *idées acquises*, puisque, même quand
elles se sont fait recevoir presque universellement, c'est toujours en devenant
autres qu'elles mêmes?" *Signes*, p. 284.

[6]"Cependant cette transformation de la connaissance de l'homme que nous
ne pouvons espérer de déterminer par une méthode rigoureuse, à partir des
oeuvres, des idées et de l'histoire, elle s'est sédimentée en nous, elle est notre
substance." *Ibid.*, p. 285.

[7]"Notre siècle a effacé la ligne de partage du 'corps' et de l' 'esprit' et
voit la vie humaine comme spirituelle et corporelle de part en part, toujours
appuyée au corps, toujours intéressée, jusque dans ses modes les plus charnels,
aux rapports des personnes. Pour beaucoup de penseurs, à la fin du XIXe
siècle, le corps, c'était un morceau de matière, un faisceau de mécanismes. Le
XXe siècle a restauré et approfondi la notion de la chair, c'est-à-dire du corps
animé." *Ibid.*, p. 287.

[8]"Freud a aperçu de mieux en mieux la fonction spirituelle du corps et
l'incarnation de l'esprit." *Ibid.*, p. 291.

[9]"Le 'petit homme qui est dans l'homme', ce n'est que le fantôme de nos
opérations expressives réussies, et l'homme qui est admirable, c'est celui qui,
installé dans son corps fragile, dans un langage qui a déjà tant parlé, dans une
histoire titubante, se rassemble et se met à voir, à comprendre, à signifier.
L'humanisme d'aujourd'hui n'a plus rien de décoratif ni de bienséant. Il n'aime
plus l'homme contre son corps, l'esprit contre son langage, les valeurs contre
les faits. Il ne parle plus de l'homme et de l'esprit que sobrement, avec pudeur:
l'esprit et l'homme ne sont jamais, ils transparaissent dans le mouvement par
lequel le corps se fait geste, le langage oeuvre, la coexistence vérité." *Ibid.*,
p. 305.

Ponty expresses the philosophical awareness of our time, as it takes form in his thought, he assigns the central position to the "body-subject" as victory over dualism.[10] For this reason we may say that this idea contains the decisive standpoint of his philosophy.

The Difficulty of Expressing the Meaning of the "Body-Subject." It is very difficult to indicate what Merleau-Ponty means by the term "body-subject." For, according to him, the "body-subject" transcends the opposition of body and spirit since we may no longer speak here of an "either or."[11] We should not say that the body belongs either to the material or to the spiritual order. It belongs to both, but not as their union, no matter how intimate such a union may be, for a union is always a meeting of opposites. The human body is a single reality, which is at the same time both material and spiritual.[12] As soon, however, as we want to express this single reality, we notice that our philosophical terminology is permeated with the dualism that in the past formed part and parcel of philosophy. This means that we are forced to speak in dualistic terms about the body which is the concrete transcendence and negation of dualism.[13] Strictly speaking, we would have to create new words to express the "body-subject." It goes without saying that Merleau-Ponty's opponents

---

[10]"La même ambiguïté qui fait passer, à l'analyse, la notion de l'esprit dans celle du corps ou du langage. . ." *Ibid.*, p. 299.

[11]"Ni le corps ni *l'existence* ne peuvent passer pour l'original de l'être humain, puisque chacun présuppose l'autre et que le corps est l'existence figée ou généralisée et l'existence une incarnation perpétuelle. . . La même raison qui empêche de 'reduire' l'existence au corps ou à la sexualité empêche aussi de 'reduire' la sexualité à l'existence: c'est que l'existence n'est pas un ordre de faits." *Phénoménologie de la perception*, p. 194. Merleau-Ponty does not speak here of the "body-subject" but of the body as a given fact, as the object of scientific research. *This* body is opposed to existence. When the matter is considered in this way, one has to agree with Merleau-Ponty that neither the body nor existence is the most primordial aspect of man. He refuses to stop at this "either or" choice.

[12]"Un roman, un poème, un tableau, un morceau de musique sonts des individus, c'est-à-dire des êtres où l'on ne peut distinguer l'expression de l'exprimé, dont le sens n'est accessible que par un contact direct et qui rayonnent leur signification sans quitter leur place temporelle et spatiale. C'est en ce sens que notre corps est comparable à l'oeuvre d'art. Il est un noeud de significations vivantes et non pas la loi d'un certain nombre de termes covariants." *Ibid.*, p. 177.

[13]"Dans ces cas de désintégration, l'âme et le corps sont apparemment distincts et c'est la vérité du dualisme." *La structure du comportement*, p. 226. According to Merleau-Ponty, the objective basis of dualism consists in this: the body, i.e., the lower established order of meaning, and the soul, i.e., the new meaning emanating from the body, can disintegrate; for instance, in the case of tiredness. In such a case tension and opposition manifest themselves. The culminating point of dualism is death.

attack him precisely on this point, alleging that dualistic terms simply cannot be avoided because dualism is an expression of experience and consequently is imposed on us by the reality itself which we want to put into words.

Descartes opposed extension to thought, matter or thing to mind or spirit. For Merleau-Ponty the body is neither a thing in the Cartesian sense nor a pure bodiless thought.[14] The human body has a mode of being of its own, by virtue of which it defies description in Cartesian terms. To indicate this mode of being, he uses such terms as "body-subject" and "ego-body,"[15] but for the careful reader it is evident that Merleau-Ponty thinks that he sees something for which he cannot find any suitable terms. For this reason it is exceedingly difficult to express the body's mode of being according to Merleau-Ponty. More than once we simply have to make use of negative expressions to indicate a positive reality.

Merleau-Ponty speaks about the *body itself*. Many have attributed to bodily being a personal, subjective character, but the reason was that they considered the body inhabited or animated by an indwelling

---

[14]It is quite possible to consider the body as a thing. It is done, e.g., in certain scientific ways of studying the body of man. However, such a view of the body is a secondary meaning of bodily being. Merleau-Ponty wants to penetrate into the primordial meaning of the human body.

[15]"Mais en reprenant ainsi le contact avec le corps et avec le monde, c'est aussi nous-mêmes que nous allons retrouver, puisque, si l'on perçoit avec son corps, le corps est *un moi naturel* et comme le sujet de la perception." *Ibid.,* p. 239. Italics ours.

"Il y a donc un autre sujet au-dessous de moi pour qui un monde existe avant que je suis là et qui y marquait ma place. Cet esprit captif ou naturel, c'est mon corps, non pas le corps momentané qui est l'instrument de mes choix personnels et se fixe sur tel ou tel monde, mais le système de 'fonctions' anonymes qui enveloppent toute fixation particulière dans un projet général." *Ibid.,* p. 294. This text contains one of Merleau-Ponty's most forceful expressions of the notion "body-subject."

"Ainsi mon oeil n'est jamais dans la perception un objet. Si jamais on peut parler de mouvement sans mobile, c'est bien dans le cas du corps propre. Le mouvement de mon oeil vers ce qu'il va fixer n'est pas le déplacement d'un objet par rapport à un autre objet, c'est une marche du réel." *Ibid.,* p. 323.

"Ce qui importe pour l'orientation du spectacle, ce n'est pas mon corps tel qu'il est en fait, comme chose dans l'espace objective, mais mon corps comme système d'actions possibles, un corps virtuel, dont le 'lieu' phénoménal est défini par sa tâche et par sa situation. Mon corps est là où il a quelque chose à faire." *Ibid.,* p. 289.

"La vision est *une pensée assujettie à un certain champ* et c'est là ce qu'on appelle un *sens.*" *Ibid.,* p. 251. In this text even the sense organ is called a "thought, subjected to a field."

"Il y a deux sens et deux sens seulement du mot exister [i.e., according to Descartes]: on existe comme chose ou on existe comme conscience. L'expérience du corps propre au contraire nous révèle un mode d'existence ambigue." *Ibid.,* p. 231.

spirit, a spiritual soul, i.e., by a principle of a different order which is most intimately connected with the body. Merleau-Ponty does not at all mean this and repeatedly denies it.[16] The body *itself,* precisely as body, is an existence and therefore of a subjective nature. The body *itself* is a subject and therefore does not derive its subjective character from a principle distinct from itself.

2. TRANSFORMATION OF THE TRADITIONAL CONCEPT OF SUBJECT

It goes without saying that Merleau-Ponty does not defend this position without essentially modifying the traditional concept of subject.[17] Subjectivity, as understood by Descartes, cannot be of a bodily nature. Descartes' concept of the body is purely quantitative, and for this reason he has no trouble whatsoever in showing that the soul has a spiritual, i.e., supra-corporeal, nature. For, to the extent that the body is more divested of content and wealth of being, it becomes increasingly evident that man is more than "body" and that many phenomena manifesting themselves in the body do not come from the body but from a principle which in one way or another is present in the body.

Classical Meanings of "Subject." For Merleau-Ponty, as we have said, the body itself is a subject. To justify this thesis, he has to begin by changing the accepted meaning of "subject." This term has a long and involved history. In Greek and medieval philosophy it possessed a dual meaning, one logical and the other ontological. It had, first of all, a logical meaning, for it was used to indicate the

---

[16]"Mais si notre union avec le corps est substantielle, comment pourrions-nous éprouver en nous-mêmes une âme pure et de là accéder à un Esprit absolu?" *Ibid.,* p. 232.

[17]A very condensed description of the "body-subject" is contained in *"L'oeil et l'esprit,"* Merleau-Ponty's last published article. It appeared originally in *Art de France,* no. 1, 1961, but has been reprinted in the special issue of *Les temps modernes,* vol. 17, nos. 184-185, pp. 193-227, dedicated to the memory of Merleau-Ponty. The description of the "body-subject" may be found on pages 196-198. Merleau-Ponty describes the body there as a "self" (*soi*) which, on the one hand, belongs to the world but, on the other, from the world takes a position with respect to this world. "Il est pris dans le tissu du monde et sa cohésion est celle d'une chose. Mais puisqu' il voit et se meut, il tient les choses en cercle autour de soi" (p. 197). The body *itself* is a "self," for "l'animation du corps n'est pas l'assemblage l'une contre l'autre de ses parties— ni d'ailleurs la descente dans l'automate d'un esprit venue d'ailleurs, ce qui supposerait encore que le corps lui-même est sans dedans et sans 'soi'" (p. 198). Because the body is a subject, it is not wholly concealed to itself: "Je dis d'une chose qu'elle est mue, mais mon corps, lui *se* meut, mon mouvement *se* deploie. Il n'est pas dans l'ignorance de soi, il n'est pas aveugle pour soi, il rayonne d'un soi'" (p. 197).

subject of a proposition expressing a judgment and as such functioned in both the linguistic and the philosophical analysis of the judgment. Any such proposition consists of two essential components, for through it we say something about something. That "about" which the statement is made is the "subject" and "that which" is stated is the predicate. The same idea lies behind the medieval use of the term "subject" to indicate the subject-matter of a science. Science was conceived as a systematic whole of judgments to be predicated of a certain "subject."

Alongside this logical meaning, however, we find also an onto-logical meaning. For a distinction was made between substance and accidents and the latter were supposed to be rooted in the subject, i.e., the substance. "Subject," moreover, was used also outside the realm of philosophical preoccupations; for example, those who fell under the power of a ruler were called his "subjects." The "subject," therefore, was anything that in any way was "subjected" to attribution, to being-influenced by an accident, to the control of authority. But it was not used to express the typically personal mode of being precisely insofar as this mode of being is distinct from thing-like being.

Subject as Person. How did this last-named modern meaning of subject arise? It is probable that the profound analysis of the cognitive relationship in the modern era has played a role in this matter. The distinction between the knower and the known received greater emphasis. That which formerly was indicated as the "subject" (matter) about which scientific statements were made began to be called also the "object" of scientific considerations, and in opposition to this object the knower came to be called "subject." In this usage the term began to acquire a meaning which is closely connected with strictly personal being. While former ages had paid more attention to the thesis that the knower is determined by the known, modern philosophy began to see that the knower co-constitutes his field of knowledge. In this way they were led to analyze the knower in order to arrive at a better understanding of the cognitive field itself. The subject was analyzed and the term "subject" referred increasingly more and more to cognitive, personal existence. Later again it became apparent that the cognitive relationship had been one-sidedly emphasized. Nevertheless, they held fast to the term "subject," but stressed that the "subject" is more than a knower: the "subject" is also a feeling, affective and emotional being, having an ethical attitude, esthetic powers and so on.[18] Finally the term "subject" came to mean personal being insofar as it is distinct from purely thing-like being. It is in this sense that the term is used today in philosophy. When we speak of "subjectivity" we intend to express that our mode of being transcends the purely thing-like character. I am a subject because my existence is not encompassed by the blind interplay of natural forces, because I assume an attitude with respect to things, because to a certain extent I take my fate into my own hands. These few remarks may serve as a succinct but incomplete summary of the long historical development of a philosophical term.

Consciousness and Subjectivity. Accordingly, fully in line with the rationalism of the West, the typically spiritual factors, such as consciousness, freedom and morality, were viewed as the fundamental characteristics of subjectivity. We would be subjects because, in knowing about the other, we would know also about our own being and our actions. In other words, the subject was conceived in a very spiritual fashion. As long as such a conception is maintained, it is difficult to assert that the body itself, precisely as body, is a subject. Before he could make this assertion, Merleau-Ponty had to modify again the meaning of the term. Thus, it is not surprising that this modification is of the highest importance for his philosophical viewpoint.

While for many modern thinkers consciousness is the center of the many aspects proper to subjectivity, the same cannot be asserted with respect to Merleau-Ponty. True, he does not quite deny consciousness to human subjectivity. He says, for example, that, if consciousness is not co-original with subjectivity, it would be impossible to understand how the subject could ever become conscious.[19]

---

[18]Cf. *Sens et non-sens,* pp. 125-26. See also Dondeyne, *Contemporary European Thought and Christian Faith,* Ch. III (Reason and the Irrational in Contemporary Thought), pp. 67-107.

[19]"Ces formules peuvent paraître énigmatiques : si la subjectivité dernière ne se pense pas aussitôt qu'elle est, comment le fera-t-elle, jamais ? Comment ce qui ne se pense pas pourrait-il se mettre à penser et la subjectivité n'est-elle pas ramenée à la condition d'une chose ou d'une force qui produits ses effets au dehors sans être capable de le savoir?—Nous ne voulons p.s dire que le Je primordial s'ignore. S'il s'ignorait, il serait en effet une chose, et rien ne pourrait faire qu'ensuite il devint conscience. Nous lui avons seulement refusé la pensée objective, la conscience thétique du monde et de lui-même. Qu'entendons-nous par là ? Ou ces mots ne veulent rien dire, ou ils veulent dire que nous nous interdisons de supposer une conscience explicite qui double et sous-tende la prise confuse de la subjectivité originaire sur elle-même et sur son monde. Ma vision par exemple est bien 'pensée de voir' . . . Il n'y a vision que

But at the same time he says that consciousness in its deepest level is so obscure that it cannot be verified, even though human existence is always, even on its deepest level, already of a subjective nature. In other words, consciousness is no longer the central characteristic of subjectivity and becomes more or less marginal. Merleau-Ponty speaks even about human subjectivity, at least on its deepest level, as "preconscious,"[20] i.e., there is no question yet of genuine self-knowledge. Complementing this statement, he adds that, on the other hand, there is no total darkness. But consciousness is so obscure that on this level we are not able to penetrate into our existence through ordinary reflection. Where our existence is conscious in the full sense of the term, we may attempt to arrive at greater clarity about ourselves by means of reflection. Our subjectivity, however, has dimensions in which we cannot penetrate through ordinary thinking, ordinary reflection.

The question which arises here is, of course: If according to Merleau-Ponty consciousness is more or less marginal to subjectivity, what then is the fundamental characteristic of this subjectivity?

3. The Fundamental Character of Subjectivity

Dialectic Relationship to Surroundings. Something has a subjective character by virtue of the fact that it has a dialectic relationship to the reality around it, changing it into its own "environment" and giving it a meaning for itself.[21] Merleau-Ponty distinguishes between dialectic relationship and causal process. In a causal process natural forces interact, but in such a way that the influence exercised by a reality can be understood from this reality itself. In causal interaction realities influence each other, but in such a way that the one is not the co-cause of the other's influence. Warm water makes a cold bottle of wine warm and the coolness of the bottle chills the water, but the cold bottle does not cause the warming power of the

---

par l'anticipation et l'intention." *Phénoménologie de la perception,* p. 463. This text is very instructive. Merleau-Ponty speaks here of "ultimate subjectivity" and the "primordial I." From the example of vision it is clear that this ultimate subject is the subject of perception, therefore, the "anonymous existence." the *"On,"* which he mentions elsewhere. Nevertheless, he does not want to deny consciousness entirely to the "preconscious."

[20]"Mais nous avons vu que la perception originaire est une expérience non-thétique, préobjective et préconsciente." *Ibid.,* p. 279. "La perception est toujours dans le mode de l' 'On'." *Ibid.,* p. 277.

[21]The purpose of his book, *La structure du comportement,* is precisely to show this point. For this reason he speaks of "structure."

water and the warm water does not cause the cooling action of the bottle. The causal interaction can be analyzed in two processes which, strictly speaking, can be understood independently of each other. The concept "causal interaction" is a thought form of certain sciences insofar as they think in an atomistic fashion and want to understand a whole from the standpoint of its elements.

In the dialectic relationship the situation is different. True, there is an interaction. Food, for instance, influences the organism, and this organism actively assimilates the food. But it is the organism itself which by virtue of its structure makes it possible to call the food "food," so that its nutritive value cannot be understood independently of the organism. Reversely, food stirs up the forces of the organism. Accordingly, the total process cannot be dissolved into two independent actions, for the one cause does not merely act on the other but also effects the other's causality which it itself undergoes.

The Subject as Center of Dialectic Relationship. However, dialectic relationship alone does not suffice to constitute subjectitvity. For the gestalt also which exists for a subject is characterized by the dialectic relationship, by "circular causality," as Merleau-Ponty often expresses it when he speaks of this dialetic relationship. In the gestalt also which appears to us within our world everything refers to everything. But there is question of subjectivity only when one element of the dialectic relationship is privileged insofar as everything else can be indicated as its "milieu" or "surrounding world." In a well-written book all chapters refer to one another, they cannot be understood independently, but make one another intelligible. Yet none of the chapters is a subject for the others, but all of them together are a whole of meanings with respect to the subject for whom the book exists. Wherever a dialectic relationship occurs, there is question of a whole of meanings. Every gestalt is a whole of meanings, but a whole of meanings exists always *for a subject.*[22]

It would be wrong, howover, to think that the subject lies outside the dialectic relationship. On the contrary, the meaning makes the

---

[22]Merleau-Ponty blames certain psychologists for considering the gestalt as an "in itself": "Le retour à la description, l'appel aux phénomènes comme à une source légitime de connaissances psychologiques interdisaient en principe de traiter la forme comme une réalité moindre ou dérivée et de conserver aux procés linéaires, aux séquences isolables le privilège que leur donne le scientisme. Mais l'école de Berlin a reculé devant ces conséquences; elle a préféré affirmer,—par un acte pur de foi,—que la totalité des phénomènes appartenait à l'univers de la physique." *Sens et non-sens*, p. 170.

subject be, and the subject constitutes the meaning. The subject, then, forms part of the circular causality, for it is through the other and makes the other meaningful. But the subject is a privileged point in the circular causality, for it is, as it were, the heart of the whole of meanings and centers everything around itself as meaning-for-itself. Accordingly, the subject at the same time is both a part of the whole of the dialectic relationship and its center. It belongs to the whole of the reciprocal relationships and simultaneously is the center of all these relations. The subject is never an absolute reality which would cast, as it were, a "surveying glance" over everything else without being involved in it. The subject is always situated and therefore influenced by its surroundings; we may even say that it owes its being to these surroundings. Nevertheless, the subject is a privileged point because everything else is a meaning for this subject.[23]

Accordingly, the subject is a meaning-giving existence. It is privileged because everything else is meaning for and through the subject. But it does not attain absoluteness because it is through the other. It rises above its surroundings because it is the center of meaning. But it lies never fully outside its surroundings. The plant is the center of an environment: we cannot say in the same way that the soil exists for the plant and that the plant exists for the soil. Likewise, we cannot say that the nest exists for the bird as the bird exists for the nest. The subject is a center of meaning.

The subject behaves also as a center of meaning, for it arranges its world around itself. In its operations a kind of "intention" manifests itself, and the operations can be understood only in the light of this intention. The subject makes its environment environment, i.e., it makes it have meaning for itself. Merleau-Ponty does not merely state this in general but analyzes also the different levels of "subjectivity" and behavior. We will consider these levels when we will analyze man in the spirit of Merleau-Ponty.

---

[23]"Si au contraire nous voulons définir sans préjugé le sense philosophique de la psychologie de la Forme, il faudrait dire qu'en révélant la 'structure' ou la 'forme' comme un ingrédiant irréductible de l'être, elle remet en question l'alternative classique de l' 'existence comme chose' et de l' 'existence comme conscience', elle établit une communication, et comme un mélange de l'objectif et du subjectif, elle conçoit d'une manière neuve la connaissance psychologique, qui ne consiste plus à décomposer ces ensembles typiques, mais plutôt à les épouser et à les comprendre en les revivant." *Sens et non-sens*, pp. 171-72. The unity of the objective and the subjective thus is the most fundamental gestalt, and all other gestalts appear within this fundamental gestalt. In the above-quoted article of *Sens et non-sens* Merleau-Ponty develops the consequences of this standpoint in a brilliant way.

4. THE BODY AS SUBJECT

Man's body is a subject in the above-described sense, but not through a principle that is distinct from the body and nonetheless present in it.[24] That the body is a subject, a meaning-giving existence, is deduced by Merleau-Ponty from the fact that there are many forms of meaning which, on the one hand, do not have the character of a reality existing independently of us but, on the other, do not result from a free and conscious giving of meaning. It follows therefore that man must already be a meaning-giving existence on the preconscious and not-yet-free level, on the level of bodily existence. Merleau-Ponty offers many examples of such meanings. A few of these may be indicated here.

Oriented Space. We may begin by drawing attention to oriented space.[25] Merleau-Ponty begins by pointing out that the concrete space in which we live is prior for us than the abstract space spoken of by Newton.[26] It is true, of course, that we have an abstract idea of endless space as the container of everything and we easily conceive this space as prior to whatever is placed into it. This idea however, is abstract and largely a product of our thought. We form this idea on the basis of the concrete space in which our life runs its course. But this "lived" space is already oriented. In this space things are for us far-away or close-by, high or low, right or left. This oriented space is a "space-for-us," i.e., it extends around us. The orientation of this space apparently is not a datum existing independently of us. For in absolute space it is meaningless to speak about far-away or close-by, high or low, which refer to space only as it is for a subject.

---

[24]"L'expérience du corps nous fait reconnaître une imposition du sens qui n'est pas celle d'une conscience constituante universelle, un sens qui est adhérant à certains contenus. Mon corps est ce noyau significatif qui se comporte comme une fonction générale et qui cependant existe et est accessible à la maladie. En lui nous apprenons à connaître ce noeud de l'essence et de l'existence que nous retrouverons en général dans la perception et que nous aurons à décrire plus complètement." *Phénoménologie de la perception,* p. 172. The expression "noeud de l'essence et de l'existence," which Merleu-Ponty uses rather frequently, indicates the meeting point of massivity and openness, fixed meaning and future, darkness and lucidity.

[25]See the chapter on space in *Phénoménologie de la perception,* pp. 281-344. For an extensive and profound analysis of this topic see Joseph A. Kockelmans, "Ruimtewaarneming en ruimte volgens Merleau-Ponty," *Tijdschrift* v. *Philosophie,* vol. 19 (1957), pp. 372-428.

[26]Merleau-Ponty presupposes that the realistic interpretation of Newtonian space has already been refuted and opposes his view especially to Kant, who conceived space as an *"a priori* form" of sensitivity which can be conceived independently of its content. Cf. *op. cit.,* pp. 281 f.

The subject, however, for which such space exists is certainly not the conscious and free subject.[27] As a thinking subject, I enjoy great freedom with respect to space. I can think, for example, that I am on the moon and look at the earth from this standpoint. But in my concrete existence I am bound by dimensions from which I cannot escape. No matter, for instance, what I think, the floor is low for me and the ceiling high. In making utensils, we have to adapt ourselves to a spatiality which we simply have to accept. Moreover, even in the world of fiction in which we give free rein to our fancy, we have recourse to the given "natural space" in our pictures and comparisons; for example, we will say that, viewed from cosmic space, the Alps resemble a mole-hill.[28]

Accordingly, there is an oriented space from which we cannot escape. It imposes itself as a necessity on our consciousness and freedom, yet it is a space that exists for us and through us. True, we are able to do something about this spatiality. For instance, space is different for us when we walk, ride a bicycle or drive a car, for what is far-away for a pedestrian is near for an automobilist.[29] However, when we do something about this experience of space, we do it from the standpoint of the "natural" situation in which we are. The original, oriented space, therefore, exists for us and through us, but not through us precisely as conscious and free subjects. As a conscious and free subject, I *find* this meaning and have to accept it.

On what level does this meaning-for-us originate? Apparently on the preconscious and not-yet-free level. Therefore, we are already meaning-giving existences on a level on which we are not yet conscious and free. On closer inspection, moreover, it becomes apparent that the oriented space of which there is question here is connected with the structure of our body or, more concretely expressed, with its

---

[27]"Ainsi comme tout être concevable se rapporte directement ou indirectement au monde perçu, et comme le monde perçu n'est saisi que par l'orientation, nous ne pouvons dissocier l'être de l'être orienté." *Op. cit.,* p. 294. Being, therefore, is always already orientated, and we cannot base this orientation on any other object whatsoever. "Et puisque cependant il ne peut être orienté 'en soi', il faut que ma première conception et ma première prise sur le monde m'apparaisse comme l'exécution d'un pacte plus ancien conclu entre X et le monde en général, que mon histoire soit la suite d'une préhistoire dont elle utilise les résultats acquis, mon existence personnelle la reprise d'une tradition prépersonnelle." *Ibid.* This text very clearly shows the body-subject as meaning-giving existence.

[28]*Ibid.,* p. 502.

[29]"Si j'ai l'habitude de conduire une voiture, je l'engage dans un chemin et je vois que 'je peux passer' sans comparer la largeur du chemin à celle des ailes, comme je franchis une porte sans comparer la largeur de la porte à celle de mon corps." *Ibid.,* p. 167.

possibilities of motion.[30] In relation to these possibilities something is distant or near, high or low, right or left. We modify the meaning of space, always on the basis of the given meaning, by developing the body's possibilities of moving, e.g., by "enlarging" the body through a bicycle or a car. The bicycle or the car is experienced as true prolongations of ourselves, as something of ourselves. The driver will say, for example, "I can just squeeze through," meaning his "motorized I." As a possibility of moving, therefore, the body already gives meaning to space; it projects a meaningful space around itself. Thus, the body is a meaning-giving existence. As possibility of moving, the body makes what is outside us space-for-us. This statement should not be understood as if we first experience this "outside" absolutely and then make it be space-for-us. No, the "outside" is precisely given as space-for-us, and it is the body which gives meaning to it and makes it be for us. For this reason we may speak of a "natural" space, but "natural" does not mean here "wholly independent of us" but "prior to consciousness and free choice." For that matter we see how with the growth of the body the meaning of oriented space becomes modified; for instance, what is high for a child is no longer high for an adult.

Sexual Meaning. Another example, which perhaps is even clearer, is sexual meaning. Reality which appears to us has sometimes an obviously sexual meaning for us. The adult woman, for instance, has a sexual meaning for the adult man, and vice versa. Certain sketches and symbols likewise have a sexual meaning, as has been made abundantly clear by the analyses of depth psychology. Commercial artists know and have to know what the meaning is of "sex appeal"; its extent can be more or less scientifically determined, and the measure of "sex appeal" which custom admits in different countries is known. Sexual meaning apparently is a meaning for us, for it is inseparably connected with the sexual character of our existence.[31] If this sexual character of our existence has not developed, or if it has not grown at the same rate as one's general development, then this same lack of development or underdevelopment applies also to the sexual meaning.

---

[30] "Les lieux de l'espace ne se définissent pas comme des positions objectives par rapport à la position objective de notre corps, mais ils inscrivent autour de nous la portée variable de nos visées ou de nos gestes." *Op. cit.*, p. 168.

[31] "Cherchons à voir comment un objet ou un être se met à exister pour nous par le désir ou par l'amour et nous comprendrons mieux par là comment des objets et des êtres peuvent exister en général." *Phénoménologie de la perception*, p. 180.

However, it is evident also that the sexual meaning is not constituted by consciousness and does not arise from freedom.[32] Our experience bears witness that the sexual meaning imposes itself on us. For this reason Christians often speak in this context of "temptation," by which they indicate a meaning that does not originate in free choice but imposes itself on freedom.[33] Accordingly, there must be in our body itself an intentionality which gives to reality appearing to us a meaning that is not freely chosen by us.

The point manifests itself very clearly when we reflect upon what happens during puberty. The child has usually constructed a world of meaning, which at a certain age can be rather coherent. It lives freely and artlessly in this world of meaning. But then, when the development of the body reaches a certain stage, a new sphere of meaning imposes itself. At first, this new meaning is not at all clearly known but merely dimly felt. The child does not know what to do with this new meaning and does not clearly realize what is happening to him. He often needs instruction to understand the character of this new meaning, and time is required before this meaning can be integrated into the life of the child who now has arrived at the age of puberty.

Here again, therefore, we find the body as meaning-giving existence. For this reason it becomes intelligible why this dimension of man always retains a measure of obscurity for us. We are never able sharply to delineate the sexual meaning and we cannot exactly indicate where it begins and where it ceases.[34] From the standpoint of certain ethical ideals it remains troublesome that the sexual meaning assails us from an obscure dimension, for it does not always fit the line of conduct which we have drawn from the standpoint of our freedom.

---

[32] "La perception érotique n'est pas une *cogitatio* qui vise un *cogitatum;* à travers un corps elle vise un autre corps, elle se fait dans le monde et non pas dans une conscience." *Op. cit.,* p. 183.

[33] "Ainsi il y a dans l'existence humaine un principe d'indétermination, et cette indétermination n'est pas pour nous seulement, elle ne vient pas de quelque imperfection de notre connaissance, il ne faut pas croire qu'un Dieu pourrait sonder les coeurs et les reins et délimiter ce qui vient de la nature et ce qui vient de la liberté. L'existence est indéterminée en soi, à cause de sa structure fondamentale, en tant qu'elle est l'opération même par laquelle ce qui n'avait pas de sens prend un sens, ce qui n'avait qu'un sens sexuel prend une signification plus générale, le hasard se fait raison, en tant qu'elle est la reprise d'une situation de fait." *Op. cit.,* p. 197.

[34] "La sexualité n'est ni transcendée dans la vie humaine ni figurée en son centre par des représentations inconscientes. Elle y est constamment présente comme une atmosphère." *Op. cit.,* p. 196.

Sensitivity as Field of Meanings. The existence of the body as a giver of meanings is discovered also when we reflect on the fields of meaning that are connected with our sensitivity. We live in a visual field, a sonorous field, a tactile field, a field of odors and flavors. These fields of meaning have sometimes been conceived in a naively realistic way as if colors, sounds, odors and flavors existed independently of man in reality itself. This conception, however, is not tenable, for it is rather obvious that these fields of meaning are connected with ourselves. In a reaction against the naive realistic view, others went to the opposite extreme and claimed that these fields exist only in our interiority, as subjective reactions to stimuli arising from the world. Under the influence of these stimuli, so it was said, we form images or representations, which exist only in us and not at all in reality. This position, however, disagrees with our experience, which tells us that the tree itself is green, the steak tasty, and the apple fragrant. It is apparent, then, that we must say that the sensitive fields of meaning are, as it were, the face which the world has for us. We are a manifold question and make the world reply in many ways. The world itself is visual in reply to our sense of sight, it is a sonorous field in answer to our power of hearing, and so on.

Here, too, the interplay of question and answer appears not to lie on the level of consciousness and freedom. We cannot help it that the tree is green and the sky blue. The interplay of question and answer, therefore, is preconscious and lies on the level of bodily existence.[34] It is connected with the structure of the body, and for this reason physiological research is able to contribute to our understanding of these fields of meaning. Here again, therefore, we find the body as meaning-giving existence. The body itself is already dialog with the world and makes this world be meaning in many ways.

A confirmation is offered by the interconnection between the many sensitive fields of meaning. Colors have a sonorous meaning and sounds have a visual meaning. Flavors and odors are interconnected. True, the supposition has been made that there is question here

---

[34]"Par la sensation je saisis en marge de ma vie personnelle et de mes actes propres une vie de conscience donnée d'où ils émergent, la vie de mes yeux, de mes mains, de mes oreilles qui sont autant de Moi naturels. Chaque fois que j'éprouve une sensation, j'éprouve qu'elle intéresse non pas mon être propre, celui dont je suis responsable et dont je décide, mais un autre moi qui a déjà pris parti pour le monde, qui s'est déjà ouvert à certains de ses aspects et synchronise avec eux." *Op. cit.,* p. 250.

of associations which we would slowly learn to make, but research has shown that the connection is too "natural" to be explained in this fashion. The interconnection is given with the body itself and consequently is constituted starting from the body itself. We do not "choose" here but discover something that is already given prior to any choice.[35]

5. Preconscious Subjectivity of the Body

The Body's Dialog with the World. Let us attempt now to summarize what exactly Merleau-Ponty wants to clarify by means of these and many other examples. We are, so he concludes, already a meaning-giving existence on a level on which we are not yet conscious of ourselves and on which we are not free. The orientation of space, the sexual meaning, the various sensitive fields of meaning and their interconnection are the result of our dialog with the world. This dialog, however, takes place at such a depth that we are unable to penetrate into it through our reflective consciousness. It is likewise impossible for us to influence this dialog by means of our free decisions. Below me, therefore, as conscious subject, there is another subject that is preconscious and prepersonal. This subject is the body itself, for all forms of meaning arising on this level appear to be connected with the structure of the body. For this reason we may not equate meaning-giving subjectivity with consciousness and freedom, but should recognize that the body itself is already a subject.

At the same time it should be kept in mind that the meaning originates within a dialog and that in a dialog both parties are active. The meaning, then, arises because the body assumes a certain attitude, it situates itself. If the body wants to see something, it has to assume the correct ocular position. As research shows, the convergence of the eyes differs according to the distance of the object to be seen; likewise, the pupils have to be dilated according to the darkness of the field of vision. In other words, the body has to situate itself if the meaning in question is to arise. Freedom and consciousness play no role in this assumption of a situation, for we do not at all know what takes place in and through our body while

---

[35] "En tant que mon corps non pas une somme d'organes juxtaposés mais un système synergique dont toutes les fonctions sont reprises et liées dans le mouvement général de l'être au monde, en tant qu'il est figure figée de l'existence, il y a un sens à dire que je vois des sons ou que j'entends des couleurs." *Op. cit.,* p. 270.

we are seeing. There is no question here of instinctive actions or of reflexes in the traditional sense of the terms. An action is instinctive when a ready-made pattern is executed, but in the case under consideration the body adapts itself to a situation in such a way that a meaning can arise. A reflex means a reaction to a stimulus, but here a reply is sought that is adapted to the situation. The body is more than a mechanism endowed with ready-made patterns of activity which would operate as soon as an external stimulus makes itself felt. The body seeks its way in the world, and in this sense we may say that it "understands" its world provided this term is not conceived as expressing conscious knowledge.[36]

Permeated with "Intentions." Accordingly, the body must be permeated with "intentions," i.e., questioning orientations. The body may feel at ease or not at ease, which is a sign that it is in the world as a questioning existence. We find in ourselves conscious intentions, questioning orientations of the conscious "I." But it is apparent that these intentions are not the only ones and not the most original intentions of our subjectivity. There are in us also preconscious intentions, to which replies are given, e.g., by oriented space, sexual meaning and sensitive fields of meaning. Our conscious intentions take up our preconscious intentions.[37] These preconscious intentions, this bodily subjectivity, of course, cannot be indicated by means of reflection precisely because they are preconscious.

Anonymous Subjectivity. For this reason Merleau-Ponty says that, although the preconscious intentions belong to subjectivity, subjectivity on this level still retains the form of the impersonal (the "*on*").[38] Or, to use another expression, there is "anonymous existence."[39] These expressions do not refer to a mythical, collective

---

[36]"Le regard est ce génie perceptif au-dessous du sujet pensant qui sait donner aux choses la réponse juste qu'elles attendent pour exister devant nous." *Op. cit.,* p. 305.

[37]"Il faut en effet distinguer mes intentions expresses, par exemple, le projet que je forme aujourd'hui de franchir ces montagnes, et des intentions générales qui valorisent mon entourage." *Phénoménologie de la perception,* p. 502.

[38]"La perception est toujours dans le mode de l' 'On'. Ce n'est pas un acte personnel par lequel je donnerais moi-même un sens neuf à ma vie. Celui qui, dans l'exploration sensorielle, donne un passé au présent et l'oriente vers l'avenir, ce n'est pas moi comme sujet autonome, c'est moi en tant que j'ai un corps et que je sais 'regarder'. Plutôt qu'elle n'est une histoire véritable, la perception atteste et renouvelle en nous une 'préhistoire'." *Op. cit.,* p. 277.

[39]*Op. cit.,* p. 275.

subjectivity in the spirit of a mysticism of nature. What Merleau-Ponty wants to say is that on this level subjectivity is not yet a conscious subject and therefore does not yet have a name. For this reason he speaks also of a "natural 'I'." The "natural 'I'," he says, understands the world before and better than the conscious "I." In the "natural 'I'" there is a kind of "logic of the world,"[40] i.e., the preconscious subject is attuned to the world, it has intercourse with the world according to meaningful norms that are not drawn up by consciousness. When, for example, I think that I have reached the bottom of the stairs while I am still actually descending, my body finds the answer to the unusual situation even before I, as conscious existence, am able to raise the problem.

Freud's Sexual Instinct and the "I"-Body. On this level subjectivity is not so much a question of "I think that" as of "I am able."[41] With this expression Merleau-Ponty wants to indicate that this subjectivity is an "understanding-in-action of the world," in which the action stands in the foreground and the understanding remains in the dark. He speaks also of "practognosis," i.e., of an understanding that is wholly submerged in action.[42] In his opinion, it was about this subjectivity that Freud wanted to speak and should have spoken when he discussed the "unconscious." Freud regularly uses the expression "sexual instinct." This term makes one think of a ready-made pattern of action which begins to operate as the occasion demands. On closer inspection, however, it becomes evident that Freud wants to speak of something quite different, for his "sexual instinct" is polymorphous. It reveals itself in all phases of man's life but always in a different form, adapted to his age. It has to pass through a long history before it arrives at the adult's sexual behavior, and there is nothing which warrants that this history will

---

[40]"Plus généralement, il y a une logique du monde que mon corps tout entier épouse et par laquelle des choses intersensorielles deviennent possible." *Op. cit.,* p. 377.

[41]"Ces éclaircissements nous permettent enfin de comprendre sans équivoque la motricité comme intentionnalité originale. La conscience est originairement non pas une 'je pense que', mais un 'je peux'." *Op. cit.,* p. 160. Cf. also *Signes,* p. 118. Note that Merleau-Ponty says that *consciousness* originally is an "I am able." In other words, there is question here of the original form of existence of *the whole subject.*

[42]"L'expérience motrice de notre corps n'est pas un cas particulier de connaissance; elle nous fournit une manière d'accéder au monde et à l'objet, une 'praktognosie' qui doit être reconnue comme originale et peut-être comme originaire." *Op. cit.,* p. 164. This text makes it very clear that this mode of being-in-touch-with-the-world lies at the origin of our *entire* existence.

run its correct course, for a man may not go beyond a primitive phase of sexuality. In other words, the so-called "sexual instinct" does not follow a ready-made path but has to seek, even to create, its way. There is no question here of a thing-like reality but of a subject which seeks its way, which situates itself, which projects its situation. What Freud really had in mind is the "I-body" of Merleau-Ponty's philosophy, but Freud did not manage to escape from the dualism and the then-current ways of thinking of the sciences. As a consequence, the perspective he had discovered could not come to full advantage within the framework of his thought.[43]

It would be useless to look for a clear and distinct description of the "body-subject" in Merleau-Ponty. In principle such a description is not possible because that which is to be described itself is obscure. Accordingly to Merleau-Ponty's philosophy, it is quite clear that the "I-body" exists, but what exactly it is cannot become really clear to us. The "I-body" is a single mode of being and not the union, no matter how intimate, of two essentially different modes of being. The "I-body" is neither pure matter, pure spirit, nor the merger of these two. This is a concrete indication that our concepts of "mechanical bodiness" and of "spirit" are abstract and one-sided forms of thinking, which are unsuitable for expressing reality in a genuine way. The Cartesian categories may seem to be clear and distinct, but their clarity is a blinding light preventing us from seeing reality in its genuine condition. Merleau-Ponty refutes Cartesianism by pointing to a reality which has escaped Descartes' schematic way of thinking. So long as we keep looking through the "either or schema" of Descartes, we cannot understand what Merleau-Ponty wants to speak about.

Perception and the Body-Subject. Merleau-Ponty's main work, *Phénoménologie de la perception,* is chiefly concerned with this mode of being, so that he could very well have entitled it also *The Body-Subject.* This body-subject, as dialog with the world, gives us our original world, that which originally appears to us. Merleau-Ponty sees perception as a function which belongs to the body. The perception which he analyzes is not primarily perception as manifesting itself in consciousness, as consciously experienced. The fact that he makes anonymous existence (the impersonal *"on"*) the ultimate subject of perception shows this very clearly. One who considers perception as

---

[43]Cf. *Signes,* pp. 288-92.

an activity of the conscious subject, one who wants to analyze it as a conscious activity would have to proceed quite differently from Merleau-Ponty. He would have to ask himself how he experiences perception, what the characteristics of perception are which present themselves to consciousness. Whoever expects such an analysis in Merleau-Ponty's masterpiece will be disappointed and understand nothing of this book's structure. For the book is an attempt to penetrate into preconscious subjectivity, into the proper subject of perception. In other words, it is not a phenomenology in the usual sense of the term, and "perception" is not understood by Merleau-Ponty in the ordinary sense of this term.

Merleau-Ponty's fundamental discovery, then, is the original and irreducible reality of the "body-subject." It follows therefore that his philosophy moves in a chiaroscuro, which resists full illumination. The author does not consider the obscure character of his philosophy a result of a defective explanation but a consequence of its very object. Quite appropriately Alquié and de Waehlens call Merleau-Ponty's thought a "philosophy of ambiguity." For its proper object is a reality that is neither mechanical matter nor spirit but the ambiguous unity of both. Merleau-Ponty penetrates into a realm that is neither wholly dark nor wholly light but an ambiguous chiaroscuro. The question that has to be faced now is how he manages to penetrate into this realm.

CHAPTER TWO

MERLEAU-PONTY'S APPROACH TO THE "BODY-SUBJECT"

1. UNSUITABLE METHODS

The Importance of Preconscious Existence for Conscious Existence. As we have seen in the first chapter, Merleau-Ponty thinks that he has penetrated into a new mode of being, that of the body-subject. It is only by starting with this reality that we will be able to come to an understanding of man.

The objection could be raised that man is not merely preconscious subjectivity, for he leads also a conscious and free life. Merleau-Ponty agrees with this, but adds that in our conscious and free life we take up again and continue preconscious life. On the level of consciousness and freedom we are able to make plans, but on closer inspection it becomes apparent that in these plans we take up again and presuppose the meaning which originated on the level of preconscious existence. For example, I plan to go hiking in the mountains and to ascend this or that particular peak. In making this plan, I presuppose that the peak is high for me and therefore demands an effort that appears attractive to me; I presuppose the body as a possibility of moving and the oriented space that is connected with this possibility; I presuppose, moreover, that I have a need to move, which I incorporate into my free plan. My conscious and free life never begins with zero, but I always start from a meaning which I find already there.[1] This meaning, however, originates within the dialog of body and world. Conscious and free existence, then, refers to preconscious existence. For this reason the study of this preconscious existence is of crucial importance if we want to understand man.

Methodic Difficulties. It is here that Merleau-Ponty encounters great methodic difficulties, for the methods traditionally used in science do not satisfy him. Hitherto the life of science has been strongly dominated by the dualism of Descartes, who made a sharp distinction between nature and mind. This dualism gave rise to the

---

[1]Cf. *Phénoménologie de la perception*, p. 502.

31

distinction between sciences of nature and sciences of the mind. Nature was supposed to be an extrinsic datum, with which we become acquainted through external perception. That which external perception teaches us is in the first instance facts. To arrive here at general knowledge, we have to take the laborious road from facts to law, we have to think inductively. The physical sciences made use, or thought at least that they made use of the inductive method. Because the mind, on the other hand, is characterized by self-transparency, the sciences of the mind use the reflective method. It consists in this that we, as conscious beings, re-flect, bend back over ourselves to discover the fundamental lines of our mental life.

These two procedures, induction and reflection, were the methods which the existing sciences were able to offer to Merleau-Ponty for his research.[2] In his view, however, the two methods are unsuitable for the realm of his investigations. Going beyond this simple rejection, he adds that they are not even appropriate for the sciences as they are *de facto* developing. At present this last remark does not yet concern us, but we will revert to it later.[3]

The Inadequacy of the Reflective Method. It is evident that he cannot make use of the reflective method. For on the level of the "I-body" our existence is preconscious, so that we cannot penetrate in this dimension through reflection. No matter how profoundly I penetrate into myself, I will never be able to witness the birth of sexual meaning, the meaning of space or of color from my own existence as giver of meanings. To some extent I am able to perceive how my conscious plans originate, but not how colors originate. Even the most profound self-observation does not make me a witness of the dialog between body and the world.[4]

Insufficiency of the Inductive Method. Induction, likewise, cannot help us. First of all, according to Merleau-Ponty, "methodology has shown that no induction is properly founded in the strict sense of the

---

[2]He speaks of the "classical distinction of induction and reflection" in *Sens et non-sens,* p. 195.

[3]According to Merleau-Ponty, the classical distinction between induction and reflection has to be revised. We have to ask ourselves: "S'il n'y a pas plutôt un seul savoir à différent degrés de naïveté ou d'explicitation." *Op. cit.,* pp. 195-96.

[4]"Entre ma sensation et moi, il y a toujours l'épaisseur d'un *acquis originaire* qui empêche mon expérience d'être claire pour elle-même." *Phénoménologie de la perception,* p. 250.

term."[5] Induction wants to pass from facts to law. This transition, however, demands that the man of science form an idea allowing him to arrange and coordinate the facts.[6] But such an idea is never found in the bare facts themselves and, likewise, cannot be verified through a crucial experiment.[7] Accordingly, in that which is called the result of an induction a role is always played by an element which does not come from inductive thinking itself. For this reason inductive thought does not find its foundation in itself.

Secondly, inductive thinking is not suitable for the realm to be investigated. Induction seeks causal connections. The law formulated by induction states that, if factor A is given, factor B has to be present also. The relationship, however, of the body-subject to its surroundings is not a relation between cause and effect. The body-subject and its surroundings constitute a connected whole of meanings, a gestalt. The body comes to be itself through its surroundings, and these surroundings are surroundings precisely as meaning for the body. One may not reason here from one factor to the other, but all factors have to be understood within the connected whole of meanings. The totality cannot be reconstructed from isolated factors, but these factors have to be understood at once within the totality. Induction presupposes that the various factors can be isolated, and this possibility is not present here.[8]

The same idea may be expressed by saying that the body enters the world not as one of the elements of a causal connection but as an *intentional existence*. It is only from the standpoint of this orientation that we can understand whether and to what extent the things around the body have meaning for it. The body does not simply undergo

---

[5] *Sens et non-sens,* p. 195.

[6] "L'induction ne parvient à ses fins que si elle ne se borne pas à noter des présences, des absences et des variations concomitantes, et si elle conçoit et comprend les faits sous des idées qui n'y sont pas contenues. On n'a pas le choix entre une description de la maladie qui en donnerait le sens et une explication qui en donnerait la cause et il n'y a pas des explications sans compréhension." *Phénoménologie de la perception,* pp. 133-34.

[7] "En physique, l'etablissement d'une loi exige bien que le savant conçoive l'idée sous laquelle les faits seront coordonnés et cette idée, qui ne se trouve pas dans les faits, ne sera jamai vérifiée par une expérience cruciale, elle ne sera jamais que probable." *Op. cit.,* p. 139.

[8] "Si le comportement est une forme, où les 'continus visuels' et les 'continus tactiles', la sensibilité et la motricité ne figurent qu'à titre de moments insépa-rables, il demeure inaccessible à la pensée causale, il n'est saisissable que pour une autre sorte de pensée,—celle qui prend son objet à l'état naissant, tel qu'il apparaît à celui qui le vit, avec l'atmosphère de sens dont il est alors enveloppé, et qui cherche à glisser dans cette atmosphère, pour retrouver, derrière les faits et les symptômes dispersés, l'être total du sujet." *Op. cit.,* pp. 139-40.

the influence of things in a purely passive way, but it situates itself while it undergoes the influence, so that it is active in undergoing it. When the body ceases to situate itself and therefore simply undergoes such influences passively it, strictly speaking, ceases to be a body. While the dialectics of the body and the world is an event that can be analyzed, the analysis in question has to be performed within the understanding of the whole.

An example may serve to illustrate the point. If light is bright, the pupils of the eye contract. Certainly, this bodily event does not occur independently of factors outside the body, for the contraction does not take place when the brightness remains the same, and there is, moreover, a controllable connection between the brightness and the contraction. What happens in the body influences the appearing world, for it is because of this bodily event that the visible world arises. But the entire event has a meaningful character and, separately from the meaning, it becomes wholly unintelligible. The body behaves in such a way that optimal "vision" becomes possible. The light makes the body seek the optimal attitude. This "seeking" of the body is more than the effect of a physical influence, and that which is effectuated by the body's attitude is not so much an "effect" of the body as a "meaning" for the body. The aspects of the event can be understood only within the whole.

2. THE METHOD OF MERLEAU-PONTY

His Trailblazing Work. As we have seen, the behavior of the body-subject is a meaningful event, and the world in which such events take place has the character of a whole of meanings. Of genuine understanding, however, there can be question only if we know how to enter into the meaningful event and into the world as the whole of meanings for the body. The question which arises here, of course, is how we can penetrate into them. As has been pointed out, we cannot enter into the meaningful event by means of our reflective consciousness and we cannot look at it from without through inductive thinking. How, then, are we to penetrate into the preconscious event?

This question brings us to one of the most remarkable problems raised by Merleau-Ponty's philosophy. He has discovered a mode of being that hitherto had largely escaped man's attention. He makes it quite clear how difficult it is to approach this mode of being, viz., the existence of the body as a preconscious subject. Nevertheless, he penetrates into this hidden mode of being—and this is one of the chief merits of his work, especially of his book, *Phénoménologie de la perception*. His main importance lies not so much in this that he analyzes our conscious acts precisely insofar as they are conscious. True, he makes valuable remarks about this matter, but others have investigated this realm more extensively. But his great achievement is that he did not only discover the hidden dialog between body and world but also managed to petetrate into it.

Here lies the reason also why Merleau-Ponty's work attracts so many psychologists and not a few sociologists. So far as the psychologists are concerned, it has become quite clear that the so-called psychology of consciousness is not able to offer a satisfactory explanation of human life. For our life has depths which play a role in everything but are not accessible to the psychology of consciousness. Efforts have been made also to view these depths in a thing-like way and to approach them by means of the method adapted to things. But man intuitively realizes that his life, no matter on what level, does not have a thing-like character. Merleau-Ponty work presents a method which recognizes both the obscure character and the subjective nature of our life.

The same line of thought applies also to sociology. Undoubtedly we, human beings, enter into conscious contacts with one another. But these conscious contacts are made possible by preconscious bonds which, however, are not thing-like. Psychologists and sociologists who are open to the genuine character of human existence and do not reduce it to aprioristic concepts realize that Merleau-Ponty's approach brings us into contact with a real and extremely important dimension of our being.[9]

Difficulty of Describing His Method. The most important chapters of *Phénoménologie de la perception* contain Merleau-Ponty's penetration into this dimension. If one asks what his method is, it is very difficult to give a satisfactory answer. The philosopher himself makes use of it but does not describe it, although here and there he gives a few brief and very incomplete indications. This situation should not cause any great surprise. Usually a method is in existence before it is reflectively described, just as somewhat similarly roads exist before they receive traffic signs or are recorded on travellers'

[9]Cf. Remy C. Kwant, "De verhouding tussen wijsbegeerte en psychologie in het denken van Maurice Merleau-Ponty," *Annalen v.h. Thijmgenootschap*, vol. 45, no. 2, Sept. 1957, pp. 164-181.

maps. Moreover, the dimension of being described and analyzed by Merleau-Ponty has only recently become an object of thought, and even Merleau-Ponty himself does not always have a clear idea of his approach to this dimension. Reading his works, one notices that he gropingly seeks his way. Despite this difficulty, let us try to indicate some characteristics of his method.[10]

Meaning is Not Absolute but Constituted. The first thing to realize is that the meaning originating in the dialog of body and world has a constituted character. As consciously living human beings we *find* this meaning, we find oriented space, sexual meaning, colors, sounds, flavors, etc. Thus we are very easily induced to see this meaning as something absolute, which lies ready-made waiting for us. Realism is inclined to see this meaning as a given reality that is independent of us. Certain forms of intellectualism see it as a projection of absolute ideas that are present in us and which we uncover through reflection. Both these interpretations have something in common—namely, the meaning in question is "given," either in objective reality or in our absolute ideas. Both, however, labor under an illusion, for this meaning is constituted within the dialog between body and the world.

It follows, then, that the analysis of the given, as it is given to us, does not lead us anywhere. The phenomenological method has often been understood as the faithful rendition of the given as it *de facto* appears to us. In that case the given becomes the absolute starting point of scientific thought. Merleau-Ponty, however, does not have recourse to such a phenomenological method, for the given itself is constituted, it has a "history." Accordingly, it has to be understood from the viewpoint of its becoming.[11]

---

[10]*Phénoménologie de la perception,* pp. 110-158, contains a fairly extensive description of his method. By means of the Schneider case Merleau-Ponty shows that neither the inductive method nor the rational-analytic method can lead us to a real understanding of the patient's illness. By way of exclusion he concludes that a new method is needed, which he calls among other names "existential analysis" (p. 158). He shows that such a method is required, that the character of the issue demands it, but does not sufficiently clarify the problem of how one should penetrate into the chiaroscuro of the body-subject, of how this darkness can be somewhat illuminated.

[11]Most descriptions of the phenomenological method contained in the current literature are rather simplistic and inadequate. All too often the phenomenon to be described is assumed to be an immediate datum and the laborious road of reduction is neglected. Authors appear to think that the knowable is, according to phenomenology, readily available for inquiry and forget that, according to phenomenology also, the inner core of our knowable world can be uncovered only in a laborious way.

This becoming, however, does not directly reveal itself to our consciousness and, on the other hand, it is, of course, entirely inaccessible to external perception. We cannot perceive how colors are formed within the dialog of the body and the world. This dialog has remained undiscovered so long by scientific thought precisely because it lies hidden from our gaze. Thus we are inclined to be satisfied with the result of this dialog and to forget about the dialog itself. The consequence is that the roots of our entire field of existence remain concealed to us.

Importance of Abnormal Dialectics of Body and World. Occasionally, however, it happens that the dialectics between body and world reveals itself somewhat. This happens when this dialectics is disturbed. So long as this dialectics runs its course undisturbedly, we take its result for granted and are inclined to see this result as a "natural world." But when the relationship between body and world is disturbed, man's entire field of existence is shaken and thus reveals its constituted and changeable character. Such disturbances may be the effect of illness and psychical deviations, or they may be caused artificially through experiments. In *Phénoménologie de la perception* Merleau-Ponty draws atttention preferably to the disturbed bodily existence. He has been reproached sometimes for this because it creates the impression that he wants to penetrate into normal existence by means of the abnormal. The analysis of deviations fills so many pages of his book that the reproach may seem justified.[12] Nevertheless, Merleau-Ponty's interest is centered on the normal dialectics between body and world. He studies disturbed existence only because, in it, the dialectics in question reveals itself to some extent, because the hesitations and gropings of the disturbed dialog offer him an opportunity to observe the body in its dialog with the world. In other words, the disturbed existence is for him only a kind of approach permitting him to penetrate into the communication of the body and the world.

Examples. Merleau-Ponty begins his analysis of the sexual character of our existence with a discussion of a famous German disabled soldier, the Schneider case.[13] This man is no longer able to take sexual initiatives, but his sexual mechanism begins to operate when the situation is such that his own initiative is no longer needed. He then

---

[12]Practically all chapters of *Phénoménologie de la perception* contain analyses of disturbed existences.

[13]*Op. cit.,* pp. 181-184.

quotes the studies of Steckel and Freud concerning frigidity,[14] followed by the clinical experiences of Binswanger.[15] In connection with this subject matter, he speaks about the phenomenon of aphasia. In this way he endeavors to throw light on sexual existence. Sexuality is a zone of our existence and, as such, it is at the same time and inseparably both of a bodily character and a free "taking up" of our bodily being. It is possible that an entire zone of our existence may be practically eliminated. In that case the corresponding bodily behavior no longer occurs, but the relevant images and free initiatives likewise disappear. The behavior of the body and the life of the mind reveal gaps. According to Merleau-Ponty, we should not seek the cause of the one in the other, for both gaps are parts of one and the same phenomenon. Because of the bodily aspect of the disturbance, the phenomenon of the illness in question becomes a condition in which we simply exist. Because of the body, the so-called inner phenomena become an existential situation.

When we go to bed, we assume the attitude of a sleeper, but when we become what we pretend to be, the attitude which we assume is really made its own by the body. It is the role of the body to perform this metamorphosis.[16] The body makes the idea a reality, the sleep behavior real sleep. The body symbolizes our existence because it realizes this existence, because it is the actuality itself of our existence. In a similar way the inner rejection of an existential zone may become bodily impotence, and only then is the illness complete, i.e, only then does it become a genuine existential situation.

Because of the body, I am open to the world, but am also able to close myself to the world. The body is my entry into the world, and all the ways in which the world is accessible to me are connected with the body. It is precisely the disturbances in the normal conditions which disclose the function of the body. In normal conditions we use the body without realizing its importance. The body is "the hidden form of self-being" and the bearer of conscious existence. While we cannot develop these ideas here more fully, the preceding remarks may serve to give the reader an idea of Merleau-Ponty's precedure.[17]

---

[14]*Op. cit.*, pp. 184-187.
[15]*Op. cit.*, pp. 187-191.
[16]*Op. cit.*, p. 191.
[17]A detailed inquiry into Merleau-Ponty's method would be very important for psychology as well as philosophy. Such an inquiry would undoubtedly throw light on the relationship between philosophy and psychology. However, it would lead us beyond the scope of this book in which we want to outline the philosophy of Merleau-Ponty.

The Schneider Case. He repeatedly appeals to the above-mentioned Schneider case, e.g., in connection with language,[18] sexuality,[19] the experience of space[20] and sense perception. He does not merely mention the case, but makes an extensive analysis, in which he tries to come to an understanding from the perspective of phenomenology.

Schneider, says Merleau-Ponty, is a disabled soldier, showing a multitude of symptoms of illness, in which it is difficult to find a pattern. His perception remains limited to that which is connected with his actual occupation, and his attention is not at all drawn to anything else. For this reason his attention shows little mobility. When something new is placed before him whose meaning a normal human being would see at once, Schneider begins by hesitatingly attributing all kinds of abstract meanings to it and in this laborious way he finally discovers the object's meaning. His field of perception has disintegrated, and many transitions have become impossible for him. The broad world of experience offers him no new meanings. He moves to the point where he is supposed to go, but pays no attention to what he encounters on his way. He does not recognize his own letters. He cannot copy a design, but has, as it were, to reconstruct the design himself. The interconnected meaning of a story escapes him, so that the story disintegrates into a collection of facts. He is unable to play with numbers, i.e., he cannot use them in all kinds of directions but can work with them only according to standardized methods. He can grasp but he cannot point, i.e., he is able to execute all the holds belonging to his actual occupation, but he cannot point to anything. He is wholly incapable of playing because he cannot place himself in an imaginary situation. A riddle and a problem of life are just the same for him. When he speaks with someone, other sounds simply do not exist for him.

How can we, Merleau-Ponty asks, find unity in all these symptoms? Schneider reveals himself endowed with a rather good intelligence, so that we cannot simply say that he has lost his mind. Likewise, not a single one of the sensitive functions is missing, so that the symptoms cannot be explained on the basis of such a defect. Yet

---

[18]*Op. cit.,* p. 228.

[19]*Op. cit.,* pp. 181 f.

[20]The analysis of this case occupies a large part of the chapter entitled, "La spatialité du corps propre et la motricité," *op. cit.,* pp. 114-172. The summary following here has been based on this chapter.

there is a certain unity in all these symptoms. With Hochheimer, Merleau-Ponty remarks that Schneider is wholly bound to the actual.[21] He lacks the freedom to move from the actual to the possible and therefore to make something else the center of his field of presence. He clings to an actual meaning, an actual occupation, an actual schema of behavior. It is useless to ask him in summer how he feels in the winter. He is not sexually impotent, but he cannot "visualize" the sexual situation when he is not actually in it. Thus he is likewise incapable of being bored.

The "Intentional Arc." From this analysis, Merleau-Ponty manages to penetrate into a fundamental function which makes a normal life possible but usually remains concealed from us. Both intellectual and perceptive life are supported by a fundamental possibility to turn our existence in the most divergent directions. Using a metaphor, Merleau-Ponty calls this function a projector which can be turned in all directions, through which we are able to direct ourselves to everything within us and outside us, and which enables us to assume an attitude toward all this. However, he continues, the metaphor of the projector is not very good, for it presupposes objects which, as wholes of meanings, exist independently of the light but can be illuminated. The function, on the other hand, of which there is question here makes all objects exist for us in a mysterious way and makes them meanings before we know them in the proper sense. Our conscious life, as it actually is, is made possible by an "intentional arc," which projects around us our past, future, our human milieu, our physical situation, our ideological situation, our moral situation— briefly put, it makes us be situated in all these respects. Thanks to this intentional arc, our life is not an arbitrary succession of actual moments but really a unity. In this way unity enters into the life of behavior, sensitive life, and here also lies the source of the unity of the senses and the intellect. In Schneider's illness this arc broke down, so that he remained a captive of actuality.[22]

The Body Organizes its World. Sometimes also Merleau-Ponty appeals to the experiments of others, interpreting them from his own perspective. A case in point is Stratton's following experiment.[23] A

---

[21]*Op. cit.,* p. 158.

[22]This paragraph is a free rendition of a condensed page of Merleau-Ponty, *op. cit.,* p. 158.

[23]*Op. cit.,* pp. 282-287.

subject is made to wear a pair of spectacles, covering his entire field of vision. These spectacles neutralize the inversion of the images on the retina. The subject has to wear these spectacles uninterruptedly for a series of days. At first, he sees an "upside down world," in which he has, of course, great difficulty in moving about. The subject evidently knows that the world has been turned upside down and on the basis of this knowledge he manages to interpret the world rationally; for instance, what he sees "up" is really "down." After some time, however, the field of vision becomes unsettled and, surprisingly, after a number of days have lapsed, everything is straightened out. The subject again *sees* the world as it is.

Merleau-Ponty asks himself how this end result is possible. It cannot be the result of the intellectual interpretation. For in this way one cannot explain why the subject, who at once interprets what he sees intellectually, needs several days before he begins to see the world again in a normal way. It remains especially unexplained why the subject's *seeing itself* becomes again normal. Likewise, there can be no question of an association between the field of vision and the field in which the subject moves, for such an association again does not explain why the subject *sees* the world as he used to before. Merleau-Ponty's conclusion is that the body itself actively organizes the field of vision. This field does not result from the causal relationship between body and the world but rather originates in a bodily project. The project in question is not fully determined by external stimuli and, accordingly, our field of vision is not a mirror-like reflexion. It is our body which *gives* us the world, in an interplay, of course, with the world, but in such a way that our body organizes its world.

In this fashion Merleau-Ponty analyzes many cases borrowed from others, giving them, however, a new interpretation.[24] Again and again he arrives at the same conclusion, albeit constantly in a different way— namely, that our body itself is already a subject, an existence, an intercourse with the world, that the body gives us a world, that the world's structure depends on the structure of our body. The reason is not that the body causally influences the world, but that the body, precisely as body, gives meaning to the world. The body is intimately permeated with meanings. Therefore, the body is not closed upon it-

---

[24]The philosopher has the right to interpret facts discovered in the pursuit of science: "Le philosophe professionel n'est pas disqualifié pour réinterpréter des faits qu'il n'a pas lui-même observés si ces faits disent autre chose et plus que ce que le savant y a vu." *Signes*, p. 127.

self, as a thing is. It is where something has to be done. The body is a possibility of a meaning-giving activity and it is only in this giving of meaning that it really is a body. When its meaning-giving activity ceases, the body is dead.

Body and "Natural World." It is through this body that there exists for me, as conscious subject, a "natural world." This natural world is not, as has been sometimes asserted, an "in itself" (*"en soi"*), a reality existing independently of us. This world is the whole of meanings resulting from the dialog between body and world. As conscious subject, I take up this world but I do not constitute it. As conscious subject, I find a world, which I experience as natural and necessary. The body plays a role in this perception and, consequently, there is naturalness, necessity, in the perceptively given.

As long as the dualistic way of thinking prevailed and thing-like existence was opposed to conscious existence, the so-called "natural world" had to be conceived either in a realistic fashion as an "in itself" which we get to know or in the spirit of rationalism as a materialization of an idea. Merleau-Ponty, however, managed to penetrate more profoundly and to find a new explanation—viz., the natural world is the result of the dialog between body and world, a dialog which precedes existence insofar as it is conscious. That which we in ourselves call "existence" is sometimes submerged in the body and at other times rises to the level of consciousness. Yet there is question here of one and the same existence. The body already dwells in the world, and my conscious dwelling in the world is a taking-up of the preconscious, bodily dwelling in the world. If I identify existence with consciousness, I am no longer able to understand myself.[25]

---

[25]It may be useful to point out that Merleau-Ponty does not always use the term "existence" in exactly the same sense. There is question of "existence" in the technical sense of this term when a reality transcends the purely thing-like, purely causal relationships. Since this is the case even with animals, Merleau-Ponty sometimes speaks about the animal as "existence." For example, "L'animal, dans une mesure variable selon l'intégration de son comportement, est bien *une autre existence*" (*La structure du comportement,* p. 137). Obviously also, the human body, as "body-subject," has an existential character: "L'expérience du corps propre au contraire nous révèle un mode d'existence ambigu" (*ibid.,* p. 231), for "Le corps n'est donc pas un objet" (*Ibid.,* p. 231). Sometimes, however, Merleau-Ponty opposes body and "existence": "Ni le corps ni l'existence ne peuvent passer pour l'original de l'être humain" (*Phénoménologie de la perception,* p. 194). In such a case the body is viewed in its thing-like character, as a whole of fixed properties, and "existence" is regarded as the overcoming of the thing-like: "L'existence est l'excès de notre existence sur l'être naturel" (*ibid.,* p. 229). Moreover, when Merleau-Ponty is confronted with "right-wing" existentialism, he uses "existence" sometimes for personal

3. THE OBSCURITY OF MERLEAU-PONTY'S PHILOSOPHY

No Systematization. The dialog between body and the world which, as it were, is the undercurrent permeating my entire existence is not directly accessible to my gaze. Merleau-Ponty penetrates into it through all kinds of by-ways. He does not succeed in presenting a clear picture of this dialog, so that there is no possibility of summarizing his conclusions in a lucid synthesis. All he can allow us is to have an inkling of something which we do not grasp. Our existence is, at least at a certain level, illuminating, but this light rises out of a darkness with which it is inseparably united. Anyone who detaches our existence as an illuminating event from the dark abyss from which it arises will never be able to understand this existence. For its fundamental lines are already laid down in the dark zone pertaining to its very essence.[26] To express the matter paradoxically, Merleau-Ponty wants to illuminate the light from the darkness to which it essentially refers.

Here lies the main reason, we may say, for the obscure character of Merleau-Ponty's philosophy. That which in our existence may be called "light," is not intelligible in itself. We may have some inkling about the dark soil in which we are rooted, but a clear synthesis cannot be offered. "Systematization" is not possible here. One who would attempt to present a systematic survey of Merleau-Ponty's ideas regarding the body-subject would merely succeed in making it obvious that he does not understand his philosophy. As Merleau-Ponty writes in the preface of his *Phénoménologie de la perception,* "There is no thought which encompasses our entire thought."[27] At first this statement may seem strange. Isn't thought conscious of itself? Don't we know that we know? "Radical reflection," says Merleau-Ponty, "is the consciousness of its own dependence on an 'unreflected' life, which is its beginning, its lasting source and its goal."[28] This "unreflected life" is also a bodily existence, also the life of the body as subject. Human thought presents itself as a light so

---

being. This variation in shades of meaning is not illogical. For "existence" always indicates the transcending of the thing-like. This transcendence, however, may take place on different levels; consequently, the term "existence" has many meanings which, however, are all interconnected.

[26]"Pour nous, la conscience ne s'attribue pas ce pouvoir de constitution universelle que si elle passe sous silence l'évènement qui en fait l'infra-structure et qui est sa naissance." *Phénoménologie de la perception,* p. 517.

[27]"Il n'y a pas de pensée qui embrasse toute notre pensée," *Avant-Propos,* p. IX.

[28]*Op. cit., Avant-Propos,* p. IX.

long as we do not reflect too profoundly on it. But as soon as we penetrate into the root of thought, thinking appears based on a darkness resisting all attempts to synthetize it rationally.

Merleau-Ponty is acquainted, of course, with Husserl's reduction. The Austrian philosopher had come to the conclusion that our current conceptions, even those accepted in the life of science, are not the original form of knowing. He wanted to bring these conceptions back to our original way of seeing and called this bringing-back "reduction." Merleau-Ponty's idea of reduction, however, is quite different from that of Husserl. Husserl thought, at least for many years, that the original experience would have the character of conscious knowledge, which, therefore, could really be brought to light. That which we would have to reach through the reduction would be a light. Merleau-Ponty, however, does not think so. According to him, our conscious life is borne by our preconscious existence; it has to be reduced to this existence and to be understood through it. But the preconscious existence neither is a light nor allows itself to be adequately brought to light. Thus his philosophy ultimately refers us to a chiaroscuro in which it is extremely difficult to penetrate. This difficulty is an added reason why Merleau-Ponty's philosophy is "the enemy of the system."

Relationship to Marx and Freud. The fundamental sphere of Merleau-Ponty's thought is related to that of Marx and Freud. These thinkers, too, thought that our original life lies submerged in the darkness of materiality. Conscious life, which Marx called the "superstructure" of our existence, has to be understood from the standpoint of its infrastructure. One who wants to know what a man is, says Marx, should not listen to what he says about himself but should observe what he really is."[29] According to Freud, our life is borne by a dark instinct. Merleau-Ponty's philosophy is related to these thinkers because he, too, sees original life as a kind of darkness.

True, there are also important differences. Unlike Freud and to a certain extent also unlike Marx, Merleau-Ponty does not admit that our life is fully determined by the dark soil from which it springs. He rejects also the scientistic tendencies revealing themselves in the works of Marx and Freud. Yet there is an unmistakeable resemblance in the trend of his thinking. It is not purely accidental that Marx and Freud are frequently mentioned in Merleau-Ponty.

[29]*Zur Kritik der politischen Ökonomie,* Berlin, 1958, p. 13.

"Accursed Lucidity." Unsurprisingly, after reading a chapter of *Phénoménologie de la perception,* one never enjoys the feeling of having acquired a clear understanding. It is almost impossible to summarize a particular chapter without betraying Merleau-Ponty's thought. He shows how that which presents itself as "obvious," e.g., motion, verbal expression, the sensitively given, space, the thing, or the natural world, is not at all so obvious. He eliminates the obviousness of everything which he considers. He shows how it points to an obscure basis and how it is constituted from there. Next, he manages almost always to quote in a masterful way experiences, psychical deviations and experiments which permit us to have an inkling about the chiaroscuro in which all the "obviousness" of our conscious life originates. He knows how to find very striking expressions which tell us something about this dark soil in which are the hidden roots of our existence. The reader feels that he has become acquainted with a valuable perspective. But as soon as he endeavors to reconstruct what he has read, he becomes aware of the obscure nature of Merleau-Ponty's explanations.

Although it is sometimes claimed that this obscurity is due to the defective and unscientific character of the philosopher's work, the reason lies really elsewhere—namely, in the obscurity of the "subject matter," as it is approached by Merleau-Ponty.[30] Whoever conceives the reduction in the same way as Merleau-Ponty is in principle unable to reach clarity.

Here lies the root of the groping character proper to Merleau-Ponty's fundamental concepts, which shocks and irritates all those who pursue the ideal of "hygienic" thinking. The philosopher is unable to satisfy the requirement that no term may be used until its meaning has been accurately described. For him such a procedure would mean to betray the dimension of human existence which he wants to consider. Writing about Sartre, he goes so far as to speak of that "accursed lucidity."[31] There is, indeed, a clarity which Merleau-Ponty cannot countenance because of the very character proper to the reality which the philosopher has to consider.

---

[30]"Toute réflexion emporte toujours avec soi des pans entiers d'expérience qui concourent tacitement à produire nos évidences les plus pures." *Sens et non-sens,* p. 195.

[31]". . . cette maudite lucidité." *Signes,* p. 33.

CHAPTER THREE

BODY AND LANGUAGE

In the preceding pages we have described Merleau-Ponty's fundamental discovery of the body-subject and we raised the question of how he gains access to this reality. In the present chapter we will devote our attention to his philosophy of language, because the ideas which he proposes in this realm are very closely connected with his philosophy of the body.

1. The Function of Merleau-Ponty's Philosophy of Language in the Whole of His Philosophy

Body and Soul or Existence. The mode of being studied in the preceding pages is not just one mode alongside many others, but occupies the very center of Merleau-Ponty's philosophy. For, from the viewpoint of this mode of being, he endeavors to understand the whole man, he sees man as a kind of unfolding of the body-subject. According to him, man is nothing else than a body-subject, provided we see this body-subject on all levels of its unfolding.

Merleau-Ponty repeatedly denies the existence of a separate principle in man, distinct from the body. Moreover, he presents his philosophy as a victory over Cartesianism. He would not be able to do so if in man, apart from the body-subject, there would be another form of subjectivity, for otherwise dualism would re-enter his philosophy by the back door. Finally, his philosophical thought shows a general tendency to reduce that which often is called the "light of the spirit" to the chiaroscuro of the body.

True, several texts could be quoted as seemingly opposed to this assertion. Merleau-Ponty often distinguishes between "body" and "existence," and even opposes the one to the other. How, then, can we say that he reduces man's entire existence to the body? The reply is that Merleau-Ponty uses the term "body" in many senses. He justifies this usage in the following way. "There always comes a moment when we withdraw from a passion, driven by lassitude, exhaustion or self-love. This duality is not a simple fact but has the character of a principle, for every integration presupposes the normal functioning of subordinate formations, which always tend to their own well-being. However, there is no question here of a duality of sub-

46

stances. In other words, the concepts 'soul' and 'body' must be rendered relative. There is, first, the body as a mass of chemical combinations which constantly interact; then, the body as the dialetics of the living being with its environment; also the body as the dialectics of the social subject with its group; even all our habits may pass as an untouchable body for the 'I' of every moment. Each of these grades is 'soul' with respect to the lower grades, and 'body' with respect to the higher grades. The body in general is a whole of already established paths, already acquired powers, it is the acquired dialectic soil on which a higher formation takes shape, and the soul is the new meaning that comes into existence."[1]

Accordingly, for Merleau-Ponty the concept "body" is a relative concept, for corporeity exists on many levels and, according as we pay attention to this or that level, we may call a certain reality either "body" or "soul." The soul, however, is never a separate reality. The soul is the higher level of the subject's self-organization. This higher level is made possible by the completion of the lower level and is supported by its equilibrium. There is question of dualism, says Merleau-Ponty, only when this equilibrium is disturbed.

The formation, then, which has already been achieved he usually indicates by the term "body," and the moving toward a higher formation he calls "soul" and even more frequently "existence." For this reason he is able to contrast "existence" with "body" and often creates the impression that he distinguishes them. But there is no question of a distinction, at least not of a real distinction. There is nothing else in man than the body-subject, and the body is a subject precisely because it constantly lifts itself up toward a higher formation, because it constantly tends to a higher mode of its own being. As the philosopher expresses it, "It is the definition of the human body to appropriate in an indefinite series of non-continuous acts 'centers of meaning' which go beyond its natural powers and transform it."[2] He adds that "language in its turn does not raise any other problem."[3] For this reason precisely the body is a subject and not a thing.[4] It is not a constant repetition of itself but takes itself

---

[1] *La structure du comportement*, pp. 226-27.

[2] *Phénoménologie de la perception*, p. 226.

[3] *Ibid.*

[4] "Le corps objectif n'est pas la vérité du corps phénoménal, c'est-à-dire la vérité du corps tel que nous le vivons, il n'en est qu'une image appauvrie, et le problème des relations de l'âme et du corps ne concerne pas le corps objectif qui n'a qu'une existence conceptuelle, mais le corps phénoménal. Ce qui est vrai

up again in a transcending way. The body, as subject, is a self-transcending movement.

Thus Merleau-Ponty may and has to make a distinction between body and existence. However, this distinction is not really a distinction between the body and "something else." It is the distinction between the body as "congealed or generalized existence" and the body as a creative taking-up of itself, between one and the same reality seen as "body" and as "soul," to use again the terminology explained above. Body and existence, body and soul are two aspects of the same reality which, however, itself also can be called "body" in a different sense.[5]

Two Meanings of the Term "Body." In Merleau-Ponty's works two meanings of the term "body" constantly intermingle. Sometimes he speaks of the body as fixed existence, as "acquisition," as a whole of established forces, as something appearing under a thing-like form, something that lends itself to the formulation of laws about itself. At other times he uses the term "body" for the self-transcending subject, the existential power which characterizes the human body precisely as human. The body, in the first sense, is achieved meaning, but, in the second sense, it is the everlasting soil from which meanings spring. If we use the term "body" in the first sense, we must admit that man is more than the body, but this "more" belongs to the body in the second sense. In the first sense, the body can become the object

---

seulement, c'est que notre existence ouverte et personnelle repose sur une première assise d'existence acquise et figée. Mais il ne saurait en être autrement si nous sommes temporalité, puisque la dialectique de l'acquis et de l'avenir est constitutive du temps." *Op. cit.*, pp. 493-94. Speaking about the subject of perception, he says: "La subjectivité, au niveau de la perception, n'est rien d'autre que la temporalité et c'est ce qui nous permet de laisser au sujet de la perception son opacité et son historicité." *Op. cit.*, p. 276. Merleau-Ponty says repeatedly that the subject is temporality, and this applies to both the subject of perception and the subject on the level of personal existence. The subject is always self-assembly from the past toward the future in the now. This clearly shows his monistic view of men and his rejection of dualism. On all levels of our existence it is true that "we are the arising of time." *Op. cit.*, p. 489.

[5]"Nous ne disons pas que la *notion* du monde est inséparable de celle du sujet, que le sujet *se pense* inséparable de l'idée du corps et de l'idée du monde, car s'il ne s'agissait que d'une relation pensée, de ce fait même elle laisserait subsister l'indépendance absolue du sujet comme penseur et le sujet ne serait pas situé. Si le sujet est en situation, si même il n'est rien d'autre qu'une possibilité de situations, c'est qu'il ne réalise son ipséité qu'en étant effectivement corps et en entrant par ce corps dans le monde. Si, réfléchissant sur l'essence de la subjectivité, je la trouve liée à celle du corps et à celle du monde, c'est que mon existence comme subjectivité ne fait qu'un avec mon existence comme corps et avec l'existence du monde." *Op. cit.*, p. 467.

of empirical sciences, but into the body, in the second sense, we can penetrate only through the existential analysis described in the preceding chapter. The body that is analyzed by the empirical sciences as a datum is, according to Merleau-Ponty, already a congealed movement of existence; consequently, it is not intelligible in itself. The sciences studying it base themselves on a foundation that is unstable. Merleau-Ponty's philosophy understands the unstable character of this foundation and thus removes the stability which the starting point of the sciences was supposed to have. He wants to make the men of science understand what they really speak about, and in this way to show the sciences what kind of truth they can attain.

Merleau-Ponty repeatedly asserts that he does not want to reduce existence to the body. One could hardly expect otherwise. He refuses to reduce man's self-movement to fixed forces, for otherwise he would attempt to understand the subject from the standpoint of the thing, and thus would lapse into a mechanistic way of thinking. He refuses also to reduce the body to absolutely conceived self-movement, for otherwise the body would become the result of something preceding it. What he wants to do is to understand fixed existence and human self-movement as aspects of one and the same reality—the body-subject.[6]

For this reason Merleau-Ponty's work has a general tendency to consider what we may call the "light of the spirit" in the darkness of being-a-body. He endeavors to discern the dark aspects of everything which we experience as light.[7] He does not deny the light but draws attention to the fact that the light exists only because and as long as we accept certain presuppositions as obvious. The evidence exists as long as we place ourselves within the "obvious" meaning of the words, but it ceases to exist as soon as we reflect upon the dark soil from which it springs. All light exists in and arises from a dark soil. The tendency of Merleau-Ponty is hardly surprising, for it lies fully in line with his fundamental thesis that man's entire being is an unfolding of the "body-subject."

Role of His Philosophy of Language. To show the truth of this fundamental thesis Merleau-Ponty would have to show that all aspects of human life can be understood in this way. This, however, he has

---

[6]For this reason Merleau-Ponty refuses also to detach facticity more or less from freedom, as Sartre does. In man facticity and freedom are aspects of one and the same reality.

[7]Cf. Remy C. Kwant, "De geslotenheid van Merleau-Ponty's wijsbegeerte," *Tijdschrift v. Philosophie,* vol. 19 (1957), pp. 217-272.

not done. For this reason we may say that his work presents a perspective that is not sufficiently developed[8] and certainly not adequately proved. Nevertheless, he has made certain attempts to show the truth of his perspective, the most striking of which is his philosophy of language.[9] His philosophy of language should not be seen as an isolated chapter of his philosophical work, but plays a very definite role in the whole of his philosophy. It functions as a kind of proof of his fundamental thesis. It is not at all a coincidence that Merleau-Ponty returns again and again to questions concerning language. In many important passages he speaks of the philosophy of language and these passages are precisely those in which he tries to approach his fundamental theme. Merleau-Ponty wants to show that the light of human existence originates in the self-transcending movement of the "body-subject." But this light exists *par excellence* in thinking, of which language is the most important instrument. If Merleau-Ponty is able to show that speech, i.e., throwing light on reality, is a phenomenon that is essentially connected with the body-subject, he confers at least a degree of probability on his fundamental thesis. Thus his philosophy of language is a crucial chapter of his entire philosophy. For this reason we will consider his philosophy of language in the light of his fundamental perspective. It should be evident that, by following this procedure, we are not unfaithful to Merleau-Ponty's was of thinking.

2. The Interconnection of Thinking and Speaking

A Simplistic View. From the role of Merleau-Ponty's philosophy of language in the whole of his philosophical thought it is obvious that he wants to show the unbreakable interconnection between thinking and speaking, because such an interconnection reveals the bodily character of thought. He admits that at first sight the opposite seems to be true. Thought seems to be universal and eternal, while language has an historical and changing character. For this

---

[8]"Désormais le creux de l'inachèvement va s'imprimer sur les mêmes textes qui nous séduisaient et nous embarassaient par le trop-plein du sens." Paul Ricoeur, "Le philosophe foudroyé," *Les nouvelles littéraires,* 11 mai 1961, p. 4.

[9]The interpretation which we give of Merleau-Ponty's fundamental perspective and to which some object, is confirmed by Paul Ricoeur's above-quoted article. Ricoeur, however, adds that Merleau-Ponty experienced increasingly greater difficulties in interpreting the forms of human existence within this fundamental framework, and that in the last years of his life he was busy with perhaps a radical revision of his basic perspective: "Ce qui rend cette interruption tragique, c'est que la base philosophique du grand livre de 1945 [*Phénoménologie de la perception*] était depuis longtemps remise en question."

reason many philosophers who have thought about the connection of thinking and speaking, consider their interrelationship as something accidental. Intellectualism was inclined to view the word as an adventitious sign, distinct from the thought expressed. Thought was viewed as lying in man's interiority, and the word as an external corporeal phenomenon.[10] Thus the meaning of a word would be distinct from this word itself. But in that case the meaning of the word, i.e., thought, does not need the word, for the thought exists already before it is expressed in words.[11] The fact that the same thought can be expressed in many languages seems to confirm this view.

This View is Untenable. On closer inspection, however, says Merleau-Ponty, it appears that this simplistic view is untenable. First of all, experience teaches us that thought needs the word. Our thought is not first internally completed and then waiting for us to find words for its expression. Thought seeks the word as its own completion.[12] To know something means that we are able to express it in words.[13] As long as our verbal expression remains vague and imperfect, our thought is likewise still imperfect. Anyone who is accustomed to teaching knows this from his own experience. As long as he is unable to explain his thoughts very clearly, there is something lacking in his understanding of the problems involved. It happens also rather frequently that a thought assumes form precisely because it is verbally explained, so that the lecturer himself arrives at a clearer understanding precisely through his verbal expression.

Merleau-Ponty appeals also to primitive consciousness, which attributes to speech the power to evoke the matter expressed.[14] This consciousness continues to be alive in certain cases; many cab drivers, for instance, dislike to hear their passengers mention punctured tubes,

---

[10]"C'est la pensée qui a un sens et le mot reste une enveloppe vide." *Phénoménologie de la perception,* p. 206.

[11]Merleau-Ponty expresses this conception as follows: "L'idée d'un *texte original* dont notre langage serait la traduction ou la version chiffrée." *Signes,* p. 54.

[12]"Si la parole présupposait la pensée, si parler c'était d'abord se joindre à l'objet par une intention de connaissance ou par une représentation, on ne comprendrait pas pourquoi la pensée tend vers l'expression comme vers son achèvement." *Phénoménologie de la perception,* p. 206.

[13]"Je dis que *je sais une idée* lorsque s'est institué en moi le pouvoir d'organiser autour d'elle des discours qui font sens cohérent." *Signes,* p. 114.

[14]"Pour la pensée préscientifique, nommer un objet, c'est le faire exister ou le modifier." *Phénoménologie de la perception,* p. 207.

as if the mere term would give rise to the puncture itself. Should we not admit in general that speech puts us into the presence of the thing spoken of? The way in which the thing is made present is most intimately connected with the way in which it is spoken of.

Finally, by means of the word we are able to appropriate to ourselves a thought that was first unknown to us. Someone who does not know what Hegel has thought is able to acquire this thought by making a thorough study of Hegel's works. This, says Merleau-Ponty, would not be possible if Hegel's thought were not present in his works.[15] How could anyone obtain Hegel's thought if this thought were not contained in his works? One could try to escape from this argument by making the remark that, for the writer as well as the reader, every word is associated with a meaning distinct from the words, and that we become acquainted with a new thought, because known words and their known meanings are connected in a new fashion.[16] However, this explanation falls short, for a new thought is not like a building constructed of old materials, but all its elements themselves receive a new meaning. In a philosophy such as that of Hegel or Merleau-Ponty most terms are given a new meaning or at least a new shade of meaning. Accordingly, in some mysterious way thought lies contained in speech.[17]

At first sight, it may seem strange that the meaning of language lies contained in the language itself. The improbable character, however, of this assertion is considerably lessened, if we pay attention to the other forms of expression used by the human body. Dancing is a form of expression, yet no one would dream of distinguishing the meaning of the dance from the dance movements. Likewise, we know very well that the meaning of a painting cannot be divorced

---

[15]*Op. cit.*, p. 208.

[16]"Cette notion du sous-entendu exprime naïvement notre conviction qu'une langue (généralement notre langue natale) est parvenue à capter dans ses formes les choses mêmes." *Signes*, p. 55.

[17]"Parfois il semble qu'il y a une rapport si intime, un rapport plus que rapport entre les paroles et les pensées; et il y a certainement chez lui une tendance à réduire, du moins à identifier pensée et parole. Mais si nous lisons la page 28 de la préface de *Signes*, nous voyons qu'il y a une transformation de la pensée en parole et des paroles en pensée; et cela nous amène à admettre qu'il y a au moins en puissance une distinction entre elles." Jean Waehl, "Cette pensée . . . ," *Les temps modernes*, vol. 17, nos. 184-85, 1961, pp. 431-432. As had already been noted by Paul Ricoeur, Jean Waehl observes here that from his basic philosophical perspective Merleau-Ponty wants to identify thinking and speaking, but that occasionaly life is richer than theory, so that there are texts in Merleau-Ponty which point to a broader perspective.

from canvas and colors[18] or the meaning of music from the sounds. In general, the meaning of an expression finds existence in the material itself of the expression. Why, would the situation be different with respect to verbal expression—words?[19]

The "Spoken Word" and the "Speaking Word." The illusion that the meaning of speech can be divorced from speech itself, arises from the fact that verbal expression, once created, can be repeated and endlessly so.[20] Once an expression has been created, it becomes a common possession and may be used by everyone. In this way one may have the impression that the expressed meaning has an eternal character. In reality, however, this so-called "eternal character" is nothing but a cultural acquisition.[21]

In an effort to clarify his perspective, Merleau-Ponty makes a distinction between the "spoken word" (*parole parlée*) and the "speaking word" (*parole parlante*).[22] The "spoken word" is the expression which, once created, has become a common possession. It is the meaning, laid down in a word, which is passed on from individual to individual and even from generation unto generation. But that which is repeated must once have been spoken for the first time. Therefore, the "spoken word" refers to the "speaking word" as its origin.

This "speaking word" is the original speech which gives meaning to words and makes them say what they have never yet said. It goes without saying that according to Merleau-Ponty the "speaking word" is more original a phenomenon and that it manifests the inner character of speech more clearly. For the "spoken word" very easily becomes "obvious" in man's social intercourse, so that the meaning existing in it is readily considered to be a natural meaning, because the word's origin has been lost sight of. In such a case one may think that our speech expresses given reality as it is in itself. In this way there arises the idea that truth is eternal, i.e., prior to man and merely expressed by speech. Thus, speech, which is really the soil in which meaning germinates, comes to be considered as an

---

[18]"Le langage constitué ne joue un role dans l'opération expressive que comme les couleurs dans la peinture." *Phénoménologie de la perception*, p. 446.

[19]For a long and profound comparison of language and painting, see *Signes*, pp. 56-95.

[20]Cf. *Phénoménologie de la perception*, pp. 459-461 and 221-222.

[21]"L'éternel, c'est l'acquis." *Op. cit.*, p. 450.

[22]*Op. cit.*, p. 229.

accidental form of expression. In the "speaking word," on the other hand, the proper nature of speech reveals itself. It is not a mere rendition of light that is already given but the source of light. Thus, it becomes apparent how much this light is connected with the words, for the light begins to exist because of the unveiling word.

It goes without saying that we should not think here solely or even primarily of the word's physical reality. In the physical order the word is almost nothing. It is the expulsion of air while the throat and mouth are in a certain position, a succession of articulated sounds.[23] The word should be seen as an intentional orientation and, as such, it cannot be divorced from that which it conveys; otherwise what we retain is nothing but empty words. But the really signifying word makes something present, and the way in which this something is made present is dependent on the words referring to it. Divorced from what it speaks of, our speech loses its meaning, but our speech makes that which is spoken of exist for us. Speech depends on that which is spoken of and, reversely, what is spoken of depends also on speech.[24]

Thought is Not Independent of Speech. It follows, therefore, that thought is not independent of speech. On the contrary, thought becomes thought in speaking. This assertion applies, of course, only to thought insofar as it comes to existence in the word. Merleau-Ponty knows also a so-called "preverbal thought," e.g., a thought existing in action, which he indicates by the term "practognosis."[25] The acting body understands its world as well as its own possibilities. This understanding is truly a form of knowledge, but this knowledge is still wholly immersed in the action itself. In walking, for example, we take into account the condition of the ground, for we do not walk in the same way through a forest and over a smooth road. This "understanding," however, of the world is not distinct from our walking itself. In many realms, says Merleau-Ponty, we acquire habits only when our body begins to understand something, i.e., when it is capable of manipulating the objects of a particular realm. One knows really how to play the organ well when the body finds its

---

[23]"Une contraction de la gorge, une émission d'air sifflante entre langue et les dents, une certaine manière de jouer de notre corps se laisse soudain investir d'un *sens figuré* et le signifient hors de nous." *Op. cit.,* p. 226.

[24]Cf. *Signes,* pp. 110-122.

[25]Cf. *Phénoménologie de la perception,* p. 164

way from the reading of the notes to the correct keys without any conscious aid of the intellect.[26] One who types well no longer needs to let his mind seek the exact location of the letters but knows it with his hands. Accordingly, there is also a preverbal kind of thought, and this thought is, of course, not dependent on the word. In the word, however, thought comes to exist in a new way and, in this new way of existing, thought depends on the word. To know something here means to be able to indicate it in a coherent succession of words. Knowledge cannot be divorced here from the words.

Descartes tried to find thought in man's interiority and believed that this so-called "inner thought" was independent of speech. He did not realize that the "inner silence" was filled with the sound of words.[27] Thus it appears that thought does not have the character of a disembodied and worldless phenomenon. Thought is embodied and is a phenomenon pertaining to the world, but a world brought to light by man. This light of the world is essentially connected with the word which unveils it. One cannot ask a mathematician that he sacrifice his mathematical terminology both externally and internally and yet retain his mathematical insight. His insight is tied up with meaningful symbols. Therefore, his light is rooted in a dark soil. As long as he remains within his symbolic language, the light exists for him and is something obvious. As soon, however, as he reflects on the soil from which this light arises, the light becomes for him a mysterious reality. It loses its obviousness. We see here again the general tendency of Merleau-Ponty's philosophy to question or rather to undercut the obvious. He does so by referring us to the not-so-obvious soil in which everything that is obvious to us is rooted.

3. THE BODY AS EXPRESSION

Existence as Giver of Meanings. In the "speaking word," says Merleau-Ponty, one can divine the presence of a fundamental func-

---

[26]Concerning the formation of habits and the body, see Merleau-Ponty's penetrating and interesting account in *op. cit.,* pp. 166-171.

[27]"Le *Cogito* que nous obtenons en lisant Descartes . . . , c'est donc un *Cogito* parlé, mis en mots, compris sur des mots et qui, pour cette raison même, n'atteint pas son but, puisqu'une partie de notre existence, celle qui est occupée à fixer conceptuellement notre vie et à la penser comme indubitable, échappe à la fixation et à la pensée." *Op. cit.,* p. 460.

tion which explains the birth of all meaning.[28]   He uses a very striking terminology on this point, saying that one "can divine the
presence of this function through and across speech."   The use
of this terminology shows that the function of which there is question here reveals itself in speech, but that it is not connected with
speech in a mutual and exclusive relationship.   As a matter of
fact, Merleau-Ponty explicitly admits that the function in question
manifests itself also in other forms of expression.   By using the
term "to divine," he clearly indicates that we do not know this
function very distinctly and are even less capable of describing it
adequately.

What is this function?   It is the creative character of our existence
as giver of meanings.   Our existence is permeated with "being," but
does not stop there.   By "being" Merleau-Ponty means that which
is already acquired, already present in its givenness, already constituted.   It is characteristic of our existence that what is already acquired is always taken up again in view of a new future.   He speaks
of a "constantly re-created openness in the density of being."[29]   Accordingly, being is always again a starting point.   What existence,
starting from being, realizes is not fixed in this being.   The new
meaning arises, as it were, in a zone of emptiness.

All this, of course, does not mean that our existence would proceed in a wholly arbitrary way.   Not everything is possible from the
starting point on which our existence relies.   The "speaking word,"
which makes use of available words to say what has never been said
before, cannot say everything in these words.   Nevertheless, what
is said was not fully fixed in the available words.   The new meaning
which comes into existence can be understood from the available
words, but it cannot be derived from them as a conclusion is deduced
from premises.

Our existence does not create meanings from nothing, for this
existence is and remains a dialog with the world.   As such, it is not
only restricted by the acquisitions connected with its own past, but

---

[28]"De là la parole parlée qui jouit des significations disponibles comme d'une
fortune acquise. A partir de ces acquisitions d'autres actes d'expression authen-
tique,—ceux de l'écrivain, de l'artiste ou du philosophe,—deviennent possibles.
Cette ouverture toujours recréée dans la plénitude de l'être est ce qui conditionne
la première parole de l'enfant comme la parole de l'écrivain, la construction du
mot comme celle des concepts. Telle est cette fonction que l'on devine à travers
le langage, qui se réitère, s'appuie sur elle-même, ou qui, comme une vague, se
rassemble et se reprend pour se projeter au-delà d'elle-même." *Op. cit.*, pp.
229 f.
[29]*Op. cit.*, p. 229.

also by the world as the field of its possibilities. As "speaking word," our existence is tied not only to the words that are available, but also to the world that is spoken of. Nevertheless, with respect to our existence as creative of meaning, the world likewise does not act as a determining factor.

Existence, as giver of meaning, manifests itself in all human phenomena, in the gestures of our hands, the mimicry of our face, the smile of the child, the creation of the artist, speech and work. It is like a wave which contracts and expands to throw itself forward beyond its own confines. The body is this power of expression. It gives rise to meaning; it makes meaning arise on different levels which continue to imply one another. The power of expression reveals itself in a very special way in language, but what it reveals there existed already before in an obscure fashion on previous levels. The body constantly more and more unfolds its own possibilities, and in doing so continually gives meaning in new ways to the world in which it dwells.

The Fundamental Fact of Merleau-Ponty's Philosophy. Accordingly, the meaning-giving power of our existence is a primordial given, irreducible to anything else. It may be called the "fundamental fact" of Merleau-Ponty's philosophy. It is presupposed by all meanings. As we have seen in the preceding chapters, it is already at work at a depth in which reflecting consciousness is unable to penetrate. It manifests itself in the fields of the senses, oriented space, sexual meaning, as well as in artistic expression and creative speech. However, it would be an illusion to think that we are able to seize our existence, as the creative power of meaning, in concepts when it reveals itself on the level on which we, as conscious beings, know ourselves. While it is true that in our speaking we consciously seek light, we do not know how we manage to say what has never been said by means of available words. We may witness the birth of a new light in ourselves, but we can never succeed in making fully clear how this light was born.

Our existence is the soil in which meaning, light, germinate. This existence is the fundamental mystery which manifests itself in everything and which is presupposed by every meaning. "Our view of man will remain superficial as long as we do not penetrate into this source, as long as we do not rediscover the primordial silence underlying the noise of words, as long as we do not describe the gesture which breaks through this silence."[30] Merleau-Ponty uses here the term "silence" for that which preceeds meaning. He speaks also of a "silent cogito," preceding the speaking of the existence.[31] By these mysterious terms he wants to express that we are unqualifiedly origin of meaning and that we will not find any absolute meaning explaining other meanings. We ourselves are ground and origin. We break through the density of being and give meaning to it. There is no meaning prior to man. Only our own silence precedes our speech as giving meaning.

4. THE SPEAKING SUBJECT

Existence as Giver of Meaning is Not an Absolute. Accordingly, we ourselves are the source of meaning in our constant dialog with the world. It is not possible to indicate any absolute meaning as the origin of all unfolding of meanings which itself would lie beyond history. For this reason Merleau-Ponty does not cease to attack the trends of thought which he calls "rationalism" and "empiricism." Rationalism views the absolute concept, the absolute category, as an unqualified starting point, an irreducible beginning. Empiricism appeals to an experience that is supposed to be characterized by necessity because it would give us knowledge of a datum which we cannot change in any way. Against these trends of thought Merleau-Ponty claims that our existence, as giver of meaning, is already at work in both category and experience. Consequently, we cannot point to any starting point that is independent of us and simply imposed on our existence as giver of meaning. Accordingly, our presence itself, as creative of meaning, is the origin of meaning.

Nevertheless, we would be unfaithful to Merleau-Ponty's thought, if we were to consider our existence, as giver of meaning, to be a kind of absolute point, prior to the historical movement within which meaning arises. Conceivably, one could say: our existence as giver of meaning is the starting point; therefore, in his reflection the philosopher will first have to consider this starting point in himself and then examine how meaning arises from this source. Merleau-Ponty refutes this conception, which goes wholly counter to his ideas, by pointing

---

[30] *Op. cit.,* p. 214.

[31] "Le *Cogito* tacite n'est *Cogito* que lorsqu'il s'est exprimé lui-même." *Op. cit.,* p. 463. See also p. 462.

out that our existence is a "speaking subject."[32] Let us attempt to explain the sense and scope of this expression.

Empiricist and Rationalistic Viewpoints. According to certain philosophies of language which are of an empiricist trend, the connection of words into sentences is a kind of natural process governed by blind laws. For many years an extremely important role was ascribed to the association of psychical entities; efforts were made to find the laws governing association, and these laws were viewed as rules that apply of necessity. In a similar way the association of words was viewed as a necessary process. To a certain extent it was possible to find support for this view in our experience, for experience bears witness that words are joined together and evoke one another, even though we do not know clearly and distinctly how this happens. Merleau-Ponty, however, objects to this view for, if the connection of words is governed by necessary laws, it is not made by a subject and, consequently, speech does not manifest a subject seeking light.

Philosophies of language, on the other hand, which are based on rationalism do not deny the subject. However, they conceive the subject as a thinking subject, having within itself concepts and categories that are prior to speech. Thus, although there is here a subject, there is no speaking subject, for the proper life of the subject, his thinking existence, precedes speech and is independent of it. Even if one knows how thinking takes places, he does not yet know how words are connected, for thinking is not tied up with speech. Thus the interconnection of words could again be explained in a mechanistic fashion.

Merleau-Ponty's View: the Speaking Subject. Against these theories Merleau-Ponty affirms that man is a "speaking subject." What he means is, first of all, that man's subjectivity, is seeking light and creating meaning, is present in speech. In other words, speech is not a natural event, running its course according to blind laws, but speech itself is a subjective event. The connection of words is a connection for and through the subject. Secondly, Merleau-Ponty wants to express that the subject exists in speech, finds itself in speech, we may even say, comes to existence in speech. The human subject is not a subject beyond and above language, a subject which views the

---

[32]"Dans la première conception [empiricism], nous sommes en deçà du mot significatif; dans la seconde [rationalism], nous sommes au delà—dans la première, il n'y a personne qui parle, dans la seconde il y a bien un sujet, mais ce n'est pas le sujet parlant, c'est le sujet pensant." *Op. cit.*, p. 206.

plurality of words, as it were, from an absolute standpoint and chooses the correct words from this absolute standpoint. The subject does not lie outside speech but lives in speech. Speaking is more than a natural event, because it is permeated with human subjectivity, and the subject is not an absolute point, because it exists in speech.

It is very difficult to realize the scope of Merleau-Ponty's viewpoint in this matter. Careful speech is characterized by coherence. A sentence, for example, is a well-rounded phrase because its meaning is coherent.[33] We could say that a sentence is a sentence because it has a meaning. A unity of meaning reveals itself in the plurality of words. What is the nature of this unity? It has often been said that it is the concept which is this unity of meaning, and that this concept precedes its verbal expression. If this is true, the understanding subject would exist in another dimension than that of the word, the understanding subject would not fall under the plurality and temporality which manifest themselves in speech. The understanding subject would, as it were, lie in an absolute point, beyond plurarity and temporality. But, according to Merleau-Ponty, the subject exists in speech. It exists, therefore, in plurality and temporality, it becomes itself in them. It does not look at the temporal event of speaking from an absolute standpoint beyond this temporality. The words of the sentence whose sound has already gone and the words that are still to come are not in the subject's mind as the present, but are his own past and his own future. If the subject stood outside his speech, he could gather his speaking, as a temporal event, before his glance just as the eye can seize many things in a single panorama. But the speaking subject cannot do this, because he himself exists in this temporal event.

Accordingly, Merleau-Ponty concludes, the subject himself is temporality. The subject extends from a past to a future. True, what has already been spoken is past, but it is the proper past of the speaking subject himself. The subject reaches out to his own past and from there projects himself to his future. The coherence of his

---

[33]"En ce qui concerne le langage, si c'est le rapport latéral du signe au signe qui rend chacun d'eux signifiant, le sens n'apparaît donc qu'à l'intersection et comme dans l'intervalle des mots. Ceci nous interdit de concevoir comme on le fait d'habitude la distinction et l'union du langage et du sens. On croit le sens transcendant par principe aux signes comme la pensée le serait à des indices sonores ou visuels,—et on le croit immanent aux signes en ceci que, chacun d'eux, ayant une fois pour toutes *son* sens, ne serait entre lui et nous glisser aucune opacité, ni même nous donner à penser: les signes n'auraient qu'un rôle de monition, ils avertiraient l'auditeur d'avoir à considérer telle de *ses* pensées." *Signes*, p. 53.

speech is the coherence of his own existence. The subject gathers himself into a living unity, but this self-gathering takes place in time and itself is temporal.[34]

The Subject is Temporality. We are now in a position to understand Merleau-Ponty's repeated assertion that the subject is temporality.[35] The subject is a coherence of life but only a temporal coherence. Even as the subject stretches out toward the world, so also does he stretch out toward his own past and his own future. The subject does not look at the dimension of time from the standpoint of a new dimension lying outside time but from his own temporality.

On several occasions we have already spoken about the coming to be of meaning. It appears now that the subject himself is involved in this coming to be, because the coming to be of meaning is the subject's own self-realization. One who writes a book does not first have a finished understanding and then, in addition, expresses this finished understanding in a book. He himself comes to be in his self-expression, at least, when he produces an original work. A writer may, of course, also repeat his own past self-expression or the self-expression of others, but in such a case there is no question of self-expression in the proper sense.

All this shows the scope of Merleau-Ponty's expression that the human subject is a speaking subject. The expression may be said to contain the core of his philosophical anthropology. The subject is not an absolute point outside the body and outside the world, outside the stream of events. The subject comes to be in the body, in the world, in the stream of events. It is the inner coherence of all this. The subject is not an absolute gaze for which all this exists, but is the unity of life consisting in the plurality of events. The subject itself has a past and a future. This statement should not be understood as if the subject were a new temporal line alongside the temporal line of events in such a way that the two lines would be co-extensive. There is only one temporal line, for the subject exists in the events themselves. This coming-to-be is a coming-to-be, a temporality, precisely because it is permeated with subjectivity, because it is the life-story of a subject. The subject is temporality as

---

[34]"Nous sommes le surgissement du temps." *Phénoménologie de la perception*, p. 489.
[35]This oft-repeated assertion is somewhat strange. While one can say that the human subject is essentially temporal, the identification of temporality and subjectivity remains peculiar.

gathering-itself-together. It is the coherence of coming-to-be, and for this reason the subject itself may succeed or fail. If the coherence of the coming-to-be is successful, the subject itself succeeds. The subject is the unification of coming-to-be, but a unification from within, which cannot be distinguished from the coming to be itself.

Philosophy of Language and Philosophical Anthropology. From these considerations it should be clear why, according to Merleau-Ponty, we can never succeed in attaining full clarity concerning ourselves by means of reflection. True, our own existence does not escape us completely, for we stretch out toward our own past and our own future. However, the past remains past, and the future is always future. According as the past is more distant, it sinks further away into darkness. This means that we ourselves sink away in darkness. Our existence never escapes us completely, for we stretch out toward our own past. Yet this means that we stretch out into a dimension which becomes progressively more obscure. This darkness belongs to our own being, and we can never bring it entirely to light. For this reason we are a chiaroscuro for ourselves; and our aspect of darkness belongs essentially to us; it is not something that is present merely as an unfortunate accident that can be overcome.

Thus, it becomes apparent that Merleau-Ponty's philosophy of language is really meant as a confirmation and proof of his fundamental perspective. One who really understands his expression that man is a "speaking subject" knows in what the core of Merleau-Ponty's philosophy of man consists and in what sense he thinks that he has overcome dualism.[36]

---

[36]For an excellent detailed study of Merleau-Ponty's philosophy of language, see B. Brus, "De taal bij Merleau-Ponty," *Ned. Tijdschrift* v. d. *Psychologie en haar Grensgebieden*, vol. 13 (1958), pp. 26-80.

CHAPTER FOUR

SUBJECT AND MEANING

1. The Sense of Meaning

The term "meaning" has been used constantly in the preceding chapters, for it would be impossible to discuss Merleau-Ponty's philosophy without making use of this concept. In the following pages we will now study more in detail what this fundamental concept means.[1]

Being and Subject. We have already seen in what sense, though not exclusively, Merleau-Ponty uses the term "being." Generally, for him the concept "being" indicates that which has been acquired, achieved, what is fixed and presents itself as something that remains what it is. In contrast to this "being," or rather within this "being," Merleau-Ponty places "existence," which opens being to a future. Existence prevents being from remaining fully at rest with itself. If man were fully "being," he would cease to be, he would be dead. According to Descartes' famous statement: "I think, therefore, I am," I know that I am because I think. Descartes, then, ascribes being to the subject, we may even say that for him the subject is being *par excellence.* However, Descartes merely touches the surface of the question and allows himself to be deceived by the inner logic of his words. For he forms a new thought *object,* while he attempts to find access to the one for whom all objects are.[2] What he touches is the objectified subject, i.e., a subject standing opposite the proper subject, and not the subject in the strict sense of the term. He touches the thought subject but not the subject which thinks everything.

Logically speaking, we have to admit, of course, that the subject is, for otherwise it would be unable to think. But this does not mean

---

[1]Cf. Remy C. Kwant, "De zingedachte van Maurice Merleau-Ponty," *Bijdragen. Tijdschrift v. Philosophie en Theologie,* vol. 16 (1955), pp. 1-31. Merleau-Ponty's most brilliant description of the concept "meaning" may be found in *Phénoménologie de la perception,* pp. 489-492.

[2]"Quant à la source même des pensées, nous savons maintenant que, pour la trouver, il nous faut chercher sous les énoncés, et notamment sous l'énoncé fameux de Descartes. Sa vérité logique—qui est 'pour penser il faut être'—, sa signification d'énoncé le trahissent par principe, puisqu'elles se rapportent à un objet de pensées au moment où il faut trouver accès vers celui qui pense." *Signes,* p. 29.

that the subject is a "being." Man is a subject, because he constantly takes up being toward a future, because he does not rest in being. Unlike Sartre, however, Merleau-Ponty does not want to conclude that, therefore, the subject is a "nothing" (*"rien"*). For Sartre, the essential function of the subject is to "nihilate," to "noughten," and consequently the subject is a "nothing." Merleau-Ponty rejects this Sartrian view because everything that has meaning for the subject would lose its central reference point if the subject were a "nothing." Man organizes a world around himself, in which things are nearby or far away, meaningful or meaningless. All these meanings, however, would make no sense if the subject were a "nothing."[3] The subject, says Merleau-Ponty, is the invisible for which everything visible is. The subject is the zero of visibility which stands open to everything visible.[4]

In the light of these remarks, it is hardly surprising that Merleau-Ponty does not make "being" the main theme of his philosophical thought. His philosophy is a philosophy of meaning rather than of being.

Realism. A first characteristic of meaning is that it always refers to a subject, for there is no meaning except for a subject. We touch here one of the fundamental features of Merleau-Ponty's philosophical perspective—he thinks that all we can speak about is being-for-us. He breaks radically with the philosophical view that is usually referred to as "realism."[5]

In a certain sense the realistic viewpoint presents itself more or less spontaneously, when one devotes himself to philosophical thinking. For there is deep-rooted awareness in us that in our acts of knowing, in our practical pursuits, briefly, in our whole life we are concerned with reality. It is not possible to describe knowledge without using the term "reality" or its equivalent. Moreover, we have the impression that the known reality exists independently of us. Whether we know reality or not, reality remains the same. In other words, the known exists independently of us. It is there,

---

[3]Cf. *Signes*, pp. 29 f.

[4]"L'autre extrémité invisible de l'axe qui nous fixes aux choses et aux idées." *Signes*, p. 29.

[5]"Le monde est inséparable du sujet, mais d'un sujet qui n'est rien que projet du monde, et le sujet est inséparable du monde, mais d'un monde qu'il projette lui-même. Le sujet est être-au-monde et le monde reste 'subjectif' puisque sa texture et ses articulations sont dessinées par le mouvement de transcendance du sujet." *Phénoménologie de la perception*, pp. 491-92.

whether we know it or not. Thus, knowledge is easily conceived as a kind of mirror-like image of objective reality.[6]

The realistic view presents itself even more obviously when knowledge is conceived as an immanent process. Living as we do in an extended world, we are inclined to localize everything. The vegetative processes of life take place "in" our blood; the circulation of the blood and the process of nutrition take place "within" the confines of our skin. Does not knowing likewise take place within us? But in that case we face the following situation: knowing is a process within us, whereas the known is outside us and exists independently of us. Combining these two ideas, we have to conclude that our knowledge is a reflexion of a reality existing outside us. Such knowledge, however, is not conceivable, unless we have in ourselves images of reality outside ourselves. Whence we arrive at the image theory, stating that man has in himself cognitive images of reality outside himself. Not only philosophy but also psychology speaks of such cognitive images; for instance, memory is often described as retaining and recalling images.

Rejection of Realism. Merleau-Ponty rejects the viewpoint of realism. In this he did not have to perform any trailblazing labor, for Hegel had already efficaciously dealt with this naive standpoint and, in addition, Sartre had already unmasked the "illusion of immanence."[7] For this reason Merleau-Ponty does not systematically attack realism, but rather assumes that it has been dealt the death blow. However, he argues against it, insofar as this realism continues to be the implicit philosophy of certain specialists in the sciences. Some of these conceive their field of inquiry as an objective reality which lies there before their eyes, and which they perceive with an objective glance. With respect to them Merleau-Ponty usually speaks of "objective thought." He sees as an example of this kind of thinking the way in which the "Gestalt"

---

[6]"Puisqu'un tableau nous fait penser à ce qu'il représente, on supposera, en se fondant sur le cas privilégié des appareils visuels, que les sens reçoivent des choses réelles de 'petits tableaux' qui excitent l'âme à percevoir. Les 'simulacres' épicuriens ou les 'espèces intentionelles' , 'toutes ces petites images voltigeantes par l'air' qui apportent dans le corps l'aspect sensible des choses, ne font que transposer en termes d'explication causale et d'opérations réelles la présence idéale de la chose au sujet percevant." *Structure du comportement,* p. 205.

[7]Sartre, *L'imaginaire, psychologie phénoménologique de l'imagination,* Paris, 1948, p. 15.

was originally understood. Merleau-Ponty attaches great value to this central concept of Gestalt psychology. Its proponents had discovered that the so-called "elemental psychology" was on the wrong track. Elemental psychology attempted to discover the fundamental elements of psychical life and reconstruct the whole from these elements, especially by means of the laws of association. But this attempt revealed itself to be impossible, for the simple reason that the whole is given to us before these so-called "elements." We experience first the whole, and from this whole we proceed, by means of analysis, to the elements. We then assume that these elements are prior and that they enable us to reconstruct the whole. Gestalt psychology, however, discovered that this cannot be done and, at the same time, managed to discover the fundamental law of the wholes appearing to us—namely, the law of the circular causality exercised among the parts. Every part influences every other part and, at the same time, in influenced by all the others. Therefore, in the whole all parts include one another and refer to one another. There is a unity of reciprocal implication.

Some Gestalt psychologists, says Merleau-Ponty, have made the mistake of understanding the Gestalt, the whole appearing to us, as an objective reality which would, independently of us, present itself to us from out of the world. In this way they still hold fast to objective thought, and fail to pay attention to the most fundamental and primordial compenetration of subject and world. Man and world imply each other. The subject is nothing else than project of a world, and the world is the living space of the subject. Man and world can be no more divorced from each other than a Gestalt can be dissolved into its elements. Merleau-Ponty makes even the remarkable statement that Gestalt psychology has to be made more profound and more radical through a Gestalt philosophy. What he means is that the holistic idea must be applied also to the most primordial compenetration, which is that of subject and world. He presents his own way of thinking as such a Gestalt philosophy.[8]

Subject as Project of the World. The subject is nothing but project of the world. In everything we are we refer to the world. We are a multiform question, but all aspects of this question are concerned with the world. The world, says Merleau-Ponty, penetrates into the very heart of human subjectivity. No matter how

_____

[8]*Sens et non-sens,* pp. 170-172.

far we penetrate into ourselves, we always find there the worldliness, the "taste of the world," which permeates our entire being.[9]

This worldiness, however, does not mean that we are part of the world in the sense of being one of the elements involved in a giant causal process. When we look at a piece of wood flung about by the waves of the sea, we may say that the wood has become part of a process in which it is totally immersed. But the same cannot be said of man, for man, no matter how deeply he is involved in the world, remains a subject for whom the world is. The relationship between man and world is not, as we have already said, causal but dialectic. This means that man, although he is interwoven with the world, nonetheless remains also a center for whom the world is there. Merleau-Ponty indicates this relationship by the terms "intentionality" and "openness."

For this reason we may not conceive human activities as immanent processes. Human existence runs its course in the world. The vegetative processes takes place within the limits of our skin, but the same does not apply to our intentional acts. Our body, says Merleau-Ponty, *is* there where something is to be done.[10] The boundaries between me and the world, drawn by objective thought, fall away for anyone who recognizes the true character of intentionality. My seeing and hearing do not take place within the limits of my skin but in the field of my existence, in the world. We have to give up the idea of localizing intentional events, and should become aware of the mystery of "openness" that we are. If we do so, all things which objective thought has placed at a distance from us approach us in a mysterious fashion :[11] we are in touch with the world, we are interwoven with the world. Realism is after all a crude way of philosophizing, which localizes intentional life and views intentional acts almost in a physical way. The most essential aspect of intentional existence, its openness, is misunderstood by such a philosophy. We may have difficulty in seeing and expressing all this because we are too much used to localizing thought. What Merleau-Ponty says about these matters presupposes that we are aware of this wonderful openness, this being-outside-himself which man is.

The Sense of Meaning. Accordingly, we are openness to the world, we are access to the world. The world, then, is open to us

---

[9]"Ce son fondamental du monde, déjà donné avec la moindre de nos perceptions." *Eloge de la philosophie,* p. 63.

[10]*Phénoménologie de lá perception,* p. 289.

[11]Cf. *Sens at non-sens,* p. 188.

because we are access to the world. For this reason self-experience and experience of the world cannot be separated. It is a contradiction to experience the world and, at the same time, to abstract from the access to the world which we ourselves are.[12] All this is contained in Merleau-Ponty's view that Gestalt psychology has to be continued in a Gestalt philosophy, that the primordial interconnection, within which all other connections exist, is the mutual implication of man and world. This primordial compenetration is the fundamental horizon within which all phenomena take place.

Accordingly, what Merleau-Ponty calls "meaning" is the appearing of the world within the openness which we are and because of this openness. Meaning, therefore, is always worldly and always human. Meaning is always worldly because we are openness to the world, we are what makes the world appear, we are the unveiling of the world. Meaning is also always human, because the appearance of the world is possible only from the viewpoint of the openness which we are. Why does Merleau-Ponty use the term *"sens,"* meaning? The reply is that the subject who is openness to the world enters the world as a question, so that the appearing world always has the character of a reply. The world always presents itself either as a reply to the question which we are and, consequently, as meaningful, or as a failure to reply and, consequently, as meaningless. It is wholly inconceivable that we would first know the things in themselves, pure objectivity, and that we would experience them as a reply only in the second place. At their very first appearance things already assume the character of a reply.

From this it follows that, according to Merleau-Ponty, the question which we are does not precede our entrance into the world. We do not, first, in a kind of interiority experience ourselves as a question and, then, go in search of a reply in the world. We are interwoven with the world, and for this reason we experience ourselves as a question precisely in the reply which we call the "world." We know the question in the answer. The visual field, for example, is the world-become-reply, but we cannot determine what it is to see by making abstraction from the visual field.

The formulas which we use here are always somewhat dangerous. For instance, when we speak of the "world-become-reply," one could

---

[12]"Elle [the analysis of time] fait apparaître le sujet et l'objet comme deux moments abstraits d'une structure unique qui est la *présence." Phénoménologie de la perception,* p. 492.

think that the world first appears to us in itself and then only becomes a reply. But such a conception would be wrong, for the world-for-us has at once the character of a reply. One could desire to know the world separately from its character as a reply. But such a desire is absurd. For it means that one wants to have access to the world, while destroying its accessibility. He would desire a world full of light without allowing any light to shine upon this world. For we ourselves are the light illuminating the world, because we are the unveiling of that world.[13]

Avoidance of Extreme Subjectivism. Many fear that Merleau-Ponty's standpoint contains extreme subjectivism. We know the world, so they say, only insofar as we make it reply to the question which we are and not as it is in itself. But such a view is plain subjectivism, particularism.

The reply is that the objection would hold if one first conceives man as a particular being, as a nature among natures, and then says that, in addition, the particular being which man is, from the standpoint of his particularity assigns a character to the world. In such a case it would be obvious that this character would be particular. Not without reason, however, does Merleau-Ponty deny a particular nature to man[14] and asserts that the characteristic feature of man is precisely that he is openness, that he makes the world appear, that he unveils the world. The statement that there is no other being than being-for-us leads to dangerous subjectivism only when we first lock ourselves up in a particular nature. But Merleau-Ponty does not do this. I am, he says, absolutely particular and absolutely universal.[15] By this statement he means that I am a body among bodies but that this "body-subject" is characterized precisely by universality, i.e., openness to everything, an openness which in principle is without limit.[16]

---

[13]Cf. *op. cit.*, pp. 494 f. Merleau-Ponty replies here to the oft-repeated objection that the world existed already before I was and will continue to be after my death. His answer is that I can say so only because of my unveiling presence in the world, which therefore always remains my field of existence.

[14]"En réalité nous n'imaginons pas, par une illusion rétrospective, une nécessité d'essence, nous constatons une connection d'existence." *Op. cit.*, p. 198. "L'homme est une idée historique et non pas une espèce naturelle." *Ibid.*, p. 199.

[15]*Sens et non-sens*, p. 188.

[16]With Heidegger, Merleau-Ponty calls our consciousness a "natural light," but he interprets "natural" in this way: even consciousness, light, openness, is a givenness and consequently facticity. Cf. *Phénoménologie de la perception*, p. 494.

The subjectivism which causes fears is the kind which connects the cognitive field with a particular being. If, however, we call the cognitive field "subjective" because it is connected with a being whose characteristic feature it is to be open to everything, then this "subjectivity" is not dangerous, it does not contain any limitation. It is difficult to see how anyone can deny such a subjectivity without contradicting himself, for he wants an accessible world without any form of access. Even though Merleau-Ponty affirms that the connection between man and world is unbreakable, he does not by that very fact close the door to the most divergent interpretations of human knowledge, and specifically, he does not say that man does not know the world itself. If it is characteristic of man to be openness, access to the world, the being-for-us of the world means that the world itself becomes manifest to the openness which we are. Merleau-Ponty repeatedly puts emphasis on the ineffable mystery that a body, i.e., a particular being, is openness to everything. Here lies the most profound reason why he denies a particular nature to man, for he conceives "nature" as something that would lock us up in particularity whereas man is precisely openness. The mystery of man is to be a body that is sensitive to what it is not. This "sensitivity" is, at the same time, absolutely particular and absolutely universal. "From the moment," writes Merleau-Ponty, "that I recognize my experience precisely as mine, that I open myself to what I am not, that I am *sensitive* to the world and the other human beings, all the beings which objective thought had placed at a distance approach me in a special way. Reversely, I acknowledge my relationship with them, I am nothing but a power to be an echo for them, to understand them, and to reply to them."[17]

Accordingly, for Merleau-Ponty meaning is not an ethereal, subjective phenomenon. The other, the world itself, becomes meaning for me, and therefore meaning is permeated with the solidity of reality. At the same time meaning is subjective because the other appears as a reply to my subjectivity, which enters the world as intentionality.

Meaning and Meaninglessness. Nevertheless, these remarks do not remove all difficulties. Significantly, the text just quoted is contained in a book entitled, *Sens et non-sens (Meaning and Meaninglessness)*. In the introduction to this work Merleau-Ponty writes: "There is not so much question of an intelligible world as of focal

---

[17]*Sens et non-sens,* p. 188

points of light, separated by shreds of darkness.[18] Both meaning and meaninglessness are present in what appears to us. Therefore, we may ask, Does not this distinction point again to man's particular character, so that we still have to admit that our world of meaning is subjective in the above-mentioned dangerous limiting sense? This objection is all the more urgent when we take into consideration that there are different levels of experience, and that we appear to transcend a mode of particularity on one level while remaining in this mode on a different level.[19]

There are many examples to illustrate the point. We are sensitive to temperature and, as such, open to the world. But a certain temperature is agreeable to us, another disagreeable, and there are also temperatures at which we are unable to live. From the standpoint of the body's sensitivity to temperature, we have here an example of the distinction between meaning and meaninglessness. The physicist, however, who studies the phenomenon of heat transcends this distinction, and the same is true of the technologist who works with high temperatures. A certain degree of light is agreeable to the eye, another is painful or torturous, and there is also a degree of light which destroys our power of sight. This distinction concerns us insofar as we see by means of the body, but not insofar as we think with our mind. Insofar as we have material wants, we live in a realm of scarcity because we are so numerous and therefore may come into conflict with one another as particular consumers of the world. In the intellectual life, however, all of us may, at the same time, fully possess the same light. Briefly, there are different realms of meaning, and our particularity manifests itself more in one realm of meaning than in another. In a higher sphere of meaning we transcend a particularity which belongs to the essence of the lower sphere.

What, then, does Merleau-Ponty mean when he says that "my experience, precisely as mine, opens me to what I am not"?[20] The term "experience" appears to be ambiguous. There is a level of experience on which man's openness is essentially partial, but there is also another level on which this partial character is transcended. Is it not necessary to distinguish these levels if we want to clarify our world

---

[18]*Op. cit.,* p. 9.

[19]Merleau-Ponty himself draws attention to, e.g., the partiality of sense experience: "La sensation ne peut être anonyme que parce qu'elle est partielle"; and "La vision est *une pensée assujetti à un certain champ* et c'est là ce qu'on appelle un *sens.*" *Phénoménologie de la perception,* pp. 250 and 251.

[20]*Sens et non-sens,* p. 188.

of meaning, and if we want to arrive at a judicious judgment concerning the subjectivity and objectivity of meaning?

Truth and Meaning. Merleau-Ponty does not deny the affirmative reply to this question. The above-quoted passage has a footnote, in which the author says: "This would be an obvious place for the accurate description of the transition from perceptive experience to explicit truth, as we find it on the level of language, concept and the cultural world. However, we hope to discuss this point in a special work devoted to the topic: the origin of truth."[21] This footnote was written after the publication of *Phénoménologie de la perception*, in which Merleau-Ponty sometimes speaks of language, concept and cultural world. The footnote shows his keen realization that the problem of truth, the problems of the different levels of meaning have not been sufficiently treated in his main work. Unfortunately, Merleau-Ponty has never published the book promised in his footnote. Thus, his work lacks an adequate analysis devoted to the different levels of meaning. He has given us a general description of meaning, but that striking mode of meaning which we call "truth," and which is *par excellence* meaning for the mind, has not received a sufficient analysis. True, in his main work he recognizes that truth is rooted in perceptive life, that the chiaroscuro of this origin always continues to be present in truth. Nevertheless, he admits that truth has characteristics of its own, which are distinct from "perceptive faith," but he has not presented us with an analysis of these characteristics.

In this respect, then, his work has remained incomplete. The "body-subject" has many levels of existence, and one of these levels is that of truth. Merleau-Ponty has never written the philosophy of this level. This is unfortunate, for according to the author himself, whenever a sentence is spoken the first words wait for their definitive meaning until the last ones have been said. The same rule applies to the chapters of a book and, of course, also to the main parts of a philosophical whole. Several important chapters of Merleau-Ponty's philosophy have not been written, and thus what he has written is still "waiting" for a definitive meaning. Because of the author's death at a relatively youthful age, his philosophical perspective will always have to remain incomplete.

---

[21]*Ibid.*, note 1.

2. The Criterion to Distinguish Meaning and Meaninglessness

The Subject is Not an Absolute Norm. Merleau-Ponty, as we have seen, makes a distinction between meaning and meaninglessness. This distinction seems to have the character of a value judgment. However, wherever a value judgment is made, the question of a norm arises. Where, then, does Merleau-Ponty find a norm to distinguish, within the field of the appearing world, between meaning and meaninglessness? At first blush, the reply does not seem too difficult. For all meaning is meaning for a subject, all meaning is meaning for man, and therefore man is the norm by which we distinguish meaning and meaninglessness.

This reply would be apodictic if for Merleau-Ponty man were an absolute point outside the field of meaning. The shoemaker who makes a pair of shoes for a particular customer finds a norm for his task outside his activities: the shoes will be good and meaningful if they fit the customer. But, according to Merleau-Ponty, man is not such an absolute point outside our realm of meaning.[22] For man belongs to the world, even though he is not there as a thing among things but as the subject around which the world is organized. Man is not outside the event called the "coming to be of meaning." Because meaning comes to be in the world, it comes to be also in life itself. Meaning does not arise in an abstract fashion, but germinates and develops in and through both the world and life, and these two aspects of its origin cannot be separated from each other. As we have seen, according to Merleau-Ponty, our life is temporality, self-gathering. Our life, too, can succeed or be a failure. Whence, we speak not only of the meaning of the world but also of that of life.

The World is Not an Absolute Norm. It would be wholly against the spirit of Merleau-Ponty's philosophy to seek, outside the movement toward meaning, an absolute point which would be able to function as a criterion of meaning and meaninglessness. Such a point cannot be found in the world. For he calls the stable part of the world "being," and precisely stability is broken by existence which takes "being" toward a future. Man is man precisely because he is

---

[22]"Faut-il même dire que le philosophe est humaniste? Non, si l'on entend par l'homme un principe explicatif qu'il s'agirait de substituer à d'autres. On n'explique rien par l'homme." *Eloge de la philosophie*, p. 61.

bored with what is already constituted.[23] Accordingly, to the extent that the world is human, it is permeated with movement. For this reason there is meaning in the world. The subject, likewise, does not offer a fixed point of reference, for the subject is temporality. The French term *"sens,"* says Merleau-Ponty, has two senses: it means both "meaning" and "direction." These two senses are connected, for meaning exists and arises always in the movement which we call temporality.[24]   Accordingly, the affirmation of a fixed point would be in direct contradiction with the fundamental principles of Merleau-Ponty.

The Question Which Man is, is Not an Absolute Norm. If, one could persist, there is no fixed point in life and in the world, insofar as they have the character of a reply, may we not find such a point at least in the question which we are? Is this question not capable of acting as a norm? The reply is again in the negative. For even the question which we are, is not an eternal reality but develops in the dialog with the world. Questioning man makes a project of the reply, but because of this reply the question itself assumes again a different form. Man always seeks light, but our search has assumed a different form from that which it had for primitive man. We need, for instance, food, but the food we need differs from that of primitive man.

The Distinction Between Meaning and Meaninglessness is Both Given and a Task. Accordingly, there is no fixed point that can function as an absolute norm either in the world, in ourselves, in the reply which we have projected, or in the question which we ourselves are.[25]   It follows, therefore, that we cannot make a distinction between meaning and meaninglessness which would have an everlasting value. We are a questioning existence, and therefore not everything has the same value; consequently, there is meaning and meaninglessness. However, this distinction is both a givenness and a task: it has to be constantly made again in a new way. What was meaningful yesterday may tomorrow again be meaningless. The distinction remains a task, even as our entire existence is a task.

---

[23]"Elle [philosophy] s'ennuie dans le constitué." *Eloge de la philosophie,* p. 79. Although this text speaks of philosophy, Merleau-Ponty points out a little later that in this matter philosophy is the expression of life itself.

[24]Cf. *Phénoménologie de la perception,* p. 492.

[25]"En morale comme en art, il n'y aurait pas de solution pour celui qui veut d'aboard assurer sa marche." *Sens et non-sens,* p. 9.

Accordingly, the situation is not such that we behold an eternal ideal, whose realization we try to bring about or rather approximate in actual life. Nothing exists for us except the developing field of meaning, to which we ourselves, as question and answer, as well as our world belong. In our groping and seeking we are not guided by an absolute light; therefore, there is no absolute and everlasting distinction between meaning and meaninglessness. We are unable to determine that something is always and permanently meaningful for every one.

Nevertheless, this inability does not mean that there is no distinction between meaning and meaninglessness. Such a conclusion would be warranted only if one were to posit that only an absolute distinction between these two is a true and ultimate distinction. But Merleau-Ponty denies this position. He admits a distinction, provided one is willing to be satisfied to view the field of meaning from the standpoint of the question which we are, provided, therefore, one places himself within the actual movement of life. Anyone who wants more will seek without finding what he wants. Such a search, however, is a sign that one wants something that is above man, that one pursues an illusion.

Thus, we see that those who claim that Merleau-Ponty is ultimately unable to make a distinction between meaning and meaninglessness, impose on this distinction a requirement which he himself, in principle, rejects in the name of man's temporality and self-becoming. The distinction in question is, for Merleau-Ponty, historical and not absolute.[26]

3. EXISTENCE AS CREATIVE OF MEANING

Philosophy and Praxis. We still have to indicate where, according to Merleau-Ponty, meaning originates and, consequently, where the distinction is made between meaning and meaninglessness. It would be better perhaps to use the term "distinguishing" rather than "distinction," for the former term can be understood in a dynamic fashion as indicating a temporal operation and not a timeless result. With Merleau-Ponty, we should distinguish especially two dimensions— namely, the dimension of real life and that of the reflective philosopher.

---

[26]"Quand donc je place hors de l'expérience progressive le fondement de la vérité ou de la moralité, ou bien je continue de m'en tenir aux probabilités qu'elle m'offre—seulement dévalorisées par l'idéal d'une connaissance absolue,— on bien je les déguise en certitudes absolues, et alors je lâche le vérifiable pour la vérité, c'est-à-dire la proie pour l'ombre." *Op. cit.,* p. 190.

Meaning comes into being in real life, there where work is done, where human beings live together, find access to one another, in the market place, in politics. Arts and sciences likewise are part of real life, for they contribute to the rise of light and meaning. Merleau-Ponty uses the term "praxis" to indicate the real life in which meaning comes into being. This term has a wider meaning for him than that of the anglicized form "practice." "Praxis" means the movement of human existence as creative of meaning, the creation of meaning in the dialog with the world. Praxis is, of course, extremely manifold, for the laborer, the man of exact science, the technologist, the politician, and the artist do not create meaning in the same way. Nevertheless, all of them, in one way or another, contribute to the rise of meaning.

Merleau-Ponty makes a distinction between philosophy and praxis. This distinction should not be conceived as if the philosopher lives in another dimension, another universe. Merleau-Ponty does not follow the view of Plato, according to which the ordinary man lives in the realm of variable shadows, while the philosopher dwells in the realm of the absolute and the necessary. The realm of thought proper to philosophy coincides with the realm of ordinary existence. However, the philosopher assumes a different attitude with respect to this realm of ordinary existence. He looks at it from a distance. He assumes a reflective attitude and attempts to discern and express the fundamental lines of this realm of existence.[27]

Philosophy as "Action at a Distance." Does philosophy make a contribution to the rise of meaning? Sometimes Merleau-Ponty calls philosophy "action at a distance."[28] At one time Merleau-Ponty was attracted by Marx' ideal of destroying philosophy to attain philosophy. Marx wanted to destroy the philosophy which lives in a sphere of its own and desired to have a philosophy which enlightens praxis and, as such, is able to contribute to life. Life, says Marx, is characterized by estrangement. The philosopher desires harmony and order. Not finding them in a world torn apart, he constructs his own world of ideas in which everything is in order—witness the great German systems of philosophy. However, such structures are meaningless, for order has to be established there where disorder is. The philosopher, then, should think about real life and contribute to

---

[27]A large part of *Eloge de la philosophie* is dedicated to an analysis of the philosophical attitude.

[28]*Signes,* p. 20.

the overcoming of its actual estrangements. Attracted at first by this ideal, Merleau-Ponty pleaded for the unity of philosophy and praxis.[29]

Gradually, however, Merleau-Ponty began to see the wholly proper way in which the philosopher views praxis—namely, in a non-practical manner. Praxis is always permeated with men's concrete aims, their contrasts and interests. Praxis always has a tactical character, for man tends to that which here and now is desirable or attainable for this or that particular group. Praxis is also influenced by the individuals' interests. If one completely mixes philosophy and praxis, they interchange not so much their virtues as their vices.[30] Praxis then borrows from philosophy weighty motives which go far beyond what they motivate, and philosophy becomes tainted by the too particular aims of praxis. In this way, praxis is given a chance to conceal its true intentions under philosophical motives. By means of philosophical motives, for example, Marxism is able to present its concrete aims as an absolute demand of history. As a result, philosophy loses its aloofness and its purifying action. Mixing philosophy and politics means that one ends up with bad politics as well as bad philosophy.

Philosophy retains its proper character when it keeps in mind that it is reflective and therefore has to remain "at a distance" from praxis. This requirement implies that its mode of thinking is ineffective. The politics of philosophers are politics which no one ever executes.[31] Truth becomes effective only when it is expressed after the manner of politics,[32] but the philosopher may not speak in this way. By sacrificing its distance, philosophy is able to become effective, but in doing so it loses its philosophical character.

The Proper Meaning of Philosophical Thinking. What, then, we may ask, is the proper meaning of philosophy? The reply is that philosophy makes us adopt a position in a human way in the coming to be of meaning. For man is not a being which may cling

---

[29]However, Merleau-Ponty has never advocated such an intimate connection between philosophy and praxis as Marxism wants.

[30]"Au lieu d'unir leur vertus, philosophie et politique échangeraient dès lors leur vices: on aurait une pratique rusée et une pensée superstitieuse." *Signes,* p. 11.

[31]"La politique des philosophes, c'est celle que personne ne *fait.*" *Signes,* p. 10.

[32]Concerning political speech Merleau-Ponty says: "Ce langage qui dit sans dire, qui touche en chacun les ressorts de la colère et de l'espoir,—et qui ne sera jamais la prose du vrai." *Signes,* p. 10.

"with a massive and bodily yes"[33] to what is already constituted, to certain forms of meaning. Man is a movement which constantly again transcends itself. If he sacrifices his distance, he really sacrifices his humanity. The distance in question is what the philosopher experiences and promotes more than all others. In this way, therefore, he contributes to a human mode of in-being. We could describe philosophy as a very striking way of practicing our being-man. Nevertheless, it lies outside the line of Merleau-Ponty's thought to expect a crucial contribution from philosophy to praxis. Marx' greatness consisted in this that he placed himself at a distance from the then current capitalistic praxis and from this distance revealed both its meaning and meaninglessness. At present, however, Marxist philosophy has become an instrument of politics in countries in which Marxism has become the established system. This situation contains a great danger, for it exposes Marxism to the fate of ceasing to be a genuine philosophy.

Accordingly, philosophy remains meaningful because of its distance from praxis, even though it has to sacrifice effectiveness in the process. As we have pointed out, in this question there is a certain development in the thinking of Merleau-Ponty. At first he tended to posit a more intimate bond between philosophy and praxis, but later he realized that it is of essential importance for both to maintain their distance.

The Intersubjective Character of the Birth of Meaning. Meanwhile it remains true that, according to Merleau-Ponty, the birth of meaning takes place in real life, and that the field of thought proper to philosophy materially coincides with that of praxis. Philosophy is a reflection on the field of real existence. For this reason Merleau-Ponty shows a lively interest in numerous aspects of real life. He has written articles about the novel,[34] painting,[35] the film.[36] The examples he quotes from literature and the way in which he elaborates them, show that he is well-read. He is well-informed about the way in which the sciences, especially those of man, develop. He follows politics closely and did not fail to make his voice heard on the occasion of important political events.[37] For this reason his phi-

---

[33]*Eloge de la philosophie*, p. 81.
[34]"Le roman et la métaphysique," *Sens et non-sens*, pp. 51-81.
[35]"Le doute de Cézanne," *ibid.*, pp. 15-45.
[36]"Le cinéma et la nouvelle psychologie," *ibid.*, pp. 97-122.
[37]A number of articles about the political situation and actual political events have been bundled together under the title *Propos* in *Signes*, pp. 308-435.

losophy impresses the reader as "true to life" and has drawn the attention also of many who are not professional philosophers. When, after the war, he attended an international congress of philosophers and was asked to write a brief report about it, he expressed his surprise to see that Karl Jaspers made the impression of being a withdrawn intellectual. How can such a person, he asked himself, reflect philosophically on real life? The philosopher has to give expression to life and, consequently, has to know life from his own experience.

At the same time, however, Merleau-Ponty's philosophy shows that he knew how to place himself at a distance from real life. In this respect also he fulfils the requirements which he himself makes. No matter how numerous and divergent the topics about which he writes, he never popularizes. He does not allow himself to be carried away by emotions and passions, not even when he describes actual events that generate widespread and deep feelings, such as, the conquest of Budapest by the Russian army.[38] Even here Merleau-Ponty remains the reflecting philosopher who gazes from a distance at the birth of meaning or meaninglessness.

The birth of meaning is not an individual but a social event. The meaning in which we exist did not begin with our own life, but we have entered into a movement of meaning which had started long before us. In other words, the growth of meaning belongs to intersubjective history. To throw more light on this movement of meaning we must now reflect on history.

CHAPTER FIVE

SUBJECT AND HISTORY

1. PHILOSOPHY OF HISTORY AND OF INTERSUBJECTIVITY

"Just as space," says Merleau-Ponty, "does not consist of isolated and simultaneous points, just as our duration cannot break loose from its connection with a common dimension in which it runs its course, so likewise is it impossible for the world in which we have dealings with one another, to be dissolved into a plurality of conscious beings existing merely alongside one another."[1] Merleau-Ponty's philosophy of history cannot be divorced from his philosophy of intersubjectivity.

Sartre and Merleau-Ponty. In this respect there is a radical difference between the philosophy of Merleau-Ponty and the perspective opened by Jean-Paul Sartre in his *Critique de la raison dialectique.* Sartre claims that the individual existence can be understood in itself, and that this individual existence is the "constituent reason" of history. He calls individual existence the totalization of the world, for, from its absolute freedom, this existence transforms the world into a field of existence of which it itself is the center, thus making the world "a whole." History is the "totalization of totalizations," i.e., men unite into a group and make the world their common field of existence. History, however, is "constituted reason," and this reason has to be understood from the standpoint of the individual existence, for this existence is the "constituting reason." By means of these involved formulas, Sartre wants to say that absolute light is to be found in the individual existence and that the common development of mankind has to be understood from the standpoint of the individual existence.[2]

By saying that there is a radical difference between Merleau-Ponty and Sartre, we do not want to assert that Merleau-Ponty's view is diametrically opposed to that of Sartre, and that he conceives individual existence as a blind result of a common development. For, how could the common development be illuminating if all the persons involved in it are blind? In this point also Merleau-Ponty remains faithful to his Gestalt form of thinking, to circular causality and the

---

[1]*Signes*, pp. 27 f.
[2]Concerning this book of Sartre, see our article, "Het Marxisme van Sartre," *Tijdschrift v. Philosophie,* vol. 22 (1960), pp. 617-676.

unity of reciprocal implication. The common development has to be understood from the standpoint of the person, and personal existence likewise has to be understood from the standpoint of the common development.

History is to be Understood from the Standpoint of Man. There would be no history if the human person were not a "movement of transcendence,"[3] a constantly self-transcending movement. Man is characterized by this that he does not cling to anything with a "massive and bodily yes," but is bored by that which is already constituted. The "body-subject" is a dialog with the world, and meaning originates within this dialog. Constituted meaning Merleau-Ponty calls "being," but existence is characterized by this that it always again transcends "being."[4]

For this reason the philosophical attitude, as described by Merleau-Ponty, is *par excellence* the embodiment of our humanity. He expresses his view about this attitude in the portrait he paints of Socrates.[5] Socrates is accused of undermining the religion and customs of Athens, of substituting new gods for the old and therefore of being guilty of treason. However, says Merleau-Ponty, this accusation is based on a fundamental misunderstanding. Socrates does not reject the gods and customs of the city but only refuses to make them absolutes. The city demands an unqualified recognition, and it is this which Socrates is unable to give. He looks, as it were, through everything and sees its relativity. While he is willing to accept everything, he cannot go beyond accepting it as a provisional value which may be overtaken by history. He understands the gods and customs and therefore sees their true, i.e., provisional, value. He wants to retain the same as his judges but in a better way. He reverses the roles, becoming the judge and making them the accused. He points out to them how they should see and accept the "city's gods" and how they should understand their common meaning.

This, however, is more than the judges are willing to grant. They do not object to revolutionaries, for everyone feels that there is something wrong with the city and, accordingly, it is in harmony with accepted customs that a few people be permitted to say so explicitly. Once the evil has been pointed out, so they think, life can undis-

---

[3]"Nous appellerons transcendance ce mouvement par lequel l'existence reprend à son compte et transforme une situation de fait." *Phénoménologie de la perception*, p. 197.
[4]"La parole est l'exès de notre existence sur l'être naturel." *Op. cit.*, p. 229.
[5]*Eloge de la philosophie*, pp. 48-57.

turbedly continue to run its appointed course. Socrates, however, places himself at a distance from everything and thus eliminates every unqualified affirmation of values. He does not know more than his judges, but he knows that there is no absolute truth and for this reason he is open to the proper truth of everything.[6] Socrates unmasks the pseudo-knowledge of his judges, and this is more than they can stand.

Such is the picture presented by the philosopher: he is someone who goes against every unqualified affirmation of truth and values; he does not exclude the affirmation, but his affirmation is such that he remains at a distance; he is unable to surrender unqualifiedly to anything whatsoever.

It was not our intention here to describe philosophy again, for this question has been considered in the preceding chapter. The reason why the description is given here lies in this that Merleau-Ponty's description touches the fundamental characteristic which makes man an historical being. "Man," says Merleau-Ponty," is wholly distinct from the various kinds of animals by this that he is not endowed with any original equipment and that he is a center of ambiguity."[7] Unlike the animal, man does not enter the world with fixed "equipment" adapted to a fixed world, but has to situate himself and to equip himself for his own existence. He projects his own situation. It is precisely in this that he differs from other beings. Thus, he surrenders his humanity when he surrenders fully to what is already constituted. For this reason Merleau-Ponty rejects also the Marxist dream of the future, for the end of history is something that is wholly inconceivable for him.[8] From this it follows that the Greco-Christian idea of an ultimate end of life to be reached either here or hereafter, cannot be reconciled with Merleau-Ponty's philosophy. Those who admit such an end conceive its attainment as the realization of man's possibilities. For Merleau-Ponty, however, it would mean the destruction of man.

From all this it should be clear that according to Merleau-Ponty history has to be understood from the standpoint of man. But this statement does not express his perspective fully, for, at the same time,

---

[6]"Il n'en sait pas *plus* qu'eux, il sait seulement qu'il n'y a pas de savoir absolu et que c'est par cette lacune que nous sommes ouverts à la vérité." *Eloge de la philosophie,* p. 55.

[7]*Signes,* p. 304.

[8]"C'est l'hypothèse d'une conscience sans avenir et d'une fin de l'histoire qui est pour nous irreprésentable." *Humanisme et terreur,* p. 99.

the individual has to be understood from the standpoint of, and within the common history of mankind.

The Individual is to be Understood from the Standpoint of the Common History. The reason why this is so lies in this that, although man is a self-transcending movement, he is nonetheless a movement which presupposes a situation. Man is not an absolute starting point. He situates himself starting from a situation in which he finds himself, and this initial situation is the result of a common history. Note that we may speak of an "initial situation" not unqualifiedly but only in relationship to the individual human being, to his personal course of life. For it is characteristic also of man that he can begin to exist in a situation which was projected before him and which he makes his own. "The whole of the beings known as 'men,' defined by the familiar physical characteristics, also possesses a natural light, an openness to being, which render the acquisitions of culture communicable to all of them and to them alone."[9] This text is very illuminating. Human beings are characterized by common physical properties, which is true also of animals. What is proper to human beings, however, and to them alone is that they possess an openness, a light enabling them to pass on their cultural achievements. Without this light no such thing as history would be conceivable. Because of this light, man is able to make his own a situation which his predecessors have created.

An example may serve to illustrate this point. When a child is born, says Merleau-Ponty, everything in the home receives a new meaning and a new destiny, for it begins to exist for the child. Everything waits, as it were, for the new giving of meaning, which will arise from the child's conduct.[10] The child gradually becomes acquainted with this situation. We may not yet speak here of a personal appropriation, as if the child made the situation its own in a personal and conscious way. The "body-subject" is an "assembly of the world" (*montage du monde*), i.e., a possibility to appropriate the world, not only the physical world but also the cultural world. The "body-subject" learns to use the common world and in this way makes the meaning of the common things its own. It appropriates this meaning without knowing it consciously. This is true not only in the realm of practognosis, i.e., the realm in which we become familiar with things through our bodily behavior, but applies also to

[9]*Signes,* p. 304.
[10]*Phénoménologie de la perception,* p. 466.

the learning of speech.[11] We enter, as it were, into common speech. We speak without fully knowing what we say. We enter into a world in which things have become strikingly illuminating, because they have a name, because they have been spoken about. We begin to live in this light, so that we appropriate this light while, nonetheless, it continues to transcend us on all sides. Speech and praxis contain a common glow of light, rendering the world accessible. We enter into this light, into this accessible world. This light and this world are for us something "obvious." It is just as "obvious" for us that the world is spoken of as that it is spatial. We do not experience a distinction between the natural and the cultural world, because these two are not given to us separately. The natural world is given to us in the cultural world, even as the canvas is given in the painting.[12]. The common world becomes our situation, and within this situation we give form and shape to our own existence.

Thus it is evident that we do not begin to exist from zero. For we begin to act in a world in which things have already been made suitable for our action, and we begin to speak in and about a world in which things have already a name. We find ourselves in an "already-constituted" situation, and enter this situation without re-experiencing the history of its constitution. It is wholly impossible for us to eliminate all cultural "obviousness," for we can eliminate the one only by basing ourselves on the other.

Personal Attitude and Facticity. The objection could be raised that Merleau-Ponty seems to contradict himself here. In the portrait he paints of Socrates to express the philosophical attitude and the fundamental characteristic of being-man implied in it, he seems to demand that we abandon everything obvious. Here, however, he seems to imply that obviousness has to be accepted. In reply we may say that the contradiction in question is only apparent. For, in the one case Merleau-Ponty says that we find natural and cultural obviousness as a facticity from which it is impossible for us to escape, and in the other case he denies that we may accept this facticity as an absolute value. The facticity is obvious as givenness, but not as an absolute value that cannot be overcome.

Merleau-Ponty uses in this connection the peculiar term "the flesh of history."[13] The term refers to the facticity in which we

---

[11]"La puissance qu'a le langage de faire exister l'exprimé, d'ouvrir des routes, de nouvelles dimensions, de nouveaux paysages à la pensée, est, en dernière alalyse, aussi obscure pour l'adulte que pour l'enfant." *Op. cit.*, p. 460.

[12]*Op. cit.*, p. 339.

have entered and is intended to convey that this facticity has its own density. It resists, he says, analysis. Facticity cannot be separated from our own attitude because it exists for us only by virtue of being appropriated by us. Nevertheless, this facticity cannot be deduced from our personal attitude, for a personal attitude can arise and exist only by virtue of our entrance into this facticity. For instance, I can say something only when I know something, but I always say more than I know, for I can speak only by appropriating "obvious" meanings which I have neither personally made nor personally reflected upon. If I had to reflect personally upon everything, I would have to make myself an absolute beginning, and this is wholly impossible. Husserl pursued a will of the wisp when he aimed at an absolute intelligibility which, according to Merleau-Ponty, is absolutely impossible. Husserl wanted an absolute evidence on which everything would have to be based, but, according to Merleau-Ponty, facticity and evidence cannot be separated from each other because every evidence arises within facticity and because of facticity.

We find here again the same perspective which we encountered when we spoke of the "body-subject." The "body-subject" is neither a mere thing nor pure consciousness, but a unity which overcomes dualism. The same applies to history, the field of historical meaning. This field also is neither wholly impersonal nor wholly personal. It is not entirely without consciousness, yet it is not fully permeated with consciousness. We may even say that, within the field of historical meaning, nothing is fully conscious and that nothing also wholly escapes consciousness. Nothing is fully brought to light, for when we bring something to light, we rely on acquired ideas which we use without bringing them also to light.[14] Nothing is wholly thing-like, for something begins to exist for us because we integrate it into our existence. As everywhere else, so here also Merleau-Ponty rejects the "either or," his philosophy is a philosophy of "both and," a philosophy of ambiguity.

2. THE MEANING OF HISTORY

Personal Existence and Common Situation. The so-called "meaning of history" should be viewed in the light of the same perspective. One could feel inclined to make a distinction between the meaning

[13]*Signes*, p. 128.
[14]"Ainsi les choses se *trouvent dites* et se *trouvent pensées* comme par une Parole et un Penser que nous n'avons pas, qui nous ont." *Signes*, p. 27.

of individual existence and that of the common development. Such a distinction, however, is not in accord with Merleau-Ponty's philosophy.[15] I give meaning to my personal existence only by taking up the common situation and giving it greater development. The common situation, on the other hand, develops because it is taken up by the individual persons. These two aspects cannot be separated. One may say at the same time that the persons make history and that the common situation develops. Here, too, there is no room for an "either or."

Let us consider, with Merleau-Ponty, the example of science. If someone is a genius, one who really makes science advance, no one can deny his personal initiative, his personal function. However, he is able to fulfill this function only because he has first appropriated to himself the common situation existing in this realm. He makes progress because he develops the common situation, that which had already been said about the world, according to the inner logic present in it. One could say that he makes thought advance, but also that thought assumes a form in him. He causes history to advance; however, it is also true that history runs its course in him. For he has the feeling that he merely has said what he had to say, what was imposed on him by the inner logic of the scientific perspective. At a certain moment a particular viewpoint is, as it were, "in the air," so that it may happen that different people in different places independently arrive at the same idea.

The "Flesh of History." Accordingly, so far as the meaning of history is concerned, there is a development which, although it does not remain foreign to the individual nonetheless exceeds him on all sides.[16] This development is neither fully thing-like nor fully personal—Descartes' famous dichotomy is utterly insufficient to express this reality. To indicate this reality, Merleau-Ponty uses the peculiar term "the flesh of history."[17]

---

[15]"Le monde communicatif n'est un faisceau de consciences parallèles. Les traces se brouillent et passent l'une dans l'autre, elles font un seul sillages de 'durée publique'." *Signes,* p. 28.

[16]"Partout il y a sens, dimensions, figures par-delà ce que chaque 'conscience' aurait pu produire, et ce sont pourtant des hommes qui parlent, pensent, voient. Nous sommes dans le champs de l'histoire comme dans le champ du langage ou de l'être." *Signes,* p. 28.

[17]*Signes,* p. 28. For this reason an all-revealing ultimate analysis is in principle excluded: "Il n'y a pas d'analyse qui soit dernière, parce qu'il y a une chair de l'histoire, qu'en elle comme dans notre corps, tout porte, tout compte." *Ibid.*

By drawing attention to this Cartesian insufficiency, Merleau-Ponty is able also to come to a critique of Marxism. The great merit of Marx consisted in this that he saw the supra-personal development of the meaning of history. He realized that by virtue of a kind of inner logic history is going somewhere. In his form of thinking, however, Marx was still too much dominated by Cartesian dualism. As a result, when he saw that the development of the meaning of history went beyond the individual person, he sometimes had recourse to thing-like ideas. These ideas did not fit in with the perspective discovered by Marx, but this philosopher was unable to keep his thinking constantly in line with the perspective which he had discovered.

As we have seen, Merleau-Ponty describes the body as *"existence figée,"* as existence immersed in materiality. The individual person increases, as it were, his bodily being by fostering skills, by cultivating habits. It should be kept in mind here that Merleau-Ponty speaks of "body" and "soul" on different levels: the body is here that which has already been acquired, and the soul is the new meaning arising from the fact that the person orients his "acquisitions" toward a new future. By developing his bodily being, what he has acquired, the individual person orients his existence in a certain direction. We could say that by doing so he commits his own freedom. Although it is always possible for him to go in a new direction, it is normal that he continues in the direction he has taken. In a similar way we could say that human beings, in their co-existence, develop a common bodily being, consisting, e.g., of their common economic life, their forms of social behavior, their language, literature, juridical forms, villages, cities, forms of art, and so on. This common bodily being is the "flesh of history." Through it, co-existence is, of course, oriented in a certain direction. Here, too, meaning and direction coincide. Because of this common orientation, history is always something whose course appears logical. Here also the rule applies that not everything can give rise to everything.[18]

Contingency of History. Here also man remains "the place of contingency." There are many reasons for this. First of all, there

---

[18]"L'histoire n'a un sens que s'il y a comme une logique de la coëxistence humaine, qui ne rend impossible aucune aventure, mais qui du moins, comme par une sélection naturelle, élimine à la longue celles qui font diversion par rapport aux exigences permanentes des hommes." *Humanisme et terreur,* p. 166. We may add that Merleau-Ponty agrees here more with the Marxist line of thought, even in his terminology, than he does in later works. We will consider this point more in detail in the chapter dedicated to the relationship of Merleau-Ponty to Marxism.

can be no question of an absolute meaning, an absolute goal, for, as we have seen in the preceding chapter, Merleau-Ponty rejects all absolute meanings and all absolute goals. Thus, there is likewise no absolute ideal,[19] which could be used as a norm governing the growth of the meaning of history. Secondly, there can be no question of any absolute necessity.[20] Of course, Merleau-Ponty rejects absolute freedom, for his philosophy is a philosophy of ambiguity. Something, then, is to be expected. He points out that the King of France and the Tsar of Russia expressed themselves in more or less the same way when, at the outbreak of the revolution, they lost their position and found their lives in danger. It is to be expected that human beings in the same circumstances will act in a similar fashion. We may even speak about an interpretation of the course of history and we may be able to suspect what the future will be. At a certain moment it may even become almost impossible that the course of history will take any other turn than the one which it actually takes. Nevertheless, there is never any absolute necessity, something like the "Greek miracle" is always possible,[21] and it may also come to pass that an obstacle, unforeseen by anyone, will threaten the course in which the common meaning develops. Thirdly, we should not forget that at a given moment a strong personality may profoundly interfere in the common course of life. Thus, history continues to have a character of contingency. One who wants to find an absolute meaning of history will either give absolute weight to a relative form of existence and thus atrophy history or reject the entire realm of human existence as purely relative, so that he loses interest in the development of historical meaning.

Human beings, however, are likely to foster illusions. The saints of Christendom believe in a supernatural guidance and think that the future is determined in the stars, i.e., in the plans of divine Providence. The heroes of the proletarian revolution thought that they fought for a future which was predetermined in reality, i.e., in Marx' infrastructure. If, however, we abstract from this illusion and look at what they have actually done, it appears that all of them have attempted to give coherence to the confusing story of events.[22] For this reason

---

[19]"Si l'on sait où l'histoire va inéluctablement, les événements un à un n'ont plus d'importance ni de sens." *Eloge de la philosophie,* p. 71.

[20]"L'histoire n'a pas de sens si son sens est compris comme celui d'une rivière qui coule sous l'action de causes toutes-puissantes vers un océan où elle disparaît." *Op. cit.,* p. 71.

[21]*Signes,* p. 304. The "Greek miracle" in question is the unexpected and marvelous rise of greek culture in its classical period.

[22]Cf. *Sens et non-sens,* p. 380.

Merleau-Ponty does not want to choose between optimism and pessimism. There is no guarantee that the course of common life will always give rise to the good, and, likewise, there is no fatal force at work in history which makes everything end in failure. In opposition to optimism and pessimism, Merleau-Ponty posits radical contingency. There are promises as well as threats. Ultimately, however, there is only one hope—namely, man,[23] as always self-transcending movement. He is the everlasting soil from which meaning springs in both the individual and the common aspects of the course of life.

The Converging Movement of History. Sometimes Merleau-Ponty speaks about the "converging movement" of history.[24] What he means by this term is the following. Like individual existence, so also common existence has many aspects. Mankind moves forward in economic and social life, in the sphere of law, in art and science, in politics and in the religious forms of life. Even as in individual existence everything is connected with everything, so also in the movement of common life.[25] The entire "flesh of history" is the existential field of the same mankind. Thus, it is to be expected that there are corresponding lines in the aspects of the development of common meaning.[26] The social groups, for instance, are not unrelated to the economic development. And because the same human existence expresses itself in philosophy and art, it is to be expected that one and the same awareness will make itself felt in both realms. In the sciences also there are always fundamental concepts which are not thematized by these sciences themselves; it would be surprising if these fundamental concepts would be unrelated to the philosophical forms of thinking. A city, likewise, has a unique sphere, to which one who knows this city well is sensitive and which, nonetheless, can hardly be expressed in concepts. Everything pertaining to Paris

---

[23]"Le héros des contemporains, ce n'est pas Lucifer, ce n'est pas même Prométhée, c'est l'homme." *Op. cit.,* p. 180.

[24]"De même il fait voir que l'habitude de distinguer les questions (économiques, politiques, philosophiques, réligieuses, etc.) comme le principe de la division des pouvoirs masque leur *rapport* dans l'histoire vivante, leur *convergence,* leur *signification commune.*" *Humanisme et terreur,* p. 133. Italics ours.

[25]"Dans la coëxistence des hommes, à laquelle ces années nous ont éveillé, les morales, les doctrines, les pensées et les coutumes, les lois, les travaux, les paroles s'expriment les uns les autres, tout signifie tout. Il n'y a rien hors cette unique fulguration de l'existence." *Sens et non-sens,* p. 309.

[26]"Si donc la philosophie et le cinéma sont d'accord, si la réflexion et le travail technique vont dans le même sens, c'est parce que le philosophe et le cinéaste ont en commun une certaine manière d'être, une certaine vue du monde qui est celle d'une génération." *Op. cit.,* pp. 121 f.

is permeated with the fundamental sphere of this city, and one who knows and loves Paris recognizes this sphere immediately. In a similar way there is a certain fundamental sphere in a period of history, and here, too, everything refers to everything. When Merleau-Ponty speaks of the "convergent movement" of history, he refers to these fundamental lines which can be discerned in all aspects of the development of a historical period.

Concreate Examples. In many essays Merleau-Ponty has endeavored to reveal this convergent movement in a more concrete fashion. He shows, for instance, that there is an agreement between the way Cézanne paints and the way the philosopher—meaning Merleau-Ponty himself—describes perception. Cézanne does not paint his apple as "finished things." The lines of the apples are not enclosures of a surface but dimensions of the apples themselves fleeing into depth. In this way Cézanne manages to make the unseen visible from the seen. His painting does not refer to something else but presents reality as our perception presents it. "Cézanne's investigations of perspective, by remaining faithful to the phenomena, discover what the psychology of our time should formulate."[27]

Merleau-Ponty has written also an interesting article concerning the connection between film and contemporary psychology. The film makes an event present. It does not do so by imitating as closely as possible a so-called "objective" event. For it wants to make what is happening present to the viewer and, for this reason, has, as it were, to make the viewer play a role in constituting the meaning of the event. The film presents an event completely when the viewer understands it. It makes the viewer see someone's thoughts in his behavior, and does not present a special analysis of these thoughts. The visual aspect and the sound aspect are one in a good film.[28] Everything refers to everything in such a film, everything includes everything. The director and the spectator, the idea and the behavior, the picture and the sound, all refer to one another. The unity of reciprocal implication, discovered by the psychologist and thematized by the philosopher, is shown by the film.

In a similar fashion, the ideas of a given period are pictured by the novelist. The novelist does not picture these ideas by describing

---

[27] *Op. cit.,* p. 25.
[28] "Un film sonore n'est pas un film muet agrémenté de sons et de paroles qui ne seraient destinés qu'à compléter l'illusion cinématographique." *Op. cit.,* p. 113.

them reflectively, but he brings these ideas to life in speaking and acting persons. It often happens that novelists, when they attempt to express their ideas in concepts, fail to do so convincingly. However, such an attempt is not what is expected of a novelist.[29]

Philosophy, says Merleau-Ponty, becomes aware of the fundamental contingency of meaning. But the same realization occurs in political life. When a country is dominated by a certain ideology, there arises the remarkable phenomenon of the "fifth column."[30] This means that in its bosom there are people who adhere to the ideology of the enemy. For this reason the country's ideology has to be protected by a secret police. Such a situation would not be possible if there were no uncertainty about the controlling ideology. Accordingly, the awareness of contingency manifests itself in philosophy of science, which emphasizes that science makes progress by stating hypotheses rather than formulating external laws. The same ambiguity exists in both political life and the life of science. Thus, politics also provides us with a new example of history's convergent movement.

3. The Unity of History

The Insufficiency of Historical Materialism. The fact that there is a convergent movement in history means that history has unity. How, we may ask, must this unity be explained? Historical materialism presents a facile solution. It teaches that one of the factors at work in history is deterministic—history is determined by the evolution of productive means.

As should be evident from the preceding pages, Merleau-Ponty cannot be satisfied with this reply. For, if this idea is applied with rigorous logic, it implies that the existential level is reduced to the thing-like. A determining factor operating of necessity has the character of a cause and, consequently, reduces man to the sphere of the thing-like. Thus, the subject, in the proper sense, which situates itself in history and in the world disappears from the scene. While Merleau-Ponty is willing to attribute an important role to economics, he does not want to describe its function as causal. Economics is not a thing but a factor of human existence. Economics is man, as dealing with the world and developing on the economic level. For this reason the economic aspect operates as a motive,

---

[29]*Op. cit.*, pp. 51-53.
[30]*Signes*, p. 300.

perhaps, even as a dominating motive, but not as a cause. Moreover, although man exists in the economic realm, he is not solely economic but exists also in all other factors contributing to the course of history.

Intersubjectivity and the Unity of History. Accordingly, the unity of history, its converging movement, does not originate from the determining influence of a single material component of history but from the subject which seeks its way in everything. However, the unifying subject may not be understood as an absolute point outside the "flesh of history." By thinking along this line, we would arrive at Sartre's theory of absolute freedom, which Merleau-Ponty rejects just as much as the idea of historical determinism. Just as the subject cannot be divorced from the body but exists in it, as subject-body, so the human subject cannot be separated from the material components of history. Moreover, as we have seen, history is intersubjective and has the character of a development of common life. Thus it is the subject, as having reached intersubjectivity, which constitutes the unity of history. Even as the subject in his bodily existence tries to become himself, so also do human beings in the "flesh of history" endeavor to find one another. The converging movement of history is the road to intersubjectivity. This intersubjectivity is not an *a priori* which precedes history but comes to be in history.

For this reason Merleau-Ponty seems to posit a kind of norm by which the actual course of events can be evaluated—namely, the recognition of man by man, the realization of intersubjectivity.[31] However, one would be seriously mistaken if he were to think here of a goal, an extrinsic ideal, whose guiding light would be outside the course of events. Within the sphere of individual existence Merleau-Ponty does not accept any extrinsic ideal enlightening the life of the individual. Man tends to humanity, but what humanity means becomes clear only gradually in the concrete course of life. In a similar way, intersubjectivity, the recognition of man by man, is not an absolute and extrinsic ideal, but the inner meaning of history. Intersubjectivity is not an absolute idea, innate in us or formed *a priori*. It is a possibility which presents itself in the actual development of history, it is a demand which it to be understood

---

[31]"Les philosophes d'aujourd'hui ne renoncent pas à la rationalité, à l'accord de soi avec soi et avec autrui." *Humanisme et terreur,* p. 204. "Qu'on maintienne et multiplie les rapports de l'homme à l'homme." *Ibid.,* p. 206. "Humanité au sens d'une relation réciproque entre les hommes." *Ibid.,* p. 165. "La reconnaissance de l'homme par l'homme." *Ibid.,* p. 203.

from the standpoint of this actual development. For the facts of history show that the individual can live as a human being only when human beings learn to exist together. Only then can the material conditions of life be made secure, only then can science and art flourish.

While Merleau-Ponty occasionally uses the term "purpose" or "goal," the sense he gives to this term is that of a possibility which delineates itself in the actual development of history. Purpose and means cannot be distinguished in the sense that the purpose is an absolute guiding light, and that the means are found in the actual course of history. Means and purpose fuse, for the course of history delineates the possibilities, i.e., the purposes, and one may speak of a purpose only when the road to this purpose presents itself really as a possibility.

Intersubjectivity and the Convergence of History. Accordingly, the convergent movement of history is the road to co-existence, to intersubjectivity. At certain moments, e.g., during a revolution, the attention may become concentrated on the economic level because it is on this level that the most concrete and most striking obstacles reveal themselves on the road from man to fellow-man. For on this level one man pushes the other out of his way and, consequently, the intersubjectivity postulated by the movement of history is rendered impossible. In such a case the economic sector really becomes the center of the development of common life. This is possible and it is likely that it happens sometimes. However, it is not the task of the philosopher to determine whether or not it actually occurs. He may show that it is possible, but it is the task of the political scientist to determine whether or not it does actually happen.[32]

From these considerations it should be clear that Merleau-Ponty was not the man to choose between East and West, between the Soviet Union and the United States. He viewed capitalism as an exaggerated particularism which is an obstacle to the growth of genuine intersubjectivity. This particularism protects privileged groups and thereby gives rise to oppressed groups, which are hardly able to attain a truly human life. Merleau-Ponty saw very clearly that such a particularism had been overtaken by the course of history. For this reason he always felt sympathy for the ideals of Marx. However, he was never able to adhere to Marx' unilateral line of

---

[32]*Phénoménologie de la perception,* p. 199, footnote 1 (extends over four pages).

thinking. Gradually he even held himself aloof from Marxism and especially refused to see the existing type of Marxism as the absolute and final solution, which could not be overtaken by history. Marxism thinks that history is unqualifiedly able to succeed and has to succeed. But such an idea is wholly foreign to Merleau-Ponty's philosophy of ambiguity.[33]

No Absolute Intersubjectivity. Intersubjectivity is a unity of life which comes into existence in history itself, which can never be finished, and which will always be threatened by new aspects of life's development. Mankind will never be able to reach more than a relative balance. Every solution bears the stamp of being merely provisional. If one wants to see history as a series of revolutions, he is dealing with a series that will never be finished. It is an illusion of Marxism to think that against its system no revolution, but only a counter-revolution, is possible. For Marxism, too, establishes a system that degenerates, so that today's progressives will be tomorrow's reactionaries.

Merleau-Ponty's perspective is disappointing to anyone who continues to believe somehow in an absolute sense of history. He offers no other prospective than the contingent movement of life, in which possibilities of good and evil delineate themselves, and which shows light spots separated by "shreds of night." Such is the fundamental situation which will never change. Absolute intersubjectivity will never be realized but, on the other hand, man is not doomed to go only from bad to worse.[34] Something can be attained, but there is no possibility to realize a day without a night. If anyone is disappointed by this, the reason is, says Merleau-Ponty, that he is blinded by an unreal ideal, that he tends to something which, in principle, cannot be attained. He himself is to blame for his disappointment. He is unable to attach value to history because he expects too much of it. Let him surrender his ideal, and then his eyes will be opened to the real meaning of history.

Intersubjectivity, Anonymity and Solipsism. What is the individual capable of doing? Even in the dimension of intersubjectivity

---

[33]A special chapter will be devoted to Merleau-Ponty's attitude toward Marxism.

[34]Merleau-Ponty throws light on the contingency of both good and evil in *Signes,* pp. 303-304. "Il n'est même pas exclu en principe que l'humanité, comme une phrase qui n'arrive pas à s'achever, échoue en cours de route." *Ibid.,* p. 304.

there is a kind of anonymity, as there is anonymity in the individual existence, of which Merleau-Ponty says that "the anonymous in me perceives." So far as history is concerned, he adds, "we find things named and reflected upon as by a Word or a Thought which we do not have but which has us.[35] It is as if a light passes through us which is not ours. Our existence is a participation in the general movement of life, which deposits a sediment in us but also in others. For this reason we are exposed to the temptation to consider our own thinking and speaking unqualifiedly as the thinking and speaking of this general movement of life. If we do so, we absolutize our own thought and thus withdraw from the dialog. The result would be to bring the course of life to a standstill in us, for we solidify it into our own particularity.

Here it becomes difficult again to recover the intersubjectivity in which we begin our existence. For each one of us in his own way is a solidification of the general movement of life and in each one of us the "flesh of history" becomes a personal existence. Thus one can readily see why Merleau-Ponty, when he makes intersubjectivity the theme of his reflection, is greatly tempted by solipsism, or at least enters into a serious discussion of it. His chapter on intersubjectivity in *Phénoménologie de la perception* makes a strange impression in the whole of this philosophy of existence, intentionality and openness. However, Merleau-Ponty realizes that our life, no matter how much it is a participation in the common movement of life, is, nonetheless, a synthesis of this common movement and that, therefore, interpersonal contact is a real problem. As could be expected, he overcomes the temptation to solipsism, albeit not without recognizing here also the relativity of the "solution."[36] For this reason, after considering the person as a synthesis of the common movement of life, we must now approach with Merleau-Ponty the problem of value and truth and especially that of their alleged absoluteness.

---

[35]*Signes,* p. 27.
[36]"Merleau-Ponty meint, dass Sartre das Wahrheitsmoment des Solipsismus zu stark betont. Er selbst versucht, dem Solipsismus von der Kommunikation aus Genüge zu tun. Kommunikation ist immer möglich, sie wird von der Negation nicht aufgehoben; auch die Weigerung, in eine Gemeinschaft miteinander zu treten, ist eine Form der Kommunikation." Reinout Bakker, "Der andere Mensch in der Phänomenologie Merleau-Pontys," *Zeitschrift f. Evangelische Ethik,* Heft 1, 1960, pp. 21 f.

CHAPTER SIX

MERLEAU-PONTY'S REJECTION OF THE ABSOLUTE

1. The Absolute and the Reasons for its Rejection

From the preceding chapters it should have become gradually clear that Merleau-Ponty rejects the absolute. We must now study this rejection and present an account of its reasons.

As we have seen, Merleau-Ponty's fundamental discovery consists in this that man is a "body-subject." No matter how much the human body may be subjective, in its most intimate aspects it remains obscure to our consciousness. What Merleau-Ponty attempts to do now is to understand man, even in the spiritual aspects of his life, from the standpoint of this "body-subject." His reduction is not so much a reduction of the obscure to light as a reduction of light to the obscure. Within this perspective absolute evidence, absolute truth and absolute value become unintelligible.

Meaning of the Absolute. Let us first indicate more precisely what Merleau-Ponty means by the absolute which he rejects. We are not referring here to the Absolute as applicable to God, for Merleau-Ponty's position with respect to God will be discussed in another chapter. The absolute in question here is something absolute within the reality appearing to us, within the sphere of light which, by virtue of our existence as giver of meaning, arises for us from the world. Considered in this sense, the absolute, as viewed by Merleau-Ponty, is a light, seen by me, of which I know *"a priori"* that it is valid for all human beings of all times, i.e., I know this validity from the very nature of this light itself and do not need to consult the views of others or verify its validity-for-others in a dialog. The absolute is that which is valid but does not owe its validity to any contingent, historical context. Its value does not depend on historical factors, but is evident in itself. For this reason it is valid forever, i.e., no matter how much the conditions change, the light in question can never become darkness, its truth can never be doubted. The absolute, then, is valid for all, it is eternal and immutable.

While Merleau-Ponty nowhere considers *ex professo* the absolute which he rejects, the preceding description is a faithful rendering

of his intentions. It is in harmony with the incidental remarks he
makes about it and especially with the arguments which he adduces
to motivate his rejection of the absolute.[1]

Light Arising from Darkness. Merleau-Ponty rejects this absolute, because all light appearing to us arises from a dark soil and is
dependent on this darkness. When, for instance, by seeing, we make
the world a field of vision, we really live in an accessible world, full
of light. So long as we live in the realm of seeing and do not reflect
upon it, the visual field, full of light, will be quite unquestionable to
us. This is confirmed by the fact that many thinkers have looked at
this field realistically and have seen it as a reality independent of us.
Reflection, however, shows that the visual field is rooted in a dialog
between body and world, and this dialog is not at all unquestionable
and necessary. Thus, it appears that the field of vision itself is likewise not at all unquestionable and necessary, and its unquestioned
acceptance gives way to wonder.

The same line of thought applies also to what we call "rational
evidence." Merleau-Ponty does not deny the light of evidence,[2] but
this light also arises from the dialog between the "body-subject" and
the world, even though the dialog in question wholly differs from that
referring to the field of vision.

The Origin of "Eternal" Truth. Thought, as we have seen in the
chapter about the body and language, exists in words. Of course,
thought may exist also in other means of expression; for instance, we
are able to think by means of chessmen or playing cards, and there is
a kind of thinking embodied in our activity. Nevertheless, thinking
is always incarnated in one way or another, and the most subtle form
of embodiment is that of speech. When, then, there is question of
evidence, it will usually be a question of paying attention to thought
embodied in words. Once the words—which pertain to the "flesh
of history"—are accepted as unquestionable, once we place ourselves
in the perspective of revealing speech, there are undoubtedly unquestionable truths. When one presupposes the sense of the terms the
feeling follows that one has to state things as one actually does. More-

---

[1]"Quand donc je place hors de l'expérience progressive le fondement de la
vérité ou de la moralité . . ." *Sens et non-sens,* p. 190. This text occurs in
an article in which Merleau-Ponty argues against the affirmation of the absolute. It is apparent that he understands by the absolute an *"a priori"* lying outside progressive experience. From his arguments, however, and from the
fundamental trend of his thought it appears, as we will see, that not even
within progressive experience is there room for absolute truth.

[2]"Il y a de l'irrécusable." *Op. cit.,* p. 191.

over, words can be repeated (the "spoken word"), and thus they become something that is quite obvious and commonly accepted. What, then, is more obvious than to form the opinion that that which was expressed, the object of the thought, is eternal and necessary? It is here that lies the root of eternal and immutable truth.

However, as we have seen, the meaning of words cannot be divorced from the words themselves. The words are intentional, they bring to light, they draw our attention fully to that which they reveal, to such an extent even that we forget about the revealing word itself and deny its function. But reflection shows that the light exists only by virtue of the illuminating word. In this way we realize how contingent the source of this light is and, consequently, also how contingent this light itself is. The light is unquestionable, irresistible, as long as we place ourselves within the unquestionable means of expression, but it loses its irresistible character as soon as we pay attention to these means of expression themselves. For then we realize that these means belong to history, that man could have created other expressive means. Consequently, the light of truth itself is subject to the same contingency.

We say, and we feel that we have to say, that two plus two equals four. This truth may appear to us as absolutely evident, provided we presuppose the meaning of these mathematical terms. When, however, we ask ourselves what really the meaning is of "two," "four," "plus" and "equals," and when we reflect on how these meanings have arisen, our evidence sinks away into darkness.

The so-called "eternal," says Merleau-Ponty, is merely the acquired. Our existence lies in an intersubjective history, and this history, as we have seen, is the birth and development of meaning. We begin to live in the meaning which our ancestors have constituted. On the basis of the acquisitions of the past we stand in the present and look toward the world. This outlook seems to us to be in many respects necessary and evident. We cannot conceive that the world would appear other than it actually does appear. The appearing world is vested, as it were, with a shroud of eternity. But this eternal shroud is acquired. As soon as we realize this, the illusion of eternity vanishes.

Mathematical Thinking and Eternal Eidos. One could think that the eternal and necessary *eidos* may be found in mathematical thinking.[3] Discussing this point, Merleau-Ponty takes the example of the

---

[3] *Phénoménologie de la perception,* pp. 439-445.

triangle and considers the well-known theorem that is controverted by Euclidean and non-Euclidean geometry. I draw a line through the top of a triangle, parallel to the base, and conclude that the three angles at the top are equal to the three angles of the triangle. There seems to be here, says Merleau-Ponty, question of necessity, of perfect lucidity. One does not deal here with a coincidence, as in an arbitrary drawing of a child, but with the clarity of the intellect. One transcends here the order of perceptive forms of appearance and enters into the domain of the necessary *eidos*. The triangle is not a perceptive phenomenon of our contingent world, but a necessary being in the realm of thought.

However, Merleau-Ponty resolutely rejects this line of thinking. According to him, when there is question of "the essence of the triangle," this expression can be understood either formally or materially. That is, either the *eidos* "triangle" is thought apart from its perceptive representation, as an eternal essence in the realm of ideas, or it is understood as the material essence of the perceptive datum itself.

The contemporary formalization of mathematical thinking may seem to indicate that we are in the presence of formal essences, separated from any perceptive representation. But, says Merleau-Ponty, such a statement cannot at all be maintained. For formalization is never inventive but always retrospective, it does not create new fields of thought but merely analyzes the connection of previously created fields. What is the character of this connection? Is it eternal and necessary? Not at all, for the character of this connection cannot be of an essentially higher nature than the things which it connects. But ultimately all perceptive data, and therefore all objects of thought, are the result of the actual dialog between existence and the world; consequently, they have a factual character. From this it follows that formalization merely discloses the factual connection which are present in the perceptive data, but do not reveal themselves there clearly and openly. "The place where certainty arises and where truth appears is always intuitive thought," says Merleau-Ponty.[4] By "intuitive thought" he means perceptive intuition.

If there is no formal essence transcending the perceptive datum, may we not speak at least of a "material essence" of the triangle? The reply again is in the negative. The implications deduced by the mathematician do not lie contained in a kind of essence or definition, but

------

[4] *Op. cit.*, p. 442.

in the figure or its construction insofar as this figure is the embodiment of an "intention." As Merleau-Ponty expresses it, "The triangle is for me a system of orientated lines, and if terms such as "angle" or "direction" have any meaning for me, the reason is that I place myself at a certain point and from there aim at another point. The system of spatial positions is for me a field of possible movements. In this way I grasp the concrete essence of the triangle, which is not a whole of objective characteristics, but the formula of an attitude, a certain modality of my grasp of the world, a structure."[5] What is at work here is man's creative imagination and not the absolute light of an idea or essence. The mathematician who studies the objective laws of localization knows the spatial relations only by projecting them, at least virtually, by means of his body. The proper subject of mathematical thinking is the "moving subject,"[6] i.e., a subject which is able to move itself from a situation in the world. Thus, we find here again the "body-subject." Merleau-Ponty's conclusion, therefore, is, "The mathematician does not transcend perceptive consciousness; on the contrary, I borrow my concept of an essence from the world of perception."[7]

2. MERLEAU-PONTY'S CONCEPT OF TRUTH

We must now devote our attention to the concept of truth. As we have pointed out, Merleau-Ponty uses expressions which make one think of absolute truth. He says, for instance, that "there is irresistible"[8] evidence and that he does not want to give up the hope of reaching truth beyond the diversity of opinions.[9] He rejects, moreover, relativism.[10] On the other hand, however, he also has expressions which seem to point to a relativistic standpoint.[11] Some of these have been quoted in the preceding pages. The ques-

---

[5]*Op. cit.*, p. 442.

[6]*Op. cit.*, p. 443.

[7]*Op. cit.*, p. 444.

[8]*Sens et non-sens*, p. 191.

[9]*Op. cit.*, p. 126.

[10]"Nous l'ayons vu: si l'on entre assez profondement dans le relativisme, on y trouve le dépassement du relativisme, et c'est ce dépassement qu'on manquerait si l'on érigeait le relatif en absolu." *Les aventures de la dialectique*, p. 77.

[11]"Certain expressions of Merleau-Ponty cannot be interpreted in any other way than that of vulgar relativism." William A. Luijpen, *Existential Phenomenology*, Pittsburgh, 2nd impr., 1962, p. 163, footnote 277.

tion therefore is, How are we to harmonize all these statements in a synthesis?

Being and Appearance. Merleau-Ponty wants to show us the road by means of a reflection on the relationship between "being" and "appearing." There are philosophers, he says, who think that they can attain the absolute light of being without having to pass through appearance. He calls this standpoint "dogmatism." Dogmatism is convinced that it is in possession of a truth that is not ambiguous, not mutable, not provisional. Others, on the other hand, the so-called "relativists," think that our knowledge is encompassed by appearance, and, in saying this, they do not conceive appearance as the unveiling of being.[12] Thus, there is room only for purely subjective opinions, and man does not have any objective foundation for anything he thinks.

These two views apparently are opposite extremes but, says Merleau-Ponty, in reality, the difference between them is not very great. For in the relativistic view one can say that our knowledge is limited to appearances because absolute being and absolute knowing are surreptitiously intended, and it is from the standpoint of this absolute being and absolute knowledge that our opinions are judged to be purely relative. In other words, relativism thinks from the standpoint of a dogmatic ideal.

Merleau-Ponty wants to refute as well as to transcend both standpoints by saying that our knowledge is concerned with "appearing being." We know being precisely as appearing, but this appearance is a manifestation of being itself. To speak in the spirit of Merleau-Ponty, we may not say that we *merely* know the appearance of being, for the term "merely" contains a reference to something more, to the impossible ideal of dogmatism. Appearance should be understood not as a limitation but as an access to being. It would be absurd to think that being would be known independently of the access to being. However, since being is knowable to us because we are open to being, our knowledge remains ambiguous and provisional.

While these expressions may sound very nice, they offer us no clarity, for they can be understood in many ways. Everything depends on how Merleau-Ponty conceives the appearance of being and

---

[12]"Cette évidence du phénomène, ou encore du 'monde', est aussi bien méconnue quand on cherche à atteindre l'être sans passer par le phénomène, c'est à dire quand on fait l'être nécessaire, que quand on coupe le phénomène de l'être, quand on le dégrade au rang de simple apparence ou de simple possible." *Phénoménologie de la perception,* pp. 454 f.

our openness to it. Let us try, therefore, to find out in what way Merleau-Ponty gives a more precise content to these expressions.

The Classical Distinction Between Rational Truth and Factual Truth. There is a classical distinction between "rational truth" (*vérité de raison*) and "factual truth" (*vérité de fait*). Rational truth seems to be clothed in a shroud of eternity, for it remains true no matter how much the situation changes. Factual truth, on the other hand, is tied to an actual constellation of factors. Anyone acquainted with the history of philosophy will recognize here the distinction made by Plato between rational certainty and variable opinion. This distinction returns again and again in manifold ways in the history of philosophy. Merleau-Ponty, however, thinks that the essential difference between the two is subject to doubt. For "there is no rational truth which does not contain a co-efficient of facticity."[13]

He refers here again to the example of Euclidean geometry. In the past this geometry was believed to be perfectly transparent and to have the character of permanent truth. Gradually, however, it became clear that this truth is connected with the factual structure of space, but that space could be constructed also in a different way. A factual "motor formula," i.e., a factual way of our dwelling in space, plays an essential role in this so-called "eternal truth." If this is so, then the distinction between these two spheres of truth disappears. For every rational truth contains factual aspects, and every factual truth appears to us within a whole of meanings which is not without intelligible coherence.[14]

The "Co-Efficient of Facticity." Accordingly, the "co-efficient of facticity" is the ground or reason why rational truth, in the traditional sense, does not make sense to Merleau-Ponty, whether as actually given or as ideal. "Our experience of truth," he says, "would be absolute knowledge only when we would be able to thematize all its motives, i.e., when we would cease to be situated."[15]

Considering this text, one could object that Merleau-Ponty himself thinks here from the standpoint of an ideal of absolute truth, for he even indicates a condition for its attainment. In reply, we may

---

[13] *Op. cit.,* p. 453.

[14] "Ainsi toute vérité de fait est vérité de raison, toute vérité de raison est vérité de fait." *Op. cit.,* p. 451.

[15] *Op. cit.,* p. 453.

say that Merleau-Ponty wants to exclude even the ideal of absolute truth, but does not always succeed in maintaining this intention. However, we do not want to discuss this point at present. The coefficient of facticity, then, which prevents the absolute character of truth, is found in the fact that we are a situated existence. Elsewhere Merleau-Ponty writes: "Reflection always contains entire zones of experience, which codetermine even our most pure evidences without themselves becoming manifest."[16] Where is this horizon of darkness which always makes itself felt but hides from our gaze? As should be clear from the preceding chapters, the reply is that this horizon of darkness is the "body-subject," which is our door of access to reality and through which being appears to us. With respect to thought, the body plays a role especially insofar as it speaks.

Speech and the Illusion of Eternal Truth. "Language," says Merleau-Ponty, "has the remarkable property of making us forget about itself."[17] It makes it possible for us to unveil reality, but does not demand any attention for itself. Thus, it produces an illusion—namely, "our certainty that we, over and beyond expression, possess a truth which can be separated from its expression and of which the expression is merely a vestment and a contingent manifestation."[18] Language creates the illusion of eternal truth and, at the same time, makes such truth impossible. "Where is this eternal truth which no one possesses? Where is the expressed that transcends the expression? And if we have the right to posit such truth, whence that lasting concern to arrive at a better expression of it?"[19]

A measure of understanding is possible now. We grasp being in its appearance. Being appears because we *make it appear*. The idea of knowledge as a mirrorlike reflexion is entirely foreign to Merleau-Ponty's philosophy. Our entire existence is to make appear. But our existence is the existence of a bodily being. Our body is a "significant center," the center of all giving of meaning and, therefore, of all appearances. We reach the highest level in linguistic expression. Language is a bodily, historical fact. As soon as we begin to think about speech, we find ourselves in darkness. Yet the same language also gives rise to the illusion of light.

---

[16]*Sens et non-sens,* p. 195.
[17]*Phénoménologie de la perception,* p. 459.
[18]*Op. cit.,* p. 459.
[19]*Op. cit.,* p. 452.

Merleau-Ponty unmasks this illusion. There is no absolute light for us because all light originates in darkness. Truth is not absolute because the thinking subject is essentially a speaking subject and therefore a "body-subject." Descartes has failed to realize this. Through reflection he thought it possible to attain to the pure interiority of the spirit and there to discover absolute evidence: "I think, therefore I am." But the inner silence of Descartes' spirit is filled with the noise of words. If he had understood this and realized its importance, he would have recognized that his so-called "interiority" belongs to the world and, therefore, is permeated with the world's darkness. The strength of Merleau-Ponty's standpoint lies especially in the fact that he does not merely reject the illusion of eternal truth but also explains why man has this illusion.

"Irresistible Resistible Evidence." In the light of the foregoing one can understand also Merleau-Ponty's paradoxical statement that "an evidence is both irresistible and resistible for the same reasons."[20] An evidence is irresistible for me because I accept as unquestionable a certain past, a certain cultural sphere, a certain way of thinking which is given to me in my language. I think within a certain tradition that is interwoven with my existence. Certain insights are therefore just as unquestionable as my existence itself. However, precisely because the evidence lies within this factual horizon, it is also, in principle, subject to rejection. "The consistency of a perceived thing, the transparency of a mathematical equation or of an idea exists only if I renounce all-sided explicitation."[21] But such an explicitation is not possible according to Merleau-Ponty. Every clarity exists for me only, by virtue of the "to make appear" which I here and now am. Thus, I am never compelled to admit a truth *solely* by the inner convincing power of an appearing object. For this reason Merleau-Ponty can justly say: "There is absolute certainty concerning the world in general but not about a single thing in particular."[22] This statement lies fully in line with Merleau-Ponty's thinking. There is no absolute certainty. What, then, about the absolute certainty concerning the world, mentioned in the above-quoted text? The reply is that the world is not an appearing object but the horizon of all objects, not a "noema," but the sphere in which all "noemata" exist. In other words, the world is not in the strict

[20]*Op. cit.,* p. 454.
[21]*Op. cit.,* p. 454.
[22]*Op. cit.,* p. 344.

sense an object of certain knowledge.[23]   Certainty cannot be absolute because it originates from the darkness of the "body-subject."

3. MERLEAU-PONTY'S THEORY OF UNIVERSALITY

The Cultural World as the Primary World.   We are now in a position to understand Merleau-Ponty's doctrine of universality. Above we have already quoted his remarkable statement: "My life appears to me as absolutely individual and absolutely universal."[24] But this and other similar texts should be read in the light of another statement—namely, that my body is not an object among other objects but is "sensitive to everything," it is that through which objects exist for me.   The root of the universality proper to our knowledge is found in the openness of the body-subject to the world.   The term "world" should be taken here concretely so as to include also other human beings, their way of acting, the patterns of society, labor, technology, etc.   Briefly, the world which reveals itself to us is, first of all, the cultural world, the humanized world, and in this world the natural world transpires as the canvas transpires through the painting.   The humanized world appears to us as the actualization of our own potentialities.   It invites us to enter this world, to dwell in it and to make it our own through our actions.   This world is also a world expressed in speech, a world in which things have a name.   By entering this world, we begin to live in language and make our own a world expressed in speech.   Thus, we begin to dwell understandingly in the world.

No a Priori Common Truth or Value.   This is the reason why the world is common.   Not a single truth or value is *a priori* common, i.e., by virtue of its own inner light.   Universality is essentially tied up with the convergent movement of history, which I have joined through my birth.   The assertion of this historicity does not mean that truth and value disappear.   If anyone considers that the truth and value arising within history are not authentic, the reason is that he has a false ideal of truth and value, which prevents him from appreciating that which *de facto* presents itself.   It is proper to value and truth and to all meaningfulness to arise within history.

This historicity does not mean that truth, value and meaning are not really mine.   I come to them because I am inserted into history,

---

[23]The world always remains "horizon" and can never be make into a "figure."

[24]*Sens et non-sens*, p. 188.

but I am inserted insofar as I actively take up this history and make it my own. My existence is a participation in an intersubjective history and, consequently, is a participation in something common. In this way, and only in this way, am I in value, truth and meaning. Truth begins to exist for me, e.g., because I am taken up into a speaking society. I am taken into this society by making its speech my own, by beginning to live in its light. This is the only light I have, and this light arises from darkness and always remains surrounded by a dark horizon.

The Classics. All this does not exclude that there is intersubjective meaning. Merleau-Ponty expresses the hope that a new "classicism" will be born,[25] i.e., that a new coherence will arise in the confused story of the growth of meaning. As this growth, so also the coherence will be intersubjective. Yet intersubjectivity, universality, coherence and classicism remain within the *factual* movement of history. There is no *a priori* evidence. This historical character of truth does not mean that we are cut off from the past because our era would possess a coherence that is entirely its own and differs radically from that of the preceding periods. For the community of which we are part is not only "synchronic" but also "diachronic," i.e., it permeates not only a certain period but encompasses the entire history of mankind. For there are "classics," men who have disclosed a viewpoint which continues to inspire us. Plato, for instance, says Merleau-Ponty, still lives among us.[26]

What does Merleau-Ponty mean by the classics? The history of thought, he says, does not make any summary statements, establishing this as true and that as false. But this history makes unspoken judgments, it deprives certain theories of their attractive power and buries them, it makes them messages of interest only to the antiquarian. Other theories, on the other hand, retain their attraction and continue to be actual, not in the sense, says Merleau-Ponty, that they are miraculously in agreement with an eternal reality, for such a punctual and lifeless agreement is not needed or even sufficient to make them truly great doctrines.

Such theories do not remain actual either because man continues to repeat them verbally. It is quite possible that man will acknowledge that the explicit statements of such a theory have been over-

---

[25] *Sens et non-sens,* p. 188.
[26] *Op. cit.,* p. 126.

taken by history. Yet underneath all such explicit statements there lies a vision of reality which man can continue to make his own and continually makes his own in ever different ways. Whoever wants to enter into dialog with reality has to consider these standpoints. Those who have created these standpoints are the "classics." They can be recognized by this that no one follows them literally, yet they continue to be sources of inspiration. The reason is that the new facts with which we have to deal can be illuminated by the classical visions. The new facts give new actuality to the old viewpoints.

According to Merleau-Ponty, then, there is no question here of an eternal truth, as opposed to "eternal falsity." History does not pronounce judgment on the classics in the sense of an ecclesiastical *"nihil obstat"* or placing on the Index of Forbidden Books. Anyone, however, who wants to continue the history of thought will have to consider these standpoints and is influenced by them. Is this or that author, asks Merleau-Ponty, Cartesian or not? Put in this way, he replies, the question is meaningless, for those who reject one or the other view of Descartes do so for reasons which, to a certain extent at least, have been borrowed from Descartes. Among the classics of thought Merleau-Ponty places also Karl Marx; hence his theory is neither a system that has been established, once and for all, nor a phenomenon that has been overtaken by history.[27]

4. THE SCOPE OF MERLEAU-PONTY'S REJECTION OF THE ABSOLUTE

"Spoken Truth." Hitherto we have followed Merleau-Ponty in his explanations of the various aspects concerning the absolute. We must now see in what sense he rejects the absolute. It is clear at once that he rejects the absolute character of "spoken truth."[28] Such truth is rooted in darkness because it comes into being through means of expression which lie in darkness. Because of the historical character of these means of expression, this truth is subjected to history.

Absolute Unspoken Truth? The question, however, is whether these spoken truths are preceded by something which somehow could be called "truth." Merleau-Ponty says somewhere that "perceptive faith" precedes "explicit truth."[29] Could we perhaps find absolute

---

[27]The last three paragraphs are a paraphrase of Merleau-Ponty's fascinating description of the classics in *Signes*, pp. 16 f.

[28]"Spoken truth" is the truth of *"les énoncés," "l'acquis,"* and *"la parole parlée."*

[29]*Sens et non-sens*, p. 188, note 1.

truth here? It would seem to be very difficult, for, according to Merleau-Ponty, perception has a pre-personal root: "the impersonal perceives in me." Thus, we may legitimately question whether this "perceptive faith" leads us into the order of truth. Other texts, however, indicate that "explicit truth" is preceded by more than a dark "perceptive faith," for the "spoken word" is preceded by the "speaking word." Elsewhere Merleau-Ponty speaks of a "silent cogito," i.e., a "cogito" that has not yet pronounced itself. Moreover, he says that the theories of the classical thinkers continue to speak "beyond their statements."[30] Especially the last text appears to refer to a real light, a light which is more important than the spoken truth and in which the truth can again and again be brought to expression.

Hardly any philosopher will attribute an absolute character to expressed thought in all respects and without any qualifications. For it is beyond any doubt that words are subjected to history. In every realm, including that of philosophy, terms may get out of use. And even when they continue to exist, they usually change their meaning in the course of history. For this reason the protagonists of absolute truth will say that words give expression to a *vision* whose inner value and everlastingness transcends the words and is only inadequately expressed by them. Moreover, when we carefully read an author and manages to penetrate into what he really has seen, it often becomes evident that he expresses himself inadequately. It may happen that the reader can express the writer's vision better than the writer himself. Merleau-Ponty admits this, for instance, when he tries to find a better expression for Freud's fundamental intuition than the one used by Freud himself.[31] Thus, we must ask, May we interpret Merleau-Ponty's theory of truth in this direction?

As appears from the preceding pages, such an interpretation would give rise to great difficulties. Merleau-Ponty generally attributes a greater value to the expression of thought than has been hitherto the custom. For him, thought becomes itself in the word. The meaning of the words cannot be separated from the words themselves. Whence Merleau-Ponty asks the challenging question: "What is the expressed that transcends the expression?"[32] True, the existence which brings itself to expression is preceded by existence seek-

---

[30]*Signes*, p. 30.
[31]When Freud spoke of the "unconscious," says Merleau-Ponty, he was on the point of discovering what others subsequently and better have called "ambiguous perception." Cf. *Signes*, p. 291.
[32]*Phénoménologie de la perception*, p. 452.

ing to express itself. But Merleau-Ponty calls this existence seeking self-expression a "silent cogito," and from the context it appears that what he means by this is not so much a light that transcends expression as a darkness which tries to reach light, which needs expression to know what it itself is.[33] How, then, would there be room here in this "silent cogito" for absolute truth? Accordingly, his numerous explicit rejections of absolute truth seem to refer not only to expressed truth but to truth as such.

This interpretation seems to be confirmed by a fundamental perspective which will be studied in the following chapter—namely, contingency, as the soil in which germinate all human meanings, including truth. A distinction can be made, says Merleau-Ponty, between necessity and contingency, but, on closer inspection, it appears that both are realms belonging to the fundamental sphere of an all-pervasive contingency.[34] How, then, could an absolute truth exist within this fundamental sphere of contingency?

Reasons for Hesitancy. Nevertheless, there are texts in Merleau-Ponty which make us suspect that such an unqualified rejection of the absolute in every form goes too far. When, with reference to the classics, Merleau-Ponty speaks of a truth which lies outside that which is expressed, which throws light on new facts, and which constantly can be placed in a different focus, there seems to be question of a kind of fundamental intuition which is more than "darkness trying to reach light." The proper light does not seem to lie here in the spoken truth but in something preceding its expression. This "something" is certainly more than "perceptive faith," for one is not a genius, a classical thinker, by living in "perceptive faith." It is more also than the "silent cogito," for in this light the spoken truth can be experienced as inadequate. This fundamental light seems to be, according to Merleau-Ponty, of a more permanent character, for, as long as human beings will continue to think, they will let themselves be inspired by this light. The classics do not die, for Plato still lives among us. Whence our question: Doesn't it seem that Merleau-Ponty, after all, still leaves room for a form of absolute truth?

As we have noted, Merleau-Ponty has never published the promised book about truth. Thus, we are dealing here with an unwritten

---

[33] *Op. cit.,* pp. 462-63.

[34] "La contingence ontologique, celle du monde lui-même, étant radicale, est au contraire de qui fonde une fois pour toutes notre idée de la vérité. Le monde est le réel dont le nécessaire et le possible ne sont que des provinces." *Op. cit.,* p. 456.

chapter of his philosophy. Yet, an implicit theory of truth is present in his works. This theory, we think, may be summarized as follows. Merleau-Ponty outlines a few basic features of his view, which, pursued to their ultimate conclusion, exclude absolute truth. He says that contingency is the soil in which all meaning germinates, and what he means by contingency is, as we will see, something more profound than the dimension in which we usually oppose necessity to contingency. If it is really true that absolute contingency is the ultimate sphere in which all meaning originates, absolute truth is unthinkable. Merleau-Ponty says also that man is the unfolding of the "body-subject" and that, therefore, all light is rooted in darkness. How could such darkness be the soil bringing forth a truth endowed with an absolute character? Merleau-Ponty refuses to divorce the meaning of an expression from the form of the expression itself; these forms of expression are historical; how then could the meaning of these expressions somehow transcend history? All this shows that in Merleau-Ponty's works there are basic features of a synthesis which excludes absolute truth. Moreover, in many passages he explicitly rejects absolute truth. For these reasons we think that Merleau-Ponty's philosophy in its synthesizing lines is a denial of the absolute.

Merleau-Ponty's Aversion to "Those who Know." On the other hand, according to Merleau-Ponty, philosophy is the "enemy of the system." When he writes, he is not like one who explains a complete system of thought to the reader. In his explanations his own thoughts constantly assume new forms. For this reason he has texts which seem to point to perspectives that hardly fit in with the explicit line of his thought.[35] Is this perhaps the reason why he has never written the book about the origin of truth? Being very open-minded, Merleau-Ponty would not have permitted even his own past to determine him fully. In an article written on the occasion of Merleau-Ponty's sudden death, Ricoeur states that Merleau-Ponty was busy with a rather radical revision of certain important parts of his thought. Unfortunately, he does not give any further details. It does not seem impossible to us that the theory of truth may have been one of these parts. For precisely with respect to his views on truth there is a divergence

---

[35]In the previously quoted article, "Le philosophe foudroyé," *Les nouvelles littéraires*, 11 mai 1961, p. 4, Paul Ricoeur writes, "De fait, la théorie du langage, que la *Phénoménologie de la perception* s'efforçait de contenir dans les bornes d'une réflexion sur le 'corps comme expression' et de comprendre comme 'geste linguistique', cette théorie du langage n'a cessé de faire éclater le cadre de la relation au monde par simple perception."

between, on the one hand, the fundamental lines he draws of his philosophy and, on the other, certain intuitions which make themselves felt in scattered passages.

Moreover, Merleau-Ponty's theory of truth does not agree with the way in which he affirms truth in his works. Quite frequently he pronounces a decisive negation with respect to certain views of the past. But this "no" cannot be more forceful than the new "yes" by virtue of which the "no" is possible.

Our attitude in this chapter has been rather hesitant. This hesitation could not be abandoned, for Merleau-Ponty himself had promised us a further elucidation of the question without, however, redeeming this promise. Yet there is one point on which Merleau-Ponty remains radical and self-consistent, viz., his firm rejection of the formulas of dogmatism. He is deeply impressed by the inadequacy of expression and for this reason remains very open to dialog. He demands the same openness of the others. He fears those who simply think that they know. He considers them even dangerous, for they would be quite ready to massacre their opponents, as he says, "piously."[36] If he is so much afraid of "those who know,"[37] are we entitled to consider the fundamental lines of his theory of truth unqualifiedly as definitive? An affirmative reply would fail to do justice to a philosopher who has never ceased to plead for openness.

---

[36]*Sens et non-sens,* p. 190.
[37]*Signes,* p. 308.

CHAPTER SEVEN

METAPHYSICAL CONSCIOUSNESS

1. MERLEAU-PONTY'S DESCRIPTION OF METAPHYSICAL CONSCIOUSNESS

In the preceding chapters we first described Merleau-Ponty's fundamental discovery of the "body-subject" and how he approaches this discovery. We then studied how the subject in his speaking comes to thinking, and devoted our attention to the subject as the origin of meaning, before undertaking a consideration of history. Merleau-Ponty's rejection of the absolute, revealing itself with increasing clarity in these studies, became the topic of the preceding chapter. We will now touch a new theme, metaphysical consciousness. Although new, this theme will, at the same time, serve to summarize the preceding topics and to give them a more profound foundation, for in his considerations of metaphysical consciousness Merleau-Ponty supplies us with a synthesis of the fundamental lines along which his philosophy proceeds. He has made it rather easy for us because he himself has written a condensed article containing his views in this matter. Thus, we will be able to follow him closely.[1]

The Rationalism of Science. Metaphysics manifests itself to some extent even in certain sciences, says Merleau-Ponty, and especially in the sciences about man.[2] For these sciences have penetrated into a new mode of being, which we neglect in our natural way of thinking. Because of our natural way of thinking, it seems obvious to us that we find ourselves in the presence of a field extending in space and time and that we can examine any part of it freely without changing its character. Thus, we conceive the spatio-temporal field of existence as an objective whole, inspected by us. Our gaze is conceived thus, as an absolute standpoint outside this spatio-temporal whole. At first, the sciences took over this view and, by systematizing it, reinforced it considerably. Merleau-Ponty distinguishes here between

---

[1] "Le métaphysique dans l'homme," *Sens et non-sens,* pp. 165-196.

[2] "Dans les sciences même elle [metaphysics] reparait, non pas pour en limiter le champ ou pour leur opposer des barrières, mais comme l'inventaire délibéré d'un type d'être que le scientisme ignorait et que les sciences ont peu à peu appris à reconnaître. C'est cette métaphysique en acte que nous nous proposons de circonscrire mieux." *Op. cit.,* p. 166.

the "major rationalism" of philosophers, such as Descartes and Kant, and the "minor rationalism" which, according to him, prevailed in the sciences. Describing this "minor rationalism," he says:

"It presupposed an immense Science, lying ready-made in things, with which our human science, once it had been completed, would coincide. No questions would then remain to be asked because every meaningful question would have been answered. It is difficult for us to conceive such a mentality, yet it belongs to a not too distant past. It is a fact that man dreamt of a moment when the mind would have caught the whole of reality in a network of relationships, a moment when the mind, having completed its task, could come to rest. Nothing would remain to be done, save to deduct conclusions from knowledge which, in principle, was complete, and to offer resistance to the last attacks of the unforeseeable through the application of known principles."[3]

It was not easy for man to abandon this myth. When the physical sciences became unbelievingly complex and, therefore, unaccessible to the ordinary man, some fostered the fond dream that certain geniuses, such as Einstein, had an almost magical access to a realm beyond the reach of the ordinary eye. Thus, they asked Einstein the most impossible questions.[4]

The Break with This Rationalism. The sciences of man as man, however, broke away from this rationalism. Later the physical sciences did the same. Merleau-Ponty refers in this connection to psychology and its discovery of the Gestalt. This discovery laid bare a mode of being which cannot be fully brought to light by a study of psychical elements and which becomes intelligible to us only when we enter it with empathy. The sciences of language have discovered the density and darkness surrounding the birth of language, but also that in this birth a role is played by a subject seeking light in darkness. The social sciences have come to the realization that the social realm is a realm of communication, and that this realm is accessible only through participation in this communication. The historical sciences are now aware that we must endeavor to bring the past to light by empathically reliving it. Everywhere the same fundamental fact reveals itself—viz., the person who studies the field of human existence is not an absolute

---

[3]*Signes,* p. 230.
[4]"Et puisque Einstein justement a montré qu'à grande distance un présent est contemporain d'un avenir, pourquoi ne lui pas poser les questions qu'on posait à la Pythie?" *Signes,* p. 245. This text is part of an article entitled, "Einstein et la crise de la raison," *Signes,* pp. 242-249.

consciousness gazing at this field from without, but an existence which empathically relives this field and makes it accessible to himself by virtue of his "in-being."[5]

Accordingly, any knowledge of man by man is not a mere external study but rather a personal re-living of what the other has experienced or still experiences. He finds ambiguous signs of an experience which is not his own and, by means of these signs, he must endeavor to resuscitate this experience. He has to make his own a structure of existence of which he cannot form a clear conception. For instance, to analyze a culture of the past, he must begin to live in the spirit of this culture. He brings it to life even as an expert pianist deciphers an unknown composition. He does so, without fully understanding the motives of every form of behavior, without becoming aware of all the hidden knowledge present in the forms in which man lived in the past. There is no question here of approaching something as an object outside us, but rather of participating in a mode of being.[6]

We exist here outside ourselves and live with others. We may speak therefore of universality. But the universality of knowledge, i.e., the fact that we extend ourselves, as it were, outside ourselves, is not guaranteed by a kind of absolute consciousness supposedly present in us and safeguarding the agreement of our thinking with that of every other subject, at least, when our thinking is "good." Universality does not arise from an inner quality of our knowledge but is achieved outside us, in the encounter, the dialog with others and with the past. We ourselves do not know how this encounter and dialog come to be, how we begin to live in a language, how we become integrated into the structure of a community, how we manage to live in the spirit of a past era. Yet we discover that we are there and that we understand from within.[7]

No Ready-Made Evidence. A new way of looking at the accessibility of reality manifests itself here. Reality is not accessible because it is a light which, as it were, lies waiting for us ready to meet our gaze. Reality is not accessible to us because we bear within us the light of of the absolute idea, that opens all doors to us as if it were a masterkey. But we discover ourselves as possibility to co-exist with everything and, thus, as access to reality. As existence, we are access to everything.

---

[5]*Sens et non-sens*, pp. 166-185.
[6]This paragraph is a paraphrase of *Sens et non-sens*, p. 186.
[7]*Op. cit.*, p. 186.

We approach metaphysical consciousness when we abandon the illusion of the object's ready-made evidence, whether it is a question of the object of sense experience or that of science, and when we discover the radical subjectivity of our entire experience and realize that this subjectivity, nonetheless, has truth value. The light arises for us through our communication with reality, through our being-together with what we are not. The term "experience" assumes a new meaning here. On the one hand, we realize that we enter into contact with reality as particular beings, and that we cannot possibly lay claim to being the norm of everything that is. On the other hand, this particular being which I am appears able to enter into contact with everything. I am not the norm of everything but I am able to communicate with everything. I am certain, therefore, that something is, and there is truth for me. Truth, however, exists because I am capacity for encounter and, therefore, I may not seek anything else than being-for-me.[8]

Examples. Merleau-Ponty illustrates the point with two examples. The first is the perception of sense qualities. When I see things, I do not have, on the one hand, consciousness of subjective states of awareness and, on the other, consciousness of objective qualities, such as blue and red. Blue and red are nothing else than modes in which I make contact with what appears to me.

The second example is that of perceiving a person. When I say that I see someone, this means that I am going to live with this behavior whose witness I am, and which is a visible realization of intentions living also in me. To perceive someone or something, Merleau-Ponty wants to say with these examples, means that I am going to live with this reality, that I, as it were, extend myself to the other person or thing. At the same time I remain myself, i.e., this particular being, but I experience in myself the strange power to live in the other, to perform the other's deeds with him, while I retain my particularity. Here lies the foundation of a truth which we cannot give up and, nonetheless, are unable to make fully our own—namely, the always repeated birth of light.[9]

The Paradox of the Universal Individual. Metaphysics is the deliberate attempt to describe the paradox that truth arises because a particular subject begins to live with the other, the paradox that a

---

[8]*Op. cit.*, pp. 186 f.
[9]*Op. cit.*, p. 187.

particular being communicates with everything. The sciences live in this paradox but do not describe it. From the moment that I discover that my experience, precisely as mine, opens me for what I am not, that the particular "I" is sensitive to the world and to other human beings, from that moment all the beings which objective thought viewed as "outside" me, as objects of observation, come close to me in a wonderful way. Or, viewed from the other side, I recognize my relationship with them, I experience that I am nothing but a power to be their echo, to understand them, to become a reply to them. My life appears to me as absolutely individual and absolutely **universal**. I discover an individual life, capable of bringing all lives of the past and the present to life and, therefore, itself capable of being brought to life, I discover a light arising against all hope, for how would I have been able to hope for this miracle?[10]

Such is metaphysical consciousness. It is, first, the wonder that the apparent contradiction becomes true reality and, secondly, the awareness that we ourselves are this miracle in the simple pursuit of our existence. In every deed we again and again confirm this miracle. Metaphysical consciousness has no other objects that those of everyday experience—this world, the others, human history, truth, culture. However, it does not accept them as ready-made data, as conclusions without premises, as if it would go without saying that they are there. Metaphysical consciousness rediscovers the radical strangeness of all things and, at the same time, the miracle of their appearance. Thus, the history of mankind is no longer the evolution of modern civilized man from a primitive human being, the growth of morality and science, spoken of all too humanly in the text books; history is no longer empirical and successive, but the consciousness of the mysterious bond emanating from me, which makes Plato still living for me.[11]

2. The Scope of Metaphysical Consciousness

Metaphysics as "Transnatural." Having followed Merleau-Ponty closely in this condensed dissertation, we must now attempt to clarify the scope of his assertions. At the beginning of his dissertation, Merleau-Ponty connects two words—viz., "metaphysical" and "transnatural."[12] He thus takes the term "metaphysical" literally as

---

[10]*Op. cit.,* p. 187 f.
[11]*Op. cit.,* p. 188 f.
[12]"Les sciences de l'homme, dans leur orientation présente, sont métaphysiques ou transnaturelles." *Op. cit.,* p. 185.

that which transcends the natural, is beyond the sphere of the natural. Specifying what he means by "the natural," he refers to that attitude, encountered in everyday life and cultivated in certain sciences, through which we accept so-called "data" as unquestionable. Living together with other human beings in the world, it seems unquestionably obvious to us that there is a world of things and men. Every science which simply accepts these data and builds on them assumes this "natural attitude." The natural attitude places the perceiving subject opposite the perceived objects. The human sciences, however, have broken with this attitude and understand that the other is accessible to me, is a datum for me, because of the fact that I exist together with the other and, as it were, "live" it. My empathy constitutes the data. Although the sciences have made this discovery, they have not made it the theme of their specific study. Such a study is made by philosophy, which thereby becomes metaphysics.

Through our metaphysical consciousness we discover that data, "the given," exist because of "giving experience," and that this "giving experience" is not a consideration at a distance but a going out from ourselves and "living" the other. Then I discover a miracle which encompasses both subject and object, I come to wonder about myself as openness and about the other as accessibility. The natural attitude is overcome, and no longer is anything unquestionably obvious.

No Transcendental Reality. It should be clear that Merleau-Ponty divests the term "metaphysics" from any reference to a reality transcending the world.[13] For him the term no longer has the Greco-medieval meaning which continues to be accepted by numerous philosophers of our time. His expression that metaphysical experience has no other objects than those of ordinary experience, should be understood literally—there is no question whatsoever of any new reality, but only of a new approach to the reality that was there already. Merleau-Ponty stated this very clearly even in his *Phéno-*

---

[13]"Faire de la métaphysique, ce n'est pas entrer dans un monde de connaissance séparé, ni répéter des formules stériles telles que celles dont nous nous servons ici,—c'est faire l'expérience pleine des paradoxes qu'elles indiquent, c'est vérifier toujours à nouveau le fonctionnement discordant de l'intersubjectivité humaine, c'est chercher à penser jusqu'au bout les mêmes phénomènes que la science investit, en leur restituant seulement leur transcendance et leur étrangeté originaires." *Op. cit.*, p. 195. We may draw attention to the fact that in this text Merleau-Ponty makes a distinction between experience and its formulation, and admits that experience is richer and more profound than its expression. He indicates here a preverbal knowledge, which remains unaccounted for in his philosophy of language.

ménologie de la perception, in the chapter concerned with the phenomenal field, the field of appearing reality. "Once it is recognized," he says, "that the phenomena have an original character in relationship to the objective world, because the objective world exists for us by virtue of the phenomena, reflection proceeds to integrate every possible object into the order of phenomena and to investigate how the objects originate from the phenomena. At exactly this moment the phenomenal field becomes the transcendental field."[14] The order of the phenomenal, precisely as phenomenal, as appearing, is absolutely original and irreducible. It is here that lies the source of everything which, no matter how, is knowable to us. We should not look for a transcendental field outside the phenomena.

No Transphenomenal Subject but a Situated Subject. Merleau-Ponty warns against a danger. One could argue as follows. The phenomenal field, which is recognized as ultimate, always extends around a subject, for whatever appears appears to a subject. If, then, the phenomenal field has an ultimate character, the same has to be said of the subject. Accordingly, as a correlate of the phenomenal field, an ultimate subject has to be admitted—namely, the subject to which everything appears. This subject would be the thinking "I" and this "I" would determine the structure of the phenomenal through the way in which it makes reality appear. Thus, the fundamental lines of appearing reality would have to be sought in the "attitudes" of the "I." Until the very end of his life, Merleau-Ponty says, Husserl pursued this line of thought.[15]

Merleau-Ponty, however, rejects this conception, thereby showing how radically he differs from Husserl. The phenomenal field, says Merleau-Ponty, does not reveal itself to a subject outside the field but encompasses also the subject, for this subject is essentially a dialog with the other. We should beware of thinking that everything else appears as facticity to a subject which itself transcends facticity. The subject and its intellect also have the character of facticity. "True, the recognition of the phenomenal as the original order condemns em-

---

[14]*Phénoménologie de la perception,* p. 73.

[15]"Il me ferait prendre possession entière de mon expérience et réaliserait l'adéquation du réfléchissant au réfléchi. Telle est la perspective ordinaire d'une philosophie transcendentale, et tel est aussi, en apparence au moins, le programme d'une phénoménologie transcendentale." *Phénoménologie de la perception,* p. 73. In a footnote to this text Merleau-Ponty remarks that Husserl formulated his program in this way in most of his writings, even in the published texts dating from the last period of his life. Accordingly, Merleau-Ponty clearly parts company with Husserl.

piricism as *explanation* of the order and of reason based on the facts and on chance in nature. At the same time, however, it allows reason and the order of the phenomenal itself to retain their factual character. If a universal constituent consciousness were possible, the density of the factual would disappear. Accordingly, if we desire a descriptive reflection which really understands the phenomenal, this reflection should not be described as a simple return to a universal reason; universal reason should not be posited as an *a priori* in the original reality itself. But we should see reason as a creative activity which itself participates in the factual character of the original reality."[16]

This text, which we have translated somewhat freely, is a plea for a *situated subject*. From the time of Parmenides, philosophy has always searched for the original. Yet it is also inclined, when it has discovered the so-called original dimension, to posit a subject to which this original order appears and to place this subject as a spectator outside this order. Husserl also, says Merleau-Ponty, has done this. He sought the original "phenomenon," but posited a subject to which it would appear. This subject was supposed to be universal reason, a transcendental subject.

According to Merleau-Ponty, however, the original subject is already situated in the order of that which appears and, consequently, it has a factual character. Wonder, therefore, encompasses both the subject and what appears to it. There is only a single field, of which everything, including the subject, is a part. "For this reason phenomenology is the only philosophy that speaks of a transcendental *field*."[17] The subject is situated in this field. Hence the field does not present itself as lying before the gaze of the subject, it is not transparent to the subject. It is in principle excluded that clear knowledge can be obtained about the entire field precisely because the knowing subject itself is situated in the field.

We arrive at metaphysical consciousness when we recognize all this, when we reduce everything, including the knowing subject and philosophical reason, to this original fact: there is a situated subject which has a factual character and to which reality appears. The subject has no privilege whatsoever of absoluteness. Openness to the other is just as much of a factual character as the other's appearance to a subject.

---

[16]*Op. cit.*, p. 74.
[17]*Ibid.*

3. THE INTELLIGIBILITY OF REALITY

A Revolutionary Thesis. The ultimate consequence of all this is that the intelligibility itself of reality is placed in the factual order. This is a very revolutionary thesis. Ever since Parmenides claimed that being and knowing coincide, are identical, philosophers have practically always started from the supposition that reality is, in principle, intelligible. For this reason the scholastics used to say that every being is true. The intelligibility of reality was considered to be a matter of principle. Yet it is precisely this that Merleau-Ponty denies. Note that he does not deny that reality is intelligible. What he claims is that this intelligibility is a *fact,* a fundamental fact, of course, but, nonetheless, a fact. This intelligibility arises because the light of unveiling existence shines on the world, or rather, belongs to the world. Since our existence is a factual datum, it follows that the intelligibility of the world is a factual datum. The nature of this intelligibility has to be analyzed as a fact. But the facts show two things: first, that man extends himself to everything, so that everything is intelligible; secondly, that our understanding is situated, so that in principle it is not possible to bring the realm of reality fully to light.

This position is perhaps the most revolutionary thesis proposed by Merleau-Ponty. It is the core of his philosophy. The previous chapters merely presaged this thesis but, now that we are making it the theme of our study, we have penetrated into the very heart of Merleau-Ponty's philosophy. Being has an inner density which resists total penetration. While nothing wholly escapes the pervading power of man's light, nothing likewise is fully captured by it. The rational order is a zone of light in the density of being. Being and light do not coincide.

We see here very clearly how philosophy, no matter how thoroughly it is renewed, always continues to revert to the same eternal issues, of which the relationship between being and intelligibility is undoubtedly one of the most fundamental and most important questions. With this question we are in the midst of metaphysics. Merleau-Ponty asks this question and his reply is the core of his philosophy. Thus his philosophy is unquestionably metaphysical. His answer is that being and intelligibility do not coincide. While he does not withdraw anything from intelligibility, he refuses to identify anything fully with it.

Its Bearing on the Limits of Knowledge. In the light of this thesis some of Merleau-Ponty's concrete analyses become easier to understand. Speaking about the "thing" he says that it is accessible to us. There is in the "body-subject" a "logic of the world" which makes things accessible. Nonetheless, the thing is a thing precisely because it retains its density. "The real," he says, "lends itself for unlimited investigation, it is inexhaustible. For this reason human objects, utensils, present themselves to us as placed in the world, but natural things are rooted in a background of inhuman nature. For our existence the thing is less a pole attracting us than a pole that repels us. We do not recognize ourselves in things and it is precisely this that makes them things. The situation is not such that we first know the perspectives of the things and that we go by means of our perspectives, our senses and our perceptions, to the things; on the contrary, we go straight to the things and only in the second place do we become aware of the limits of our knowledge and of ourselves as knowers."[18] These limits do not consist in this that we can point to a datum which escapes our knowledge, for the self-contradiction of such an assertion is quite evident. But the limits consist in this that being and intelligibility never coincide, that being always appears to have a density through which, no matter how much it is known, it again and again eludes our knowledge. We do not have to choose, says Merleau-Ponty, between the omnipresence of consciousness and its bond to a situation, for both are true at the same time.[19]

Here lies the ultimate reason why Merleau-Ponty constantly rejects the two trends of thought which he calls "realism" and "idealism," and why he says that these trends, despite all their differences, ultimately amount to the same. For both affirm that reality is, in principle, intelligible. Realism views intelligibility as an "in itself": reality in itself is intelligible and our understanding is a reflex mirroring of this reality. Idealism teaches that we find the key to reality in ourselves, in our ideas, and that with the help of this key everything can be unlocked. The two currents of thought explain intelligibility in different ways but agree that reality is intelligible.

It goes without saying that in this question, which is of crucial importance, Merleau-Ponty deviates radically from Husserl, who until the end of his life held fast to the hypothesis that reality is intelligible. As we have explained, it is precisely this hypothesis that is denied, in the sense indicated above, by Merleau-Ponty.

---

[18] *Op. cit.*, p. 374.
[19] *Op. cit.*, p. 383.

"Metaphysics is the Enemy of the System." From the preceding considerations it should be evident also why, according to Merleau-Ponty, "metaphysics is the enemy of the system." For, "if the system is an orderly arrangement of concepts which simply brings together all aspects of experience into a synthesis, then the system destroys metaphysical consciousness and, moreover, at the same time morality. If, for instance, one wants to base the fact of intelligibility or of communication on an absolute value or on an absolute thought, there are two possibilities: either this absolute does not solve any difficulty, so that intelligibility and communication continue after all to find their foundation in themselves, or the absolute becomes involved in them, but then it corrupts all the human means through which we verify or justify something."[20]

Note that Merleau-Ponty speaks of "the *fact* of intelligibility," and says that this fact cannot find its ground in an absolute thought. These words are to be understood literally. Intelligibility is a fact and no absolute ground can be assigned to this fact. The insight that all being is intelligible is, according to Merleau-Ponty, not a genuine insight but an *a priori* which renders us blind to the true structure of our understanding.

The attempt, moreover, to place the basis of intelligibility in an absolute thought is meaningless. For, whether there exists any absolute thought or not, I can make a judgment only from my own standpoint and, no matter how rigidly I try to control myself, my standpoint can be wrong. Despite all the affirmations of the absolute, it continues to be just as difficult to come to an agreement with myself and with others. No matter how convinced I am that such an agreement is in principle attainable, in actual fact I have no other real grounds to believe in the possibility of the agreement than the experience of certain agreements reached by man. Consequently, my so-called belief in the absolute is reduced to nothing else than my experience of agreement with myself and with others. And if I want more than this, if I want to make an absolute principle the basis of my factual agreement, then I destroy that to which I want to give a firm foundation. For, if I am convinced that I possess absolute truth, I have the right to place my opinions above the dialog with the others because my opinions are sacred, absolute, I have the right to impose my opinions on others and even to use violence against them, if they

---

[20]*Sens et non-sens,* p. 189.

refuse to accept my views. Thus, I destroy the dialog, the only true way toward agreement.

4. METAPHYSICAL CONSCIOUSNESS DIES WHEN IT TOUCHES THE ABSOLUTE

When, however, I understand that truth arises only through my groping in the world, in my effort to enter into dialog with others, when I understand that the concepts "truth" and "value" lose all meaning outside this perspective, then the real world regains its importance as the field of truth. Then also there is evidence, there is a distinction between true and false, between good and evil, provided I do not seek the absolute. For metaphysical consciousness dies when it comes into contact with the absolute.

This last statement presupposes the entire perspective of Merleau-Ponty's philosophy and, outside this perspective, it is wholly unintelligible. Being becomes intelligible and comes to be meaning, says Merleau-Ponty, because of man's presence. Intelligibility and meaning belong to the factual order. They are not given once and for all but develop according as we become more open to being. This openness develops in a common history, in our dialog with one another. Being becomes meaning because we make it being-for-us. Being-for-us is identical with intelligibility and meaning. But the aprioristic belief in absolute intelligibility and absolute meaning makes us blind to intelligibility and meaning as they are *de facto* given to us. This belief undermines the real dimensions in which we live. It is possible, of course, that the affirmation of the absolute becomes harmless because it is simply stored somewhere in a corner of our consciousness, i.e., we simply go on with our groping existence in the world. In that case this affirmation does not play any role and is not dangerous. But if this affirmation fulfills a function in our search for truth, then it destroys the dimension in which intelligibility and meaning arise and thus becomes the death of metaphysical thought.

The Radical Contingency of All Meaning. "The contingency of everything existing," Merleau-Ponty continues, "and of everything that has value is not at all an unimportant truth for which one willy-nilly has to make room somewhere in a little corner of the system. This contingency is the fundamental condition on which a metaphysical view of the world is possible.[21] Because of his basic perspective, Merleau-Ponty could hardly arrive at any other conclusion than that

---

[21]*Op. cit.*, p. 192.

contingency is the ultimate sphere of everything. There is an unbreakable connection between his view about metaphysical consciousness and his affirmation of the radical contingency of all meaning.

All meaning is connected with man. There is intelligibility because man, as dialog with the world, has risen to the level of rationality. Our existence, as giver of meaning, is the center of Merleau-Ponty's philosophy. But the very presence itself of man as giver of meaning is a contingent fundamental fact. We are unable to account in any way for this fact, for any account would have to start from human meaning. Every argument needs a starting point, every justification needs a foundation. No matter what starting point or what foundation we may want to use, it always belongs to the meaning existing for us, and this meaning presupposes man. How, then, could we justify that which every justification presupposes? Man's presence, therefore, in the world is a fact for us and not more than a fact. For this reason every meaning, every intelligibility has a factual character; for this reason we live in the fundamental sphere of contingency. Wonder about this fundamental fact of contingency is the ultimate that can be reached by the philosopher. Through this wonder everything that is "unquestionable and obvious" is suddenly plunged into the sphere of fundamental contingency. The development of our discussion concerning the world, the flowering of arts and sciences, the growth of a common world, the entire course of history, the rise of mankind and of the world of human meaning, all this is encompassed and illuminated by philosophical wonder.

The Ultimate Perspective. It would be wrong to seek in man, as is done by certain forms of humanism, the explanation of all this. For man is included in the above-mentioned wonder, he is the very center of it. "Nothing can be explained by way of man, for he is not a strength but a weakness in the heart of being, for he is not a cosmological factor but the place where all cosmological factors, through never ending change, alter their meeting and become history."[22] Man is not a strength but a weakness in the very heart of being. He is at the very heart of being, for there is no other being than "being-for-us,"[23] and consequently we are its center. Yet nothing

[22]*Eloge de la philosophie,* p. 61.

[23]"Le fait métaphysique fondamental est ce double sens du *cogito;* je suis sûr qu'il y a de l'être,—à condition de ne pas chercher une autre sorte d'être que l'être-pour-moi." *Sens et non-sens,* p. 187.

can be explained by way of man, for man himself is the phenomenon causing the greatest wonder, he is the heart of the entire order of phenomena. When we begin to wonder about something and reflect more profoundly on this wonder, the wonder will ultimately always be concentrated on man himself. Thus man is not at all an explanatory principle.

"That decisive moment," writes Merleau-Ponty, "when material particles, words, events let themselves be animated by a meaning, whose contours they showed without containing them, and, most of all, that fundamental sound of the world which makes itself heard even in the least of our perceptions and of which knowledge and history are echoes—to establish these as facts against any naturalistic explanation is the same as to divest them of every sovereign necessity."[24] The philosopher dwells in the miracle of the birth of meaning, and this is for him the ultimate perspective. He raises wonder above every explanation. This is metaphysical consciousness. Within this basic sphere all terms, such as being, meaning, intelligibility, history, explanation and science, acquire a new sense. Merleau-Ponty refers to himself as the "philosopher who does not know." With this expression he wants to indicate the philosopher who has come to realize that wonder is the ultimate fundamental attitude of thinking. He asks himself how it is possible for the philosopher who does not know to speak with the one who knows, by which he means especially the orthodox Marxist and the Christian. Modest as the expression may be, Merleau-Ponty goes even further and is also the one who has come to realize that absolute knowledge is impossible, that so-called "knowing" is only an illusion of knowing. He is also the one who realizes that, because of his not-knowing, he has found access to genuine truth.

Unanswered Questions. Even after this study of Merleau-Ponty's basic perspective, there remain many unanswered questions, questions arising within the very perspective opened by Merleau-Ponty. In his first work, *La structure du comportement,* he analyzes different forms of behavior, as they actually occur within our world. He assumes the attitude of the objective observer of the world of behavior and makes distinctions in it. He distinguishes syncretic forms of behavior which are connected with certain stimuli, removable forms of behavior in which the behavior becomes more like an answer to

---

[24]*Eloge de la philosophie,* p. 63.

a situation, and finally the symbolic forms in which the situation can be expressed. By way of the various levels of behavior he finally ascends to man. He appears in this work to approach man as a certain being in the order of beings. He calls the animal likewise an "existence," thus indicating that the animal, like man, changes the world into a field of meaning. How is it possible for Merleau-Ponty to approach the world in this way, if the world is accessible to us only as a human field of meaning? As Paul Ricoeur correctly remarks, there are certain perspectives in this work which Merleau-Ponty has neglected in his later years.[25]

Even within the framework of his later work certain questions arise. Merleau-Ponty has never conceived man's giving of meaning in a purely active sense, as may appear even from his repeated rejection of idealism. The giving of meaning takes place in a dialog with the other. For this reason he says, e.g., that the contours of the meaning things have, delineate themselves even in the things themselves without being contained in them. He describes the dialog between the eye and the world. Things present themselves as a vaguely put question; our seeing provides a first reply; then the question can assume a sharper form; and finally a clear reply is made in the color which assumes a fixed form.[26] Accordingly, we should not speak solely of giving a meaning but also of accepting a meaning. But does this not imply that things are already a kind of potential meaning? For, otherwise, how could they lend themselves to a dialog with our existence?

In man we find a *"montage du monde,"* i.e., man is marvellously adapted to the world. But the opposite also is true: the world is marvellously adapted to man. Merleau-Ponty, it is true, always presupposes this, but he never makes it a theme of his considerations. Yet, doesn't the world's adaption to man allow us to speak of a kind of potential intelligibility present in things? And is this intelligibility not presupposed by the sciences? Doesn't the scientist always have the feeling that he discloses what was already present in the world, at least as a promise? Of course, it is impossible for us to look at what it is like independently of our knowledge. But doesn't the miracle itself of our knowledge, of our giving of meaning, show that the world in itself is already knowable? Of course, we cannot

---

[25]See the article quoted in footnote 35 of Chapter Six.
[26]*Phénoménologie de la perception*, p. 248.

deduce factual knowledge from knowability, but we may conclude
from factual knowledge to knowability. Yet this viewpoint, which
inevitably imposes itself within the whole of Merleau-Ponty's philosophy, has not been developed by him. He does not ask the questions
which we have formulated here, yet it seems to us that these questions
are inevitable.

Accordingly, we doubt that "metaphysical consciousness," as
described by Merleau-Ponty, is the final word within the context of
what he could and should have said. Some questions remain, even
after his final answer, and these questions are not extrinsic to the
perspective disclosed by Merleau-Ponty.

CHAPTER EIGHT

THE ATHEISM OF MERLEAU-PONTY

1. THEISM AND ATHEISM

The two preceding chapters, in which we have considered Merleau-Ponty's denial of the absolute and his conception of metaphysical consciousness, clearly presaged his atheism.[1] However, the question was not explicitly considered there because this aspect of Merleau-Ponty's philosophy is so important that it deserves a special study.

Merleau-Ponty's Familiarity with Christian Faith. It cannot be said that Merleau-Ponty is not well-informed about religion. Because of the milieu in which he grew up, he was especially acquainted with the Catholic faith. In his youth he was a faithful Christian, and by youth we do not mean merely his childhood years. He reveals himself rather familiar with Catholic doctrine, as appears especially when he confronts his theories with those of the Catholic Church and also occasionally in other texts. For instance, when he wants to illustrate the presence of reality itself in sense experience, he makes a reference to the Catholic teachings about the real presence of Christ in the Holy Eucharist. The way in which he develops the comparison shows that he knows what he is speaking about.[2]

Moreover, he has closely followed the development of Catholic doctrine in France and knows what is taking place in this respect. A rethinking is taking place, he says, in comparison with which the modernism of the beginning of the twentieth century pales into insignificance.[3] Accordingly, Merleau-Ponty places himself delib-

---

[1]The thesis that intelligibility belongs to the order of facts indissolubly connected with man implicitly contains the germ of atheism. For God is always conceived as the one who understands all reality. If there is a God, then, reality must be intelligible and, reversely, there cannot be a God if intelligibility is a fact indissolubly connected with man.

[2]"Comme le sacrement non seulement symbolise sous des espèces sensibles une opération de la Grace, mais encore est la présence réelle de Dieu, la fait résider dans un fragment d'espace et la communique à ceux qui mangent le pain consacré s'il sont intérieurement préparées, de la même manière le sensible a non seulement une signification motrice et vitale mais n'est pas autre chose qu'une certaine manière d'être au monde qui se propose à nous d'un point de l'espace, que notre corps reprend et assume s'il en est capable, et la sensation est à la lettre une communion." *Phénoménologie de la perception*, pp. 245 f.

[3]*Signes*, p. 307.

erately in opposition to religion. However, he never assumes an aggressive and irreverent position. He mentions his views in this matter only occasionally, and never in such a way that religion is dragged in artificially or in a forced way. He does not use any language which the religious-minded would have to consider insulting.

In devoting the following pages to Merleau-Ponty's atheism, we want to state explicitly that we will consider it only insofar as it manifests itself in his published works. We will abstain from mentioning events of the philosopher's personal life to throw doubt on his atheism or explain why he was led to his position.

Merleau-Ponty's Refusal to Call His Philosophy Atheistic. Sometimes doubt is expressed about Merleau-Ponty's atheism on the ground that he refuses to qualify his philosophy as atheistic. This refusal has sometimes been interpreted in the sense that he wants to keep the problem of God's existence open. However, such is not the case. He refuses the qualifier "atheistic" because he refuses to describe his philosophy from the standpoint of a negation.[4]

Some have an inclination to think, he says, that every philosophy which does not culminate in the affirmation of God is to be reduced to a denial of God, so that, broadly speaking, there would be only two kinds of philosophical thinking, viz., that which affirms the existence of God and that which denies this. Merleau-Ponty refers here to, e.g., Henri de Lubac and Jacques Maritain. De Lubac wants to study an atheism which really wants to replace what it destroys and, therefore, begins by making room for such a substitution, i.e., it begins by committing theocide.[5] Maritain, on the other hand, studies a phenomenon which he calls "positive atheism." Merleau-Ponty does not cease to point to the strangeness of this terminology, which closely resembles a contradiction. However, Maritain quickly identifies this positive atheism as "an active struggle against whatever is called God," as an "antitheism," an "act of faith in reverse," a "refusal of God" and a "challenge addressed to God."[6] Merleau-Ponty acknowledges that there is such an "antitheism," but, he says, it is a theology in reverse and therefore not strictly a philosophy. If one's thinking proceeds from this standpoint, it is indeed characterized by what it opposes and consequently has a theological nature. But one who describes all philosophical thinking in this fashion acts as if the whole

---

[4]*Eloge de la philosophie*, pp. 58 f.
[5]*Eloge de la philosophie*, p. 58.
[6]*Ibid.*

of philosophy can be reduced to a discussion between theism and atheism, between recognition of God and deification of man. Both these "isms" accuse each other of estrangement. The atheist says that man, by recognizing God, deprives himself of the truth that is proper to man. The theist thinks that the atheist appropriates what pertains only to God. They forget, says Merleau-Ponty, to ask themselves whether we really have to make a choice between the recognition of God and the deification of man.[7]

The a Priori *of Theism and Atheism.* Whoever puts the question in this way, says Merleau-Ponty, proceeds from a wrong, or at least doubtful, starting point, for he assumes that there is an absolute explanation of the reality in which we live and that, therefore, philosophical thinking is a search for the ultimate explanation and basis of this reality. Anyone who is guided by this *a priori* will indeed have to make the choice. Either he will have to accept God as the ultimate explanation or he will have to seek the absolute explanation in man and the world. He will have to recognize God or attribute divine properties to man or the world. He will have to choose between genuine theology or a "theology in reverse."

However, it is this fundamental attitude itself which Merleau-Ponty attacks. The others assume that there has to be an absolute explanation of the reality in which we live and, consequently, that this explanation has to be found either outside our world or in our world. But this starting point is false. Merleau-Ponty is against any absolute explanation and even against the search for one. It is not a coincidence that, when he speaks about the problem of God, he attacks at the same time the Christian affirmation of God and Marxism. Both seek something absolute. The Christian places this absolute in God, the Marxist in matter and his dream of the future. The Christian believes in God as in the Absolute Being, the Marxist believes that man will ultimately be to the full extent. Merleau-Ponty is against any affirmation of the absolute, whether outside our world or within it.[8]

Basis of Merleau-Ponty's Atheism. In view of these explanations it should be conceded to Merleau-Ponty that his philosophy is

---

[7]"On oublie de se demander si le philosophe a à choisir entre la théologie et l'apocalypse du Wonderland ou la 'mystique du surhomme', et si jamais aucun philosophe a installé l'homme dans les fonctions métaphysiques du Tout-Puissant." *Op. cit.,* pp. 59 f.

[8]"La philosophie, elle, s'établit dans un autre ordre, et c'est pour les mêmes raisons qu'elle élude l'humanisme prométhéen et les affirmations rivales de la théologie." *Op. cit.,* p. 60.

not marked by the denial of God. However, doesn't it follow from these same explanations that his thought is characterized by an even broader denial, viz., the denial of the absolute as such, no matter where one seeks it? The philosopher, replies Merleau-Ponty, is guided by what he really sees. But he sees that the world constantly begins again, that every acquisition is a starting point, that the future is never determined by the past, that man does not have a fixed destiny, that our relationship with one another and with nature has not been set once and forever, that human freedom is the ever-lasting soil in which meaning germinates.

The philosopher has become wise through the past and recognizes that no one knows what human freedom is capable of. We do not know what the world would look like if it were no longer dominated by scarcity and mutual competition.[9] The philosopher does not see anywhere absolute meaning, but he witnesses the constant birth of meaning. This dimension reveals itself to him, and it is in this dimension that he wants to think. Where is the core of this dimension? The reply is, of course: in man, the giver of meaning. However, man, the giver of meaning, is not nature, not a set of fully fixed characteristics. Man is man precisely because he transcends all determinateness, because he is self-transcending movement. Meaning is born, precisely because everthing human escapes all fixedness, precisely because one can never explain what orginates in man, since man transcends the possibility of explanation. A natural occurrence can be explained for the very reason that it is infrahuman.

Thus, Merleau-Ponty refuses to consider man as an explanatory principle. If humanism is viewed as a mode of thinking which wants to explain the human order by way of man, Merleau-Ponty refuses to be called a humanist. For man is precisely someone whose future cannot be understood from his past. Man is self-transcendence, and for this reason it does not behoove him to take delight in his own being. He is bored by the constituted, by that which has already been achieved and, therefore, also by his own being. In this way we are back at our starting point, viz., Merleau-Ponty's fundamental idea of contingency. But this contingency now appears to be positively charged. It is the birth place of meaning, it is a constant self-transcendence, a source of hope. We may even say, "the only

---

[9] *Op. cit.,* p. 60.

source of hope," for we base our hope, according to Merleau-Ponty, on that which does not have a determinate destiny, the transcendence of all destiny.[10]

This contingency does not allow man to take delight in what he is and therefore opposes itself to a deification of man. Yet the same contingency deprives theology also of its living space. For theology establishes man's contingency only to base it on a necessary cause, i.e., to get rid of it. Theology makes use of philosophical wonder to motivate an affirmation which puts an end to wonder.[11]

2. THE SCOPE OF MERLEAU-PONTY'S ATHEISM

God as Explanatory Factor. These words of Merleau-Ponty are decisive. Let us attempt to determine their scope. His fundamental intuition consists in this that he sees man as a being transcending the determinism of nature. In man it is not possible to deduce his future from his past. He is the creative origin of meaning, and for this reason he transcends "explanation." What kind of explanation is in question here? Evidently, the kind which we meet with in the order of the things of nature. This order is controlled by deterministic necessity. Man, however, transcends this order. Merleau-Ponty's perspective amounts to this, that human events cannot be explained in the same way as the processes of nature. In other words, he affirms a dimension which transcends nature. Now, he continues, if God is affirmed as the cause of everything, including man, we destroy what we want to explain.

Thus, it follows that Merleau-Ponty starts from the assumption that God would be an explanatory factor in the same way as nature is an explanatory factor, that God would be cause in the same fashion as nature is a cause. He says that theology uses philosophical wonder to arrive at an affirmation which puts an end to philosophical wonder. Theology explains contingency in such a way that it gets rid of contingency. God's causality, then, destroys contingency. If God is affirmed, everything reverts to the causal order; hence there is no longer any room for creative freedom, for existence as the giver of meaning.

---

[10]*Op. cit.*, p. 61. Merleau-Ponty formulates this same thought also elsewhere, but it is here that its profound scope becomes apparent.

[11]"Car la théologie ne constate la contingence de l'être humain que pour la dériver d'un Etre nécessaire, c'est-à-dire pour s'en défaire, elle n'use de l'étonnement philosophique que pour motiver une affirmation qui le termine." *Op. cit.*, p. 61.

Merleau-Ponty and Sartre. It must be admitted that the causality of nature and freedom as giver of meaning exclude each other. Man cannot be reduced to the processes of nature without destroying this freedom. Whoever lets man be absorbed by nature will inevitably end with determinism. Merleau-Ponty thinks that the affirmation of God likewise denies creative freedom, human giving of meaning, and therefore history. Accordingly, he does not know any other causality than that of determinism. His argument in this question is not original, for Sartre had already put forward the same idea. This argument is that one has to choose between God and free man. Affirming God means the implicit denial of free man, of history. Safeguarding human freedom and history leads logically to the denial of God.

It may seem strange to the reader that we do not make a distinction here between Merleau-Ponty and Sartre despite the fact that there is such a marked difference in their views concerning freedom. Sartre affirms, even in his latest book, an absolute freedom, while Merleau-Ponty denies this. For, according to Merleau-Ponty, freedom is never an absolute starting point and always remains ambiguous.

While we do not deny this difference between Sartre and Merleau-Ponty, we wish to point out that it does not play any role insofar as the basis of atheism is concerned. Whether freedom is absolute or not, Sartre and Merleau-Ponty agree that human freedom and divine causality cannot be harmonized. We may add that there are faithful Christians who are of the same opinion. Gabriel Marcel, for example, does not want to call God a cause in any way, because he believes that it is not possible to affirm causality without affirming also determinism.[12]

A Univocal Concept of Causality. From the preceding pages it should be evident that Merleau-Ponty makes use here of a univocal concept of causality. All causality has a deterministic character.[13] In this point his philosophy reveals a serious defect. We call something a cause insofar as it makes something else be. Things of nature make one another be, and for this reason we call them causes. But we, human beings, also make one another be. In a successful colloquy, for instance, we make one another fruitful, and through mutual

---

[12]Marcel, "Dieu et la causalité," *De la connaissance de Dieu, Recherches de philosophie,* Paris, 1958, pp. 27-33.
[13]We wonder whether Merleau-Ponty, in rejecting the intelligibility of being, does not likewise understand intelligibility in a univocal sense.

affection we fill one another's needs. There is not only interaction between man and world but also between man and man. This mutual interaction of man and man is the core of our human co-existence. There is question here of really making one another be, of real causality. On this level, however, causality and freedom are not opposed to each other. In human existence causality receives a higher meaning; it is not merely not opposed to freedom but even presupposes it. It is impossible for me to make my words bear fruit in the other, if he is not willing to listen, if does not open himself to me. We cannot make each other happy, if we do not turn to each other. We cannot help one another unless we are willing to be helped. This dimension is hardly or not at all analyzed by Merleau-Ponty. He does not devote his attention to causality as it manifests itself on the level of human co-existence. This chapter is missing in his philosophy. Hence, he does not have the right simply to identify causality with deterministic causality. While we do not want to enter here into discussion with Merleau-Ponty's atheism, we must draw attention to this weak link in his argumentation.

The a Priori *of Merleau-Ponty's Atheism.* From the preceding explanations it becomes apparent that Merleau-Ponty's atheism is based on an affirmation and on an *a priori.* First of all, on an affirmation. He sees creative freedom, existence as giver of meaning. The fundamental fact of his philosophy is the affirmation that the subject is the origin of meaning. The subject, even as anonymous existence, is origin, cause. Here lies the most profound difference between a thing of nature and a subject. A thing of nature is cause, but a subject is origin. In the case of a natural thing one can foresee what it will produce, but no such prediction is possible with respect to a subject.

Secondly, Merleau-Ponty's atheism is based on an *a priori.* This *a priori* is that the affirmation of a cause, even a divine cause, destroys the above-described origin. Man is no longer able to be origin, if he has God as his cause. If God is the Lord of history, history itself can no longer be original. Note that Merleau-Ponty can conclude to atheism only on the basis of both the affirmation and the *a priori,* taken together. Consequently, his atheism is ultimately based on an *a priori* which he does not render sufficiently secure.

It is the same, says Merleau-Ponty, to raise man, as origin of meaning, above every naturalistic explanation and to divest him of every sovereign necessity.[14] In this text he treats the theological ex-

[14]*Eloge de la philosophie,* p. 63.

planation as if it were exactly the same as a naturalistic explanation. His thinking on this point is wholly univocal.

Influence of Traditional Theology. It cannot be denied that theology itself has been the occasion suggesting this line to Merleau-Ponty. Far too often theologians have viewed God's causality as a prolongation of natural causes. Natural processes have often been made the starting point of the proof of God's existence. By describing God as the apex in the order of causes, one opens the way to viewing Him as a kind of supercause of nature. It is striking, moreover, that for such a long time no need was felt to analyze causality, making-be, as it reveals itself in the mutual dealings of man with man. Yet this approach seems to be the only way leading us to a causality which does not exclude but rather include freedom.

Unsurprisingly, theology itself has long wrestled with the difficulty of harmonizing God's causality and human freedom. A theory, such as that of "physical predetermination," which claims that God beforehand *determines* the free action of man in a "physical" way (though the term "physical" did not have then the meaning which it has now), does not seem very suitable to remove the objections of contemporary philosophers against divine causality. Briefly put, in the light of the traditional theology, which Merleau-Ponty may have studied in his younger years, it is not surprising that he has presented this kind of an argument.

Elimination of Contingency as a Problem. In the same work Merleau-Ponty faces also de Lubac's objection, that he does not merely deny God but also "eliminates the problem that gives rise to the affirmation of God in our consciousness."[15] What Father de Lubac means is that the affirmation of God usually arises from the consciousness of contingency proper to everything. The contingent demands a ground and, therefore, there must be a God. Merleau-Ponty replies that the philosopher does not deny the problem of contingency and does not neglect it. On the contrary, the philosopher makes it radical and raises it above the "solutions" which choke it.[16] The scope of this reply should be clear from the preceding considerations. Merleau-Ponty does not deny contingency but makes it the core of his thought. The subject is a subject precisely because he is the free and contingent origin of meaning. Thus, the affirmation of contingency

---

[15]*Op. cit.,* p. 62.
[16]*Ibid.*

is the heart of Merleau-Ponty's philosophy. And, according to him, this contingency is such that in principle it excludes every explanation. In this way he radicalizes contingency.

On the other hand, it is apparent also that, strictly speaking, Merleau-Ponty fails to reply to de Lubac's objection. De Lubac did not at all reproach Merleau-Ponty for denying or eliminating contingency, but merely pointed out that he eliminates contingency, not as a fact, but as a problem, as a question demanding an explanation. De Lubac's point is unquestionably true, for Merleau-Ponty views contingency as a fundamental fact that is raised above all explanations. In other words, he fails to meet the point raised by de Lubac. Yet it is precisely here that lies one of the crucial questions of our time—viz., is man, as origin of meaning, a final fact that resists all further explanations or does he contain a reference to a higher reality? According to Merleau-Ponty, man in dialog, of course, with the other, is the origin of all meanings, the origin therefore also of all questions, and this origin cannot be made the object of a question. This is precisely the point raised by Father de Lubac's objections.

Understanding and Accepting Religion. The philosopher, Merleau-Ponty continues, is quite capable of understanding religion. For religion is one of the expressions of the "central phenomenon," i.e., of the mystery lying at the heart of appearing reality, the miracle that meaning arises and appears. But, he continues, to understand religion and to accept it are not the same but almost opposites.[17] In this point he refers again to his analysis of Socrates. The Greek philosopher did not deny the "gods of the city" but brought them to their proper truth. He accepted them, not as the city's rulers did with a "massive and fleshy consent," but he accepted them with understanding. Socrates divested the values of society from the absoluteness with which they were posited and considered them, therefore, as relative forms of expression, which in principle are subject to being overtaken by the course of history. In this sense Merleau-Ponty claims to understand religion in its source, i.e., as an expression of the fundamental mystery in which we live.

However, he realizes that religion, understood in this way, is, in the eyes of religious man, the denial of religion. In this way he affirms his fundamental viewpoint—he wants to think from the stand-

---

[17]"Ce n'est pas la même chose, c'est presque le contraire de comprendre la religion et de la poser." *Ibid.*

point of the mystery which the birth of meaning is and, by viewing everything from this standpoint, he places himself in metaphysical consciousness. This fundamental viewpoint has greater value for him than all theories claiming to be its explanation. While he is willing to understand all these explanations, he is unable to accept any of them. They appear to him too naïve in relation to that which has to be explained.

Radical "Critique of Idols." Anyone with an open mind, says Merleau-Ponty, will have to acknowledge that the above-described philosophical attitude is meaningful. Philosophical negativity has a positive meaning, i.e., it is proper to the spirit to combat unjustified absolutes. Here Merleau-Ponty quotes again Jacques Maritain, who points out that the Christian affirmation of God is a constant struggle against idols, i.e., against man's deformations of God. The saint, says Maritain, may be described as an "integral atheist" with respect to a god who would be nothing else than a safeguard of the natural order, who would sanction both the good and the evil of the world, who would approve slavery, the suffering of little children and the misery of the oppressed, who would sacrifice man to the world, who would be, to summarize it all, nothing but the "absurd emperor of the world." The Christian God, however, Maritain goes on, is the radical denial of the above-described god, for He is accessible to man's prayer.

In his reply Merleau-Ponty says that the philosopher is in agreement with the movement of thought expressed in Maritain's ideas, and he admits that this struggle against idols is characteristic of Christianity. But he asks himself whether Christianity is able to be rigorously logical in its critique of idols. For the Christian himself has recourse to the idea of the "Necessary Being," formed by the reflection of some philosophers. If God is the Necessary Being, isn't He also the "Emperor of the World"? And if He is not this "Emperor," does He not cease to be the maker of the world? So it seems that the Christian has to stop his critique of idols at a point where reason would logically want to continue. It is the philosopher, says Merleau-Ponty, who is radical in his critique of the idols.[18]

In another striking passage, Merleau-Ponty elaborates his standpoint as follows. "Catholicism, especially in France, is busily engaged in a rigorous investigation, in comparison with which the modernism

---

[18]*Op. cit.,* pp. 64 f.

of the beginning of our century appears sentimental and vague. At the same time, however, the hierarchy re-affirms the most worn-out formulas of explanatory theology, which are to be found in the Syllabus against modernism. One can understand the attitude of the hierarchy: it is true that one cannot think at the same time from the standpoint of the contingency of human existence and abide with the Syllabus. It is even true that religion is unbreakably connected with a minimum of explanatory thought. In a recent article François Mauriac indicated that atheism could have an acceptable meaning, if it would go only against the God of philosophers and men of learning, the 'thought God.' Without this 'thought God,' however, without a divine thought that is infinite and lies at the origin of the world, Christ is a human being, His birth and His suffering cease to be divine acts to become symbols of the general human situation. It would be unreasonable to expect from a religion that it understands mankind, according to the beautiful expression of Jean Giraudoux, as the *'cariatide du vide.'*[19] Thus, we are faced with a return to an explanatory theology, the return to a renewed affirmation of the Most Real Being, with all the consequences of a massive transcendence from which religious reflection endeavored to escape. There is again a distance between, on the one hand, the Church with its sacred treasure of truth, its mysteries about the invisible and unverifiable and, on the other, real human communication; again there is a 'short' between the heaven of principles and the earth of concrete existence; again philosophical doubt becomes a formality; again all adversity is called 'Satan,' and again is the battle against adversity won beforehand. Occultistic thinking scores a goal."[20]

3. Merleau-Ponty's Evaluation of Christianity

In an article entitled, *"Foi et bonne foi,"* incorporated into *Sens et non-sens,*[21] Merleau-Ponty performs a critical analysis of Christianity, which, as we have said, for him means especially Catholicism. He endeavors to perform this analysis from within. It is very instructive to see how a philosopher like Merleau-Ponty evaluates Christianity. For this reason we will outline this article here.

---

[19] The "caryatide" is a column in the shape of a woman. Thus, the expression "caryatide of emptiness" means an upward moving force which in principle has no fixed purpose, a movement without a fixed destiny, a movement which lies in the horizon of nothingness.

[20] *Signes*, pp. 307 f.

[21] Pp. 351-370.

Hervé's Critique of the Church. Merleau-Ponty wrote his article on the occasion of a discussion between Jean Daniélou and Pierre Hervé. Daniélou argued that the Christian could side with those who struggle against the ruling powers for a new freedom of mankind. To this Hervé replied that, while the individual Christian may do so, the same cannot be asserted of Christianity as a whole. According to Merleau-Ponty, Hervé is right. There have been Christians who took the side of freedom and went against established authority. Even the official documents of the Church sometimes contain passages favoring this line. However, the texts that take the opposite view are far more numerous. Above all, the Catholic Church is not a collection of texts and individuals, but an apparatus, an institution, a movement, and as such it is endowed with its own inner logic. Taken as a whole the Catholic Church functions as a reactionary power, certain pronouncements and individual Catholics notwithstanding.

When Engelbert Dollfuss established the first Christian-social government of Europe in Austria and began by bombarding the workers' sections of Vienna, Hervé was a young man, says Merleau-Ponty, whom the demands of his faith had driven to a leftist viewpoint concerning political life. A magazine of Christian inspiration addressed a protest against the bombardment to Miklas, the Austrian President. One of the most influential religious orders, so it was said, would support the protest. Invited to a meal by some members of this order, Hervé to his utter amazement heard it said at this meal that, after all, the Dollfuss' government was the established authority and that, as such, it had the right to make use of force. As citizens, Catholics could, of course, think what they wanted but, precisely as Catholics, they could not make any reproaches to Dollfuss. Hervé had never been able to forget these words, although at the time he merely told the speaker that his remarks showed how right the workers were who thought that in social questions one can never fully count on Catholics.[22]

Hervé's critique, so Merleau-Ponty continues, is incomplete. It views the attitude of individual Catholics against the background of the entire Catholic Church as an institution and of papal diplomacy. Thus, this critique passes from the order of ideas to that of facts; consequently, it does not really convince. For how can a Catholic who thinks progressively separate Catholicism from the way in which he himself thinks and feels? Daniélou, Merleau-Ponty argues, will

[22]*Op. cit.*, pp. 351 f.

admit that the past of the Church does not plead in favor of his own view, but he will add that the Church has to be brought back to its own truth. He will accuse the past and demand of the future that it hunger and thirst again for justice. He will want to bring the external face to face again with the inner core of the Church, he will want to make Catholicism sensitive again to the voice of its conscience. He will be able to think that the conservatism of the past has been an unfortunate incident and that a radical change can take place on this point.[23]

For this reason Merleau-Ponty wants to present a more profound critique of Christianity by showing that religious conviction through its own inner logic has of necessity to lead to conservatism. He is convinced that the Christian attitude of life itself contains something which leads the Christian to a conservative attitude. Let us see how he presents this critique.

Belief in an Internal and in an External God. Catholicism, Merleau-Ponty argues, believes at the same time in an internal and in an external God. It is this formula which, he claims, explains the contradictions present in the Christian attitude of life.

Catholicism believes in an internal God. Truth, says Saint Augustine, dwells in the inner man and God is more intimate to us than we ourselves are. God is spirit, and my self-experience as a spirit gives me an inkling about God. God is the fullness of the light which I myself am at my best. God knows everything I know, for He is the fullness of knowledge. My experience of my knowledge makes me suspect what an omniscient God is. To obey God does not mean that I bow before a strange power, for God is, as it were, an extension of the best that I am. If I let myself be guided by what really is light in me, I cannot become estranged from God, and if nonetheless I become estranged from Him, then this is a sign that it was not a light that guided me. God should be served in spirit and truth. External violence cannot lead anyone to God, for He is found through the inner attitude of life.

In this way religion is placed in a dimension of eternity, making it inviolable. What has value in the first place is the internal intention. Activity is merely the execution of this intention. Value lies in the motive. God is the fullness of goodness, to which the world cannot really add anything. God remains good and adorable, no matter what

---

[23]*Op cit.*, pp. 252 f.

happens to the world. In everything that occurs in the world we can find rest by turning to God. Through our bond with God we are in the core of our existence raised above the world. In this perspective anything happening in the world is merely of secondary importance.[24]

Catholicism believes also in an external God, for through the Incarnation of God the perspective has been radically modified. God has become manifest in the external. He has been seen at a certain place and at a certain moment of history. God is no longer found by entering into oneself but by looking for Him in a real past, by discovering and interpreting a real event outside us. Christianity now becomes the opposite of spiritualism. God has entered history and continues to live in it. The world and history are no longer useless, for they are the place where God comes to be. It is now as if God is no longer sufficient unto Himself. Sin is now something fortunate because through it man has been given such a redemption. Religion is now no longer a departure from history but an entrance into historical reality.[25]

Ambiguity of Christianity. Christianity and Catholicism, accuses Merleau-Ponty, never hold fast to either the internal God or the external God, but float between the two. One has to abandon himself and lose his life but, by doing so, he finds it back in a different order. Faith is trust; therefore, one leaps into the dark, but knows at the same time whom one trusts and in this way remains secure. The Catholic Church is based on the Incarnation of Christ, yet it condemns those who do not accept a rational proof of God's existence. It rejects a Christian reflection which wants to rely solely on the Christian experience achieved in the course of history. It does not reject this experience entirely, but submits it to the judgment of intellectual speculation and of Thomism.[26]

Christianity accepts the Incarnation of the Son, but continues to accept also the Father who is above history. The Spirit guarantees that God remains present in history but, in spite of this, there remains a gaze looking at history from without. History is unable to develop

---

[24] *Op. cit.,* pp. 354-57. Merleau-Ponty says, e.g., "Il [God] est absolument cette clarté, cette lumière que je suis dans mes meilleurs moments." *Ibid.,* p. 355. Note that such expressions do not take sufficiently into account the analogy of philosophical notions. The way God exists is something that human consciousness cannot at all visualize.

[25] *Op. cit.,* pp. 357-60.

[26] *Op. cit.,* pp. 360 f.

fully according to its own inner dynamics, but stands still under the eternal gaze of Infinite Knowing which again makes whatever happens something of secondary importance only.[27]

On this basis Merleau-Ponty attempts to understand the ambiguous attitude of Christianity. Insofar as the Christian thinks along the lines of the Incarnation, there is progress in history and the Christian can be a revolutionary. The recognition, however, of the eternal, transcendent kingdom of the Father makes the Christian conservative. Within the development of history sin can be a good, but under the absolute gaze of the Father it remains absolutely forbidden. Because of the Father's infinite perfection, perfection lies behind us and not in front of us. The Christian may accept existing evil, but he can never pay for progress with evil. He may adhere to a revolution that has been made; he may overlook the crime of this revolution but he will not make revolution. For revolution remains a revolt against the established order as long as it is not successful. Precisely as a Catholic, the Catholic has no feeling for the future. The future must have become a present before he can adhere to it. For the will of the Infinite is mirrored by the things of this world.[28]

Fortunately, Merleau-Ponty continues, the will of God is not always perfectly clear, and this uncertainty leaves a certain margin of freedom, allowing a Catholic, as a citizen, to adhere to a progressive movement. Even so, he will not devote the best of his talents to this movement, for, as a Catholic, he is rather indifferent to the movement of history. His presence always implies a measure of absence. He is not entirely conservative because God's perfection always transcends the contingent manifestations of His will. He is not fully progressive because history is to a certain extent merely something of secondary importance to him. The Catholic is a bad conservative and a bad progressive.

There is one case in which the Church recommends revolt—namely, when the established power violates the divine law. However, it has never yet actually happened that the Church for this reason alone has revolted against the legitimate power. What has happened is that the Church has favored revolutionaries because they protected its temples, its ministers and its possessions. God will have fully entered history, says Merleau-Ponty, only when the Church feels just as much obligation toward all men as toward its ministers, only when

[27] *Op. cit.*, pp. 361 f.
[28] *Op. cit.*, pp. 362-64.

it worries just as much about the dwellings of a threatened city as about its temples. There is such a thing as a Christian revolt, but it manifests itself only when the Church itself is threatened.

The Church demands for itself the courage and heroism of the faithful and thus does not leave them full freedom to fight for historical progress. In other words, the Church makes its faithful live in a double order. For this reason the Church is conservative. It is here, says Merleau-Ponty, that lies the true nucleus of Hegel's and Marx' theory of estrangement. Merleau-Ponty agrees with them that Christianity estranges man from the world and from history. Strictly speaking, the Christian religion itself says so explicitly, for no one can serve two masters. One is really attached only to that to which he is fully attached.

It is true that Christians believe also in the Incarnation of God and consequently in the progress of history. For this reason they are able, at least from time to time, to approach a revolutionary attitude. It is not difficult to find individual Christians as examples illustrating this point. And there is no reason to assume that these persons do not devote themselves wholeheartedly to the cause. In such a case they let themselves be guided by their historical thinking. Yet they are unable fully to remove from themselves the ambiguity implied in their religion. There always remains something in this religion through which the revolution may become a suspect phenomenon. When they actually support the revolution, they have to forget temporarily something that lives in them.

4. EVALUATION OF MERLEAU-PONTY'S CRITIQUE OF CHRISTIANITY

Let us summarize here first the two perspectives opened by Merleau-Ponty in his *Eloge de la philosophie* and *Foi et bonne foi*. In the former he argues that man is origin, free, contingent origin, and that the affirmation of God, of a supreme origin, does violence to this original character of man. In *Foi et bonne foi* he says that the doctrine of incarnation invites man to be origin because from the moment of God's incarnation history becomes a genuine development of meaning. But Christianity continues to affirm also the absolute God, who as eternal wisdom is above history and gazes at it with an all-encompassing glance. This affirmation becomes an obstacle for the Christian, preventing him from becoming seriously involved in the development of meaning. Accordingly, the Christian faith contains a possibility of progressiveness, but this possibility is impeded by the recognition of the eternal and absolute.

The Reserve of the Philosopher. We would be mistaken if, from Merleau-Ponty's critique of Christianity, we would conclude that he demands of the philosopher and of man in general an unqualified attachment to history. The reproach that the Christian stands in the development of meaning with a certain reserve is, therefore, all the more surprising because Merleau-Ponty requires a measure of reserve also of the philosopher and of man in general.

Philosophy, so he says, limps.[29] It dwells in history and in life and wants to establish itself in their center, there where they have the character of origin, where meaning is born. Moreover, philosophy is expression, and it can be this only by not coinciding with that which is expressed, for something can be expressed only if one places himself at a distance from it. The philosopher is not the grave man who focuses his attention on a single thing which he affirms without any reserve. The most resolute philosophers always want something that appears contradictory: they want to build but by tearing down; they want to abolish but by preserving. For they always see the multiple aspects of one and the same reality; they stand at a distance; they always have something at the back of their mind when they argue. The philosopher cannot argue in the same way as one who is fully involved in action, for he is much too sensitive to the arguments of his opponent. He does not want to push his viewpoint too vigorously as one pushes self-interest in practical matters, for he wants to attain truth and even his opponents may be able to contribute to this attainment.

The philosopher devotes his full attention to the serious man, e.g., the important man, the religious man, the passionate man, but the way in which he approaches them shows that he is not like them. He may act sometimes, but in that case his deed is a sign of his philosophical standpoint. Philosophizing in the proper sense does not lie on the level of action, but is a reflection on it. It places itself at a distance. Machiavelli is not at all Machiavellian, for he describes the sly ways a prince should take, but a sly man hides his tricks. The philosopher explains why opposition may in some cases and on certain conditions become treason, for circumstances may arise in which all must act together and opposition should remain silent. Thus, the

---

[29]What follows here expresses the ideas found in *Signes,* pp. 79-86.

philosopher's language is not that of the rulers, for they simply say that treason is committed, while the philosopher uses terms indicating that he remains "at a distance." He becomes involved in such a way that one feels in his approach the possibility of unfaithfulness. For he motivates his faithfulness, and the consideration of these motives could conceivably lead him to the opposition. The philosopher's adherence is never "massive and fleshy." He is never fully what he is.

The Reserve of Man. However, Merleau-Ponty continues, is all this really characteristic of the philosopher only or is the philosophical attitude the unfolding of something that is present in every man, or at least should be present in everyone? The reply is that it is or should be a general characteristic of man. For in man himself there is a difference between the one who understands and the one who chooses; consequently, every man is divided in himself even as the philosopher stands at a distance from life. Man chooses in a chiaroscuro, and it is not possible to justify the choice absolutely. One who chooses as man knows that he is groping in the dark. He understands the ambiguity of his choice. To involve oneself as man, it is necessary to remain at a distance. The "massive and fleshy 'yes'" is not only unphilosophical but also inhuman.

Yet all this is no excuse for either man or the philosopher to abstain from action. For action has to be taken at the moment when there is question of the birth of meaning. He who, because of the semi-darkness in which we move, abstains from acting until everything is clear, is capable only of being a follower, of adhering to the achievements of others. He does not make history but merely takes over the history made by others. It is proper to the situation of man that he walks in a chiaroscuro. At the same time, however, man knows this. When he becomes involved, he places himself at the same time at a distance from himself. In this aspect also philosophy is an expression of life.

The Core of Subjectivity. The question could be asked whether a philosopher who thinks this way about life and philosophy has the right to reproach the Christian's aloofness. Doesn't Merleau-Ponty himself plead in favor of the distance for which he blames the Christian? We may even go further and ask whether Merleau-Ponty philosophically justifies the distance which in his view is an essential characteristic of man.

The distance with respect to the situation, with respect to the choice made by man, is one of the most essential themes of Merleau-Ponty's philosophy. For his philosophy is a philosophy of the birth of meaning. But it is precisely because he is capable of placing himself at a distance that the "body-subject" becomes an existence which projects a history. The body-subject becomes the origin of light by giving expression to meaning, by making meaning value, and especially by passing from perceptive meaning to explicit truth. All this, however, is wholly impossible without the above-mentioned distance. If man were unable to place himself at a distance from situation and world, he would cling to his situation like an animal; he would not be able to project a history. Sartre saw this very clearly and therefore refers to human existence as "nihilation," placing the "being" of things in opposition to the "nothingness" of consciousness. Merleau-Ponty speaks of the "other extreme of the axis which connects us with things and ideas."[30] But, unlike Sartre, he refuses to refer to this other extreme as a "nothingness." For if consciousness were "nothingness," we could not speak of nearby and far away; the relief of the entire order of being would disappear, and there would be no reason to speak any longer about dimensions and openness.

Merleau-Ponty approaches here the question of what the human subject really is in the depth of his being. His essence is not thing-like being, for through his subjectivity man transcends the thing-like. It is not the "nothingness" of Sartre, for this "nothingness" does not at all explain how we have access to being. Because of our core of subjectivity we are in the world in such a way that we are able to place ourselves at a distance, express ourselves, make history.

In what does this "core of subjectivity" consist? In *La structure du comportement* Merleau-Ponty says that the animal is another existence, but in his later works he writes that man is absolutely distinct from the animal. And the reason is precisely that he can place himself at a distance from his situation. Thus, the question concerning this core of human subjectivity becomes all the more urgent. Yet Merleau-Ponty does not reply to this question, at least not in his published works. All we can find are incidental remarks, mostly of a negative character.

He says, for example, that "there is no inner man," and he is opposed to the "abyss of the self." However, a systematic investigation

---

[30] *Signes,* p. 29.

of this question is lacking in his published works. He has not even made human consciousness the topic of an analysis, although consciousness is a fundamental characteristic of being-man. True, he studies consciousness in its intentional directedness, i.e., he follows the direction, indicated by consciousness, toward the world, toward the past and the future. Nevertheless, when we speak of conscious orientation, a distinction should be made between the aspect "orientation" and the aspect "conscious" even though consciousness is seen as essentially intentional or oriented. If this distinction is not made, one cannot distinguish consciousness from any other orientation. Even if consciousness is orientation, it is nonetheless conscious orientation and, therefore, has to be examined precisely as consciousness.

The same applies to freedom. Against Sartre, Merleau-Ponty argues extensively that our freedom is not absolute but has an ambiguous character, that complete freedom for man does not make sense because our freedom always starts on the road on which we are already travelling. But, whether our freedom is absolute or not, it is nonetheless freedom. Again, however, Merleau-Ponty offers us no solid study concerning the innermost character of freedom.

Insufficiently Founded Argument. In his article *Foi et bonne foi* Merleau-Ponty says that the affirmation of the absolute God is connected with the affirmation of man's interiority. From his being-in-truth the religious man affirms absolute truth. But, if the affirmation of God takes place in a dimension which Merleau-Ponty has not investigated, how, then, can he exclude this affirmation as absolutely as he does? Would not the philosophical justification of his position demand that the denial of God be preceded by an inquiry which he has never made? It seems to us that Merleau-Ponty's standpoint in this question is a conclusion based on insufficient premises.

This doubt extends also to the way in which Merleau-Ponty argues. The affirmation of God's causality, he says, contains a denial of the fact that man himself is origin. But, is it excluded that there can be a causality which allows the effect to have the character of origin? It would seem that the reply has to be in the affirmative when we consider how we, as human beings, influence one another. Parents educate their children, and this education implies the exercise of influence. Yet good parents educate in such a way that the child itself becomes origin of meaning. To educate well means that justice is done to the child precisely as an inner source of meaning. Likewise, he who expresses love evokes the beloved's love but in such a way that this love comes from within, for otherwise it would not be love. We have here a mode of causality which does not prevent the "effect" from being-origin but, on the contrary, evokes and promotes its originality. Merleau-Ponty has never made this dimension the object of his study and, therefore, an essential link is missing in his argumentation.

It is not our intention here to offer a counter-argument, but merely to investigate the conclusive power of Merleau-Ponty's train of thought. In our general critical inquiry into Merleau-Ponty's philosophy we will revert to this question and assign to these critical remarks their proper place in a more general framework.

Catholic Lack of Creativity. Those who know Merleau-Ponty's work thoroughly will remark that what we have done here is to express precisely what he complains about in reference to contemporary thinkers in general and Christians in particular—namely, that they combat one another from traditional standpoints without creatively developing their own viewpoint. To philosophize, he says, is to search. Today, however, hardly anyone is searching. Almost everyone simply accepts a tradition and continues to defend it. Yet, one would have to start philosophizing because there are things to see and to express. In its stead, the basis of philosophical reflection is sought not in the truth or values one sees but in the vices or errors of standpoints which one rejects. We execrate many things but adhere to very few. Our thinking is a rearguard action.

This condition, says Merleau-Ponty, is in harmony with the general characteristics of our time, which is a period of decay. In such a period ideas cease to be fruitful. They degenerate into the justification of what is established, into relics, points of honor. What is pompously called the "movement of ideas" can be reduced to the sum total of our nostalgias, our resentments, fears and phobias. All this is typical of a decaying order, exposed to the threat of a world-wide movement which threatens to subvert everything.[31] This description reminds us somewhat of Marx' analyses.

The same situation, Merleau-Ponty continues, exists also with respect to the approach to the problem of God. Unlike Thomas Aquinas, Anselm and Descartes, no one, or hardly anyone, proves the existence of God. Contemporary studies simply presuppose the proofs. They limit themselves to refute the denial of God either by seeking in

[31]*Eloge de la philosophie,* pp. 57 f.

the new forms of thinking gaps through which the affirmation of God can be smuggled in or by simply rejecting these forms as atheistic.[32]

In this respect Merleau-Ponty is largely right. Creative thinking is not sufficiently pursued by Catholics. All too frequently the established systems are simply repeated, and new forms of thought are criticized from without. Too few thinkers are involved in the growth of light that illuminates our era. It is difficult to find in Catholic writings a philosophical study of God, which endeavors to discover the road to God from modern standpoints.

Nevertheless, we may and must point out that Merleau-Ponty's line of thinking in this respect is incomplete and, therefore, unsatisfactory. He undermines what constitutes for the religious man the starting point of his affirmation of God and his living with God. Of course, we cannot blame Merleau-Ponty for not raising certain problems, for every philosopher has the right to determine for himself what he wants to reflect upon. However, this right does not allow him to draw conclusions from insufficient premises. Without performing an analysis of the subject, one may not reject any statement that is based in part also on such an analysis. Once more, we are not trying to construct here our own philosophy, but merely to throw light on the insufficiency of Merleau-Ponty's analyses.

---

[32] *Op. cit.*, p. 58.

CHAPTER NINE

MERLEAU-PONTY AND PHENOMENOLOGY

1. INTRODUCTION

The fundamental lines of Merleau-Ponty's thought have been outlined in the preceding chapters. We must now turn our attention to his position with respect to trends of thought that are related to his thinking but nonetheless distinct from his philosophy. In doing so, we cannot make arbitrary comparisons, but have to study those forms of thought which, according to Merleau-Ponty himself, are related to his way of thinking, even though he shows a certain aloofness in their respect. Thus, we will successively study his position in reference to phenomenology, the sciences, Marxism, and the views of Sartre.

A Methodic Difficulty. The objection could be raised that the chapters concerned with this position should really have been presented at the beginning of this book. For it would seem to be a logical procedure first to indicate the relationship of Merleau-Ponty's theory with other views, and then only to present a systematic outline of his philosophy. As a matter of fact, many writers proceed in this fashion when they consider the views of a particular philosopher.

Nevertheless, we think that the method followed here is most appropriate. For the position a philosopher assumes with respect to other trends of thought flows from the inner nature of his thinking and, consequently, has to be understood in the light of his own thought. Now that we are acquainted with Merleau-Ponty's thinking, we will understand why he takes a certain position with respect to Husserl, the sciences, Marx, and Sartre. At first, Merleau-Ponty himself did not know clearly how his thought was related to that of other thinkers. For instance, his position with respect to Sartre is much more clearly defined in *Les aventures de la dialectique* than in *Phénoménologie de la perception*. His relationship to Marxism likewise shows a clear development, leading him constantly farther away from this trend. But these developments in his position with respect to other philosophers certainly are the result of the inner development of his own thinking and can be understood only in this light.[1]

The Order Followed in These Chapters. Difficulties also could be put forward against the order followed here. This order is not chronological, i.e., first phenomenology, then Marx, and then Sartre, nor logical, for we confront Merleau-Ponty first with a philosophical trend, then with the evolution of the sciences, and finally again with two philosophers.

Yet there is a reason for the order followed here. We first confront Merleau-Ponty with phenomenology because Merleau-Ponty himself qualifies his philosophy as a phenomenology. He appears to feel most closely related to this trend of thought. Secondly, his position with respect to the sciences can be understood only from the standpoint of his phenomenological attitude. Husserl constantly confronted his thinking with the sciences, and it is precisely on this point that Merleau-Ponty has been strongly influenced by Husserl. We then confront Merleau-Ponty with Marxism. There is question here not merely about a confrontation with a trend of thought but also and especially with a political movement. Finally, we will compare Merleau-Ponty with Sartre. At first these two were closely allied and seemed to belong even to the same group, that of existential and phenomenological thinkers with Marxist leanings. They published their articles in the same periodical. Gradually, however, they

---

[1]In a very penetrating article, "Situation de Merleau-Ponty," *Les temps modernes*, vol. 17, nos. 184-85, pp. 377-398, Alphonse de Waehlens discusses Merleau-Ponty's relationship to Hegel, Hussserl, Heidegger, and Marx. He opposes the opinion that in *La structure du comportement* the influence of Hegel is predominant and that *Phénoménologie de la perception* has a more Husserlian inspiration. The two works, says de Waehlens, are in perfect harmony because both are dominated by Merleau-Ponty's fundamental idea— viz., the concept of "form" or "Gestalt," understood as "meaning." Merleau-Ponty recognizes several levels of meaning and, with Hegel, he says that the lower levels come to fullness in the higher levels. Nevertheless, this does not mean that everything has to be ultimately reduced to thought, because thought remains rooted in perception and therefore can never become the Hegelian absolute Idea. In other words, Merleau-Ponty understands "meaning" in the Husserlian rather than the Hegelian sense. On the other hand, he is not simply a follower of Husserl. For Merleau-Ponty's radical affirmation of man's being-to-the-world overcomes many of Husserl's hesitations concerning the meaning of the "world" and man's worldly character. In Merleau-Ponty's later years, says de Waehlens, one could observe a certain way of getting closer to Heidegger, but in such a way that the affirmation of the autonomy of being remained foreign to Merleau-Ponty. These remarks indicate only a few points of the rich and clear analysis presented by de Waehlens, which we are unable to relate here fully. De Waehlens concludes, and we fully agree with him, that Merleau-Ponty is simply an independent thinker who has absorbed many influences without, however, falling into eclecticism.

began to go their own way. Thus, it is reasonable that, after analyzing Merleau-Ponty's phenomenological way of thinking and attitude toward Marxism, we devote our attention to his relationship to Sartre within this trend of thought.[2]

Why No Confrontation with Existentialism. Finally, the question could be asked whether an essential factor is not omitted here, viz., Merleau-Ponty's relationship with existentialism. In reply, we may point out that in some philosophers existentialism and phenomenology have fused. The fundamental concept of existentialism is the idea "existence," while the basic idea of phenomenology is undoubtedly the concept of intentionality. Existence, in the technical sense, means that consciousness is not closed in itself but is a relationship to the other, whether person or thing. Existentialism emphasizes that this relationship should not be conceived as a thing-like relation. In Kierkegaard the main emphasis was placed on the relation of consciousness to God. The same is likewise often the case in Gabriel Marcel. Jaspers also emphasizes the fact that our existence transcends the world.

This aspect of transcendency, however, disappears entirely in Sartre and Merleau-Ponty. Existence is nothing else than "project of the world"; the world is the horizon of the possibilities of existence. Merleau-Ponty understands intentionality also as a dialectic relationship with the world. He does not at all conceive it as the relationship of consciousness to an absolute "noema," divorced from its horizon of being by the fact that being has been "placed between brackets" (*Einklammerung des Seins*). Thus, existence and intentionality are really the same insofar as Merleau-Ponty is concerned. Moreover, precisely the existentialists who represent a trend of thought that is distinct from phenomenology, such as Kierkegaard, Marcel and Jaspers, are hardly or not at all quoted by Merleau-Ponty. "Right wing" existentialism has had almost no influence on him. True, he quotes Ludwig Binswanger, but refers not so much to his philosophy as to his studies in the realm of psychopathology. All this indicates that there is no reason to confront Merleau-Ponty with existentialism.

---

[2]Sartre also is counted among the phenomenologists. His earlier works readily lend themselves to this inclusion; for instance, the subtitle of *Being and Nothingness* is *An Essay in Phenomenological Ontology*. In this book as well as in other works, Sartre presents many brilliant phenomenological analyses. Nevertheless, there remains in him an undertone of rationalism, which becomes constantly more vigorous. His latest book, *Critique de la raison dialectique*, has hardly any traces of the phenomenological style of thinking and approach to philosophy.

2. INTENTIONALITY

After these preliminary considerations we may now begin our confrontation of Merleau-Ponty with phenomenology. Generally speaking, he is considered to be one of the greatest phenomenologists of our time. Let us point out first that no doubt is possible about the fact that he belongs to this style of thinking. The *Avant-Propos* of *Phénoménologie de la perception* reads like a kind of "phenomenological act of faith." Secondly, Merleau-Ponty has developed phenomenology in a way that is characteristically his own.

Merleau-Ponty and Hegel. That Merleau-Ponty does not want to bind himself fully to the trend of thought stimulated by Husserl becomes evident from what he writes about Hegel on the occasion of a conference given by Jean Hyppolite at the institute for Germanic studies in Paris, on February 16, 1947. Hegel, says Merleau-Ponty,[3] lies at the source of everything outstanding in the realm of philosophy achieved in the last one hundred years. He is the origin, e.g., of Marxism, the philosophy of Nietzsche, phenomenology, German existentialism, and psychoanalysis. Hegel launched the first effort to investigate the realm of the irrational and to integrate it into reason, more broadly conceived; and the continuation of this attempt remains the main task of our century. Hegel is the inventor of that reason which is more encompassing than the intellect. This reason showed itself capable of respect for the variety of psychical attitudes of different human beings, for the different civilizations, the different methods of thinking, and the contingency of history. Nevertheless, despite its reverence for these differences, this reason does not forsake its task of finding unity in plurality, of understanding everything and thus giving everything its own truth.[4]

However, the successors of Hegel place more emphasis on what they reject in his heritage than on what they owe to him. If we do not want to abandon hope for a truth which transcends the difference of positions, if, despite our lively feeling for subjectivity, we want to remain faithful to our desire for a new classicism and an organic culture, then our most urgent task is this: we have to reconnect the ungrateful theories with their Hegelian origin which they are trying

---

[3]"L'existentialisme chez Hegel," *Sens et non-sens,* pp. 125-139. These two paragraphs are a paraphrase of pp. 125-126.

[4]See the penetrating formulation of this problem in Albert Dondeyne, "Reason and the Irrational in Contemporary Thought," *Contemporary European Thought and Christian Faith,* Pittsburgh, 1958, pp. 67-107.

to forget. For in Hegel we find a language common to all, and a crucial confrontation of the different theories can be made in this language. We do not mean that Hegel himself embodies the truth which we seek. Hegel's work lets us hear a variety of voices; none-theless, all the oppositions encountered among us can be found in this one life and this work of a single man. To interpret Hegel means to assume a position with respect to all philosophical, political and religious problems of our century.

These words of Merleau-Ponty should make us prudent. He wrote them after the publication of his main work. True, later he expressed himself with more reserve about Hegel,[5] yet he retained his great respect for the German philosopher. Thus, Husserl does not constitute an absolute beginning or even an absolute norm for Merleau-Ponty. He himself situates his work in a much broader historical perspective. In general, we may say that Merleau-Ponty uses the fundamental concepts of phenomenology, but interprets them in his own way. This personal interpretation can become so important that one may legitimately ask whether the core of his philosophy is fully indicated by calling Merleau-Ponty a phenomenologist. In the following pages we will show this point in relation to some of the fundamental ideas of phenomenology.

Husserl's Intentionality. The most important category of phenomenology is undoubtedly that of intentionality. Our consciousness, says Husserl, is always consciousness *of* something. For this reason there are in every conscious act two poles, often indicated by the terms "noesis" and "noema." The choice of these terms shows that Husserl's phenomenology devotes most of its attention to the cognitive acts, even though it does not in principle limit itself to these acts.

By means of his theory of intentionality Husserl wants to say that consciousness is not first something in itself and then enters also into relationship to something else. The relationship to the other enters into the very essence of the conscious act. Thus, it follows that consciousness is codetermined by the term to which it is related.

---

[5] "L'historie universelle de Hegel est le rêve de l'histoire. Comme dans les rêves, tout ce qui est pensé est réel, tout ce qui est réel est pensé. Il n'y a rien à faire pour les hommes qui ne soit déjà compris dans l'envers des choses, dans le système. Et le philosophe leur fait bien cette concession d'admettre qu'il ne peut rien penser qui n'ait été déjà fait par eux, il leur accorde ainsi le monopole de l'efficience. Mais, comme il se réserve celui du sens, c'est dans le philosophe, et en lui seul, que l'histoire rejoint son sens. C'est le philosophe qui pense et décrète l'identité de l'histoire et de philosophie, ce qui revient à dire qu'il n'y a pas identité." *Eloge de la philosophie,* pp. 67 f.

We arrive at an understanding of a conscious act by analyzing the term to which it is directed: we understand the "noesis" through the analysis of the "noema." For this reason Husserl distinguishes different "realms" in the intentional correlate of our life, and by means of these realms he distinguishes our various conscious acts. When, against all forms of relativism, he wants to show the existence of something absolute, he does so by pointing to something absolute in the intentional correlate of our conscious acts. Accordingly, against all forms of subjectivistic thinking, Husserl emphasizes the importance of the object. This return to the objective explains in part the enthusiasm which greeted the phenomenology of Husserl.

Husserl, however, always held fast to the conscious character of human intentionality. The subject pole or "noesis" has always remained a conscious act for him. No matter how much this conscious act is overgrown with all kinds of conceptions, opinions and interpretations, no matter how much we have forgotten what we originally are, man's original acts always remain conscious acts.

Merleau-Ponty's Pre-conscious Intentionality. Taking over Husserl's idea of intentionality, Merleau-Ponty follows him in opposing the self-contained consciousness. Regardless of how deeply we penetrate into ourselves we always find there the reference to the other. However, for him, the orientation, characterizing us in the depth of our essence, is no longer, at least not first of all, a conscious directedness. As he writes, "Unlike what classical idealism thought, the relationship of subject and object is no longer that *cognitive relationship* in which the object always appears as constructed by the subject, but is a *relationship of being,* through which, to use a paradox, the subject *is* his body, his world, his situation, and in a certain sense enters into *interaction* with it."[6] For Merleau-Ponty, intentionality becomes an ontological relationship. At its deepest point intentionality is, as we have already seen, pre-conscious, and in its proper core it is not self-experience.

Of course, Merleau-Ponty does not deny that at a certain level human intentionality begins to have a conscious character. But it is striking that he has never made this conscious intentionality the main theme of his philosophical thought. His attention goes mainly to our pre-conscious intentionality and, when he speaks of conscious

---

[6]*Sens et non-sens,* pp. 143 f.

intentionality, he does so as a rule only to show that the conscious level is supported by the pre-conscious level.

Moreover, Merleau-Ponty very sharply indicates how far removed he is from Husserl—even though he does not explicitly mention him—when he says that consciousness originally is not an "I think" but an "I am able."[7] For Merleau-Ponty, the original subject is a power to give meaning, and consciousness seems to become something marginal. We cannot quite say that it is something accidental, for Merleau-Ponty realizes very clearly that consciousness cannot develop from the wholly unconscious. For this reason he says that consciousness has to be present from the very beginning, for that which does not think of itself from its very inception can never attain to such thinking. Strictly speaking, however, in the depth of our intentional life consciousness sinks so deeply into darkness that it becomes imperceptible. We are unable to bring it to light through reflection. Merleau-Ponty hovers between the affirmation of the pre-conscious and the realization that consciousness itself has to be also original, without being able to arrive at clarity. He himself concedes that his formulas remain enigmatic.[8]

Difference Between Husserl and Merleau-Ponty. Accordingly, the original intentionality is not yet characterized by the distance between a subject and an object. Merleau-Ponty himself says that this distance is connected with expression and especially with the word. Distance arises only on the level of consciousness and freedom. Hence the original intentionality is pre-objective. In its innermost nucleus our existence is fused with the world. Husserl, on the other hand, has always affirmed the distance between "noesis" and "noema." "Insofar as every thought demands a thought object," he says, "and this object has a relationship to the pure 'I' in the cognitive act, we find a remarkable polarity in every act: on the one side, the 'I'-pole and, on the other, the object as counter-pole. Each of these two is an identity, but the character and origins of these two identities are radically different."[9] Husserl does not know a

---

[7]"La conscience est originairement non pas un 'je pense que', mais un 'je peux'." *Phénoménologie de la perception,* p. 160. Note that he does not say: "consciousness is *rooted* in an 'I am able,'" but in its innermost depth "consciousness *is* an 'I am able'."

[8]*Op. cit.,* p. 463.

[9]*Ideen zu einer reinen Phänomenologie und phänomenologische Philosophie,* Zweites Buch, *Husserliana,* vol. 4, The Hague, 1952, p. 105.

subject that is not at a distance from the world but fused with it. He even admits a distance between the pure 'I' and the body, for he says that the pure 'I' realizes that the objects of sense experience imply a relationship to the body. In other words, the pure 'I' looks at the relationship between objects of experience and the body and consequently has to be to some extent outside this relationship.

Thus, we see that Merleau-Ponty's intentionality differs from that of Husserl. For him, intentionality is a dialectic relationship within which meaning originates. It is an interaction through which an organism makes its material surroundings its situation. It is a remarkable mean between the causal relationship existing between things and the subject-object relationship spoken of by Husserl. For this causal relationship lies hidden in the darkness of things, and Husserl's subject-object relationship lies in the light of consciousness. In this respect also Merleau-Ponty's philosophy is a philosophy of ambiguity. The above-mentioned term "mean" is not intended to indicate a kind of conciliatory attitude. What Merleau-Ponty hopes to do is to overcome the traditional opposition of subject and object by affirming a new mode of being.

3. EIDETIC REDUCTION

Meaning of Reduction. Another important topic of phenomenology is so-called "reduction." For Husserl, to reduce means to bring the immediately given back to the essential, the original. This assertion should not be misunderstood. Husserl is a phenomenologist, i.e., someone who, as the very term indicates, wants to give expression to that which appears, the phenomenal. This implies that he cannot reduce the phenomenal to anything else than that which appears. However, Husserl is not a philosopher who is simply satisfied with the phenomenal as it appears to us here and now. Our consciousness is not purely passive with respect to the phenomenal, for we make things appear to us, so that the way in which they appear depends also on ourselves.

A very simple analysis, e.g., of a human act of looking at something, suffices to show this point. All looking takes place within a field of vision. However, the presence of a visual field is not enough to speak of real looking. To look requires that within this field something comes forward as a figure. What, then, is the "something" that stands out as a figure? The reply depends very much on the human being who is looking. When, for example, father, mother and their boy walk through the streets, they look within the same visual field, but they see quite different things. The boy looks at the playing children, the toys and candy in the stores; the mother looks mostly at the shops and the dress of other women; the father sees what is connected with his usual occupation and field of interest. What we, modern men, see is connected also with our common history. Our looking is influenced by the sciences and technology. The analysis presented here of a single example applies to all our intentional acts. In other words, much is arbitrary in that which appears to us immediately.

Husserl's "Eidetic Reduction." For this reason Husserl is not satisfied with a consideration of the immediate phenomenal world. He wants to penetrate into that which is essential, necessary in the phenomenal field. He attempts to do so by means of the "eidetic reduction." "Eidetic" comes from the Greek, *eidos,* which means, especially in the Platonic tradition, "essence." In other words, the eidetic reduction is a reduction of the concrete and immediate phenomenon to its essential nucleus. Husserl is convinced that in the concrete phenomenon there is an essential core, consequently, an element of necessity, and it is to this element that he wants to penetrate. Especially in the first period of his philosophical life Husserl placed great emphasis on the eidetic reduction. We must look, he says, at the concrete phenomenon from all sides; we have to ask ourselves what in this concrete phenomenon could be omitted, leaving it nonetheless essentially the same. In this way we must attempt to disengage the essential core from the accidental. Note that both aspects, the essential and the accidental, belong to the phenomenon itself; the essence is not something lying behind the phenomenon. Husserl applies this procedure to mathematical figures, e.g., the triangle, cultural things, such as a table, and also to man himself.

Husserl, then, is convinced that an essential nucleus is present in the phenomenal, and that this nucleus can be discovered through analysis. This nucleus lies in the sphere of the necessary, for the essential cannot be otherwise than it *de facto* is. It appears to us and therefore can be grasped. Our search for it should not be guided by current definitions, but we should see the phenomenal essence itself. Once this essence is seen, we have to express what we have seen. Husserl's works, including those of his later years, contain many examples of such a search for the essential core. He is con-

vinced that this core is the same for all men. By virtue of the
essential core present in the phenomenal, there exists for us necessary
and intersubjective truth.

Merleau-Ponty on the Eidetic Reduction.   From the preceding
study of Merleau-Ponty's philosophy it should be sufficiently clear
that his perspective leaves no room for a necessary and universal essential nucleus.   Consequently, an eidetic reduction in the same sense
as that of Husserl is out of place in his thought.   True, in the *Avant-
Propos* of his *Phénoménologie de la perception* Merleau-Ponty endeavors to assign a place to the eidetic reduction within his philosophical perspective.[10]   He acknowledges that it is necessary to penetrate into our factual existence by way of essential description.
Conceptual determinations (*fixations conceptuelles*) are strictly
indispensable.   We are able to reflect on our existence only by becoming provisionally to some extent detached from it, by making it the
object of a philosophical inquiry, by making the fact of our existence
an essence.   In this way we arrive at a sphere of "separate essences."
They arise especially through language, for linguistic expressions fix
reality.   This phase, however, says Merleau-Ponty, is merely transitional.   The order of fixed essences has to be reconnected with the
living stream of reality.   The essence is not the goal but merely a
means, for it is the living stream of existence itself that we want to
understand.   "The necessity of having recourse to essences," to quote
him verbally, "does not mean that philosophy makes them its object.
On the contrary, this necessity arises from the fact that our existence
is too much locked up in the world to know itself at the moment when
it plunges into the world.   It needs the realm of ideality to know and
conquer its facticity."[11]

Our existence is too much a chiaroscuro to permit us to know
ourselves by simply pursuing it.   For this reason we have to pass
through conceptual fixation.   But this fixation is only a means, a
transitional phase.   Merleau-Ponty quotes Jean Waehl, who says that
Husserl "separates the essences from existence."   What Jean Waehl
means is that Husserl sees the essences as absolute points in the fluid
world of the phenomenal and that he separates these absolute points
from the flowing stream.   Merleau-Ponty combats this opinion,[12]
for he views the entire order of essences merely as a provisional con-

[10]*Op. cit.,* Avant-Propos, pp. IX-XII.
[11]*Ibid.,* p. IX.
[12]*Ibid.,* p. X.

ceptual fixation, imposed on us by the character of language. It is our task to overcome this fixation.

The Difference Between Husserl and Merleau-Ponty. Accordingly, the determination of the essential core, which for Husserl is one of the goals of philosophical reflection, is for Merleau-Ponty merely a phase of thinking that has to be overcome by living thought. Thinking makes use of words; it exists in words, and by using words we fix the phenomenal. In this way Merleau-Ponty attempts to assign a place in his philosophy to the eidetic reduction. However, we may ask, does his attempt not amount to this that he strips this reduction of the importance and scope it had in Husserl's thinking? Merleau-Ponty says that to understand religion and to affirm it are not the same but almost exactly the opposite. Understood and interpreted religion is no longer affirmed religion. We would like to apply these words also to his interpretation of Husserl's eidetic reduction. He understands it, he situates it within his own style of philosophical thinking, but by doing this he strips it of the meaning it had in Husserl's thought.

The ultimate reason for Merleau-Ponty's position in this matter is not difficult to find. Husserl was convinced that there are necessary and absolute grounds within our field of thought. But, for Merleau-Ponty this field has no room for necessity and absoluteness. Because Husserl's eidetic reduction presupposes necessity, Merleau-Ponty had to interpret it in such a way that necessity is no longer presupposed. For this reason he was forced to strip it of the meaning it had in Husserl's thinking.

It is easy to illustrate the point by means of an example. Husserl is convinced that there is a human essence. He knows also that this human essence has many aspects, such as corporeity and consciousness. He attempts to penetrate into the essence of man and the essential aspects of being-man. This attempt is made by means of the eidetic reduction. Philosophy would reach one of its goals, if through this reduction it could penetrate into the essential nucleus of man.

According to Merleau-Ponty, however, there can be no question of a human essence. True, in man everything is connected. It is not purely accidental that the same being walks erect and has a thumb that can be placed opposite the other fingers.[13] In both these aspects of man one and the same grip on the world reveals itself. In this

---

[13] *Op. cit.*, p. 198.

sense there is nothing accidental in man, for everything in him is connected with everything. However, this coherence is not guaranteed by any essence, but is a Gestalt, in which everything is interconnected.[14] For this reason, despite all this connection, man is permeated with contingency. Man is an historic idea and not a species of nature.[15] Thus, Merleau-Ponty is unable to apply here the eidetic reduction wanted by Husserl, for there simply is no essense to be discovered through this reduction. All we can do is understand an existential interconnection, for which we need conceptual fixations. Our terms constantly threaten to fixate human existence; hence we should be careful always to connect the words we use with the object spoken about, which is of a dynamic character.

Accordingly, it goes without saying that the sphere of Husserl's thinking differs enormously from that of Merleau-Ponty's work. A considerable mental passage has to be made when, after reading Husserl, one takes up the writings of Merleau-Ponty. Husserl's works, e.g., his *Ideen zu einer reinen Phänomenologie und phänomenologischen Philosophie,* contain many well-developed eidetic reductions.[16] He attempts, for example, to determine the core of being-a-thing and being-a-body. He tends to come to clearly-defined concepts, although he remains the eternal seeker who is never satisfied with established determinations. It would be useless to look for such attempted eidetic reductions in Merleau-Ponty. On reading his work, one senses that for him things are in principle beyond conceptual fixation.

4. Placing Being "Between Brackets"

Husserl knows also another form of reduction, the so-called "transcendental reduction," which became important especially in the later period of his philosophical life. This new reduction has two aspects. It is, first of all, a placing of being "between brackets" (*Einklammerung des Seins*) and, secondly, an attempt to penetrate to that which is original in our intentional life. We will consider here successively these two forms of reduction and devote attention to the position which Merleau-Ponty takes with respect to them.

---

[14]*Sens et non-sens,* p. 309.

[15]*Phénoménologie de la perception,* p. 199.

[16]As we will see, at the time when Husserl wrote this book he knew already other forms of reductions, which gradually began to occupy a more important place in his philosophy than the eidetic reductoin.

Husserl and Descartes' Starting Point. Invited to deliver a series of lectures in France, Husserl made a new and intensive study of Descartes. The results of this study were laid down in his book, *Cartesian Meditations.*[17]   By way of this famous methodic doubt, Descartes had arrived at the *Cogito* which abstracts from the reality of the world. Descartes wanted to find a certainty leaving no room at all for any possible doubt. This certainty, says Descartes, cannot be found in our sense perception, for the facts indicate that the senses deceive us sometimes; consequently, we are not certain that they do not always deceive us. Moreover, says Descartes, we sometimes confuse reality and dreams. How, then, can we be certain that we do not always dream and, therefore, live permanently in a world of dreams? Thus, we are not absolutely certain of the reality of the world. Is there anything that remains unaffected by this doubt? Yes, says Descartes, for I am absolutely certain that I think and that I have ideas, even though I do not know whether anything corresponds to these ideas. In this way Descartes thought that he had discovered an absolute and indubitable starting point.

This Cartesian starting point profoundly impressed Husserl. He, too, wanted to think in this perspective albeit with a different aim from that of Descartes. We must analyze, so he says in his above-mentioned book, the phenomenal precisely as it appears to us. But in that case it is only of secondary importance whether the phenomenal has any real content. There are many essences in our mind which do not have any real content, e.g., mathematical and logical entities. Yet they, too, should be of interest to the phenomenologist. He has to analyze the phenomenal, whether or not it has any real content. For this reason it is useful to abstract from the real content of the phenomenal, to place its being between brackets.

Thus, Husserl does not deny being, but no longer directs his attention to it. In doing so, he reacts especially against the empiricist and positivistic trends, which far too easily see the phenomenal as the expression or mirrowing of reality, and make the real content of our ideas the criterion of their value. For this reason Husserl abstracts from the question of reality and limits himself to the phenomenal precisely as phenomenal. Thus, the primary object of his phenomenological analysis is that which appears to our mind, regardless of its real content.

---

[17]English edition published by Nijhoff, The Hague, 1961.

By taking this position, Husserl comes close to the starting point of Descartes' philosophy, albeit in a different way and for a different purpose. Husserl's way is different, for he does not doubt reality, but merely limits himself methodically to the phenomenal precisely as phenomenal. His purpose also is different. Descartes withdrew into his absolute certainty in order to find there a valid starting point leading to absolutely certain knowledge of real being. He withdrew, as it were, into the fortress of interiority with the intention of leaving it as soon as possible for real being. Such is not Husserl's intention. What he wants is to analyze the structure of the phenomenal, precisely as appearing, and to penetrate into the nature of our intentional acts to which the phenomenal corresponds.

After placing being between brackets, Husserl still has a whole field-of-presence of appearing "noemata." He brings order into this field, marks its different zones, establishes the proper character of each of these zones, etc. Briefly, it is here that he finds his work. Many of Husserl's analyses are concerned with this field of presence stripped of reality.

It is a well-known fact that many of Husserl's students, who had given an enthusiastic welcome to his phenomenological way of thinking, refused to follow him on this road. They feared the danger of idealism, and this fear was not altogether unfounded. For Husserl himself speaks sometimes of "transcendental idealism," by which he means a kind of methodic idealism. There is no, or hardly any, question of a theory of being in Husserl, i.e., of any interest in the real character of reality.

Merleau-Ponty and the Methodic Reduction. The above-described aspect of Husserl's philosophy is something which has always remained foreign to Merleau-Ponty. There is hardly a trace in his works of this methodic reduction of such a pronounced Cartesian inspiration. For Merleau-Ponty, the human subject, the body-subject, is simply real mutual compenetration with a real world. No matter how profoundly we penetrate into the subject, we always find the world, the real world in it. If we were to place the real content of the world between brackets, we would have to do the same for the subject, for the subject is nothing else than project of the world, mutual compenetration with the world.[18]

---

[18]"La première vérité est bien 'Je pense', mais à condition qu'on entende par là 'je suis à moi' en étant au monde. Quand nous voulons aller plus loin dans la subjectivité, si nous mettons en doute toutes choses et en suspens

The "Transcendental Subject." To this must be added that Husserl's thinking on this point is spiritualistic in a way which Merleau-Ponty cannot accept. For, after this reduction there remains for Husserl a subject to which a field of presence appears. This subject, which he calls a "transcendental subject," is a thinking subject, to be distinguished from the concrete, empirical subject living concretely in the concrete world. For the concrete subject which eats and drinks itself is an appearing phenomenon with respect to the transcendental subject. Because of the character of his philosophy, Merleau-Ponty cannot accept such a spiritualistic subject. For him, this subject is an abstracted illusion of a way of thinking that has lost sight of its roots. Admitting such a subject is an expression of uprooted thought.

The objection could be raised that Merleau-Ponty comes close to Husserl's thinking when he says that there is no other being than being-for-us. For, doesn't this expression mean that he withdraws within the phenomenal precisely as phenomenal? The reply is entirely in the negative. This expression of Merleau-Ponty merely means that being, reality, is accessible to us only by virtue of our unveiling presence. However, we are an unveiling of the world, of the real world. Merleau-Ponty has never doubted, placed between brackets, the reality of the world. The reality of the world is for him a fundamental certainty, given together with the character of our being. When he speaks about the perspectivistic character of our experience, and remarks that not a single concrete thing is fully given to us since it can always reveal itself in a different way, he makes the curious remark that a subsequent observation can falsify the preceding observations of the same object. Consequently, we are never absolutely certain concerning any particular thing. About the world in general, however, we are absolutely certain.[19]

5. The Discovery of the Original Phenomena

Husserl's Reduction of the Constituted to the Constituent. It is striking that the transcendental reduction discussed in the preceding paragraphs has never found great favor among the philosophers who

---

toutes nos croyances, nous ne réussissons à entrevoir le fond inhumain par où, selon le mot de Rimbaud, 'nous ne sommes pas au monde', que comme l'horizon de nos engagements particuliers et comme puissance de quelque chose en général qui est le fantôme du monde. L'intérieur et l'extérieur sont inséparables. Le monde est tout au dedans et je suis tout hors de moi." *Phénoménologie de la perception*, pp. 466 f.

[19] *Op. cit.*, p. 344.

seek their inspiration in Husserl. However, as we have already pointed out, the phenomenological or transcendental reduction has still another aspect—namely, the return to the original—and this aspect is more important. Even within the transcendental field not all phenomena are equally important for Husserl. For we must distinguish constituted and constituent phenomena, founded and founding phenomena. The constituted or founded phenomena are not original but have arisen from other phenomena. They have an "intentional history," i.e., they have been constructed by intentional consciousness. Examples of them may be found in all scientific phenomena, for scientific phenomena are not original but constructed or constituted by the scientific attitude of mind. For instance, Newton's absolute space, empty space devoid of anything but in which things can be located, is not an original correlate of consciousness. This absolute space is a concept of scientific consciousness.

As we have indicated, Husserl wants to bring clarity into the realm of phenomena. He believes that this can be done only by reducing the constituted or founded phenomena to constituent or founding phenomena. His ideal is to penetrate into the most profound, most original phenomena and from there to understand the field of the phenomenal. Thus, the scientific phenomena have to be reduced to prescientific phenomena, and among the latter we must seek to discover the fundamental phenomena. Husserl aims at the ultimate, the irreducible. In many masterful analyses he endeavors to execute his self-appointed task without, however, ever being satisfied with himself. He constantly delves deeper, but his philosophical endeavor never seems to reach bottom. He assigned the task of realizing his ideal to phenomenology and seems to have thought that this task was capable of being executed. Its execution, he hoped, would provide a permanent basis not only for philosophy but also for the entire life of science. With genuine passion he labored his whole life at this task and he demanded of his students that they take it over.

The Terminus of the Reduction: Absolute Philosophy. What, we may ask, is the nature of these so-called "grounds," which Husserl endeavored to discover? They lie concealed under the constituted, the founded, yet they are phenomena, i.e., correlates of consciousness.

Their phenomenal character should be evident even from the fact that Husserl, as we have pointed out, placed being between brackets and limited himself to the phenomenal field in order to penetrate into these fundamental phenomena. These phenomena, then, are supposed to lie in the ideal field in which the transcendental 'I' places itself. Thus, the terminus of the reduction is something that is a light to the mind, even though it is buried under superficial phenomena. For this reason Husserl always aimed at absolute evidence, absolute knowledge. He endeavored to find *the* philosophy, which would give definitive clarity to the searching mind. He could not be satisfied with subjectivism and relativism. Even at the very beginning of his philosophical career he wanted to refute all kinds of relativism by pointing to absolute moments in man's cognitive life. Despite all the subsequent modifications of his philosophical inquiries he never abandoned this ideal.

Merleau-Ponty's Rejection of Husserl's Ideal. Like Husserl, Merleau-Ponty accepts a kind of transcendental reduction and he also wants to reduce the constituted, the founded to the original. However, these Husserlian notions undergo an essential change in Merleau-Ponty's philosophy. For, according to him, the original lies buried in a dimension of darkness in such a way that it cannot be brought to light. Our existence is interwoven with the world, is a dialog with the world. This dialog reaches its most profound point there where the first and most original meaning arises, a meaning that is preconscious and pre-personal. Whatever is in our consciousness, whatever comes to light, becomes lucid, originates also in this darkness. As we have seen, man is able to obtain a measure of knowledge regarding this dark depth. He is able to divine something about the mysterious dialog between the body-subject and the world. However, according to Merleau-Ponty, an absolute illumination of the phenomenal field is in principle impossible. All man can do is to erect some pointers in a darkness which resists full illumination.

Thus, Merleau-Ponty rejects the very ideal aimed at by Husserl. His fundamental philosophical aim itself differs radically from that of Husserl. Despite a certain similarity of terminology, these two philosophers differ essentially on this point. We have the impression that Merleau-Ponty is well aware of this, but tries to conceal the difference through his interpretation of Husserl. He quotes Husserl when it suits his interpretation, but omits numerous texts that do not permit his view.[20] The fundamental sphere of his philosophy differs from that of Husserl. The difference manifests itself very clearly when one reads the works of these two men. Merleau-Ponty does not and cannot believe in a definitive form of philosophical thought. He rejects absolute insights that would be valid for all. He does not admit any ultimate knowledge to which the entire history of philosophical thought would be tending. Husserl's tendency to an ideal of intelligibility is wholly foreign to Merleau-Ponty.

Merleau-Ponty and Phenomenology. By considering a few of the important topics of phenomenology we have shown that there is a deep-seated difference between Husserl and Merleau-Ponty. While Merleau-Ponty takes up the phenomenological themata and speaks the language of phenomenology, he has his own unique interpretation. Undoubtedly, phenomenology has exercised great influence on him, but the reverse is also true. Merleau-Ponty's fundamental discovery is, as we have said, his theory of the body-subject. It is in the light —or should we say, in the darkness?—of this discovery that he interprets all phenomenological data.

How, one may ask, should we characterize Merleau-Ponty, the philosopher? As the philosopher of the body-subject or as phenomenologist? What is the crucial element of his philosophy, the discovery of the body-subject or his phenomenological inspiration? In reply let us quote a text of Merleau-Ponty. "Phenomenology," he says, "may be practised and can be recognized as a way of thinking, as a style. It exists as a movement before it becomes fully conscious of itself as a philosophy. It has been pursued for a long time already, and one may find its disciples everywhere, in Hegel and in Kierkegaard, of course, but also in Marx, Nietzsche and Freud."[21] If phenomenology as a way and style of thinking is present in all these philosophers, it evidently is a way of thinking that can be pursued in very divergent fashions. Merleau-Ponty himself has used it in a wholly personal way. He is and remains himself even when he speaks the language of phenomenology. He cannot be classified as belonging to any particular school of thought.

---

[20]Sometimes, however, Merleau-Ponty admits that his philosophy differs from that of Husserl. See, e.g., *op. cit.,* p. 73, footnote 1.

[21]*Op. cit.,* Avant-Propos, p. II.

A man is a philosopher only, writes Merleau-Ponty, when he thinks and writes simply because there are things to see.[22] Because human beings are dependent on one another, we have to let those who have thought and written before us help us when we want to say what we see. Nevertheless, we must pursue philosophy, for we have our gaze fixed on the things that are to be seen. This is what Merleau-Ponty himself does. He is an original philosopher and, therefore, remains personal even when he lets himself be inspired by others. He is not satisfied with simply explaining one or the other trend of thinking. He is simply himself, even when he accepts the aid of others in being himself. Such a thing can be affirmed only of great and independent philosophers. Any generation has at most a few of these.

---

[22]"Car philosopher, c'est chercher, c'est impliquer qu'il y a des choses à voir et à dire." *Eloge de la philosophie,* p. 57.

CHAPTER TEN

MERLEAU-PONTY AND THE SCIENCES

1. MERLEAU-PONTY AND SCIENTISM

Phenomenology and, especially, Merleau-Ponty have sometimes been reproached, albeit undeservedly, for making derogatory remarks about the sciences. Yet Merleau-Ponty explicitly and repeatedly acknowledges his dependence on them with respect to very important points of his philosophy.[1] He does not create a bigger gap between science and philosophy, but points to their intrinsic interconnection. He even goes so far as to say that, in his opinion, philosophy is and should be implicitly present in the sciences. The specific task of philosophy is to thematize the implicit philosophical visions embodied in the life of science.

The Unsituated Scientist. Nevertheless, it remains true that Merleau-Ponty sharply criticizes the way in which the sciences are sometimes pursued. He does so, however, not because he is against science, but because of and insofar as a faulty philosophy underlies the pursuit of the sciences. What he attacks is not the sciences but scientism, i.e., the philosophical interpretation which the sciences make of themselves and which profoundly influences their procedures.

Scientism is ultimately a certain theory concerning the relationship between the man of science and his field of scientific inquiry. The man of science is viewed as a spectator and his field of inquiry as an external datum. The scientist's gaze is supposed, as it were, to be directed from without to his field of study. The man of science is not situated with respect to his field.

Scientism in this sense does not necessarily have to be conceived as a kind of naive realism. For the naive realist, the cognitive field is a reality outside man, which is mirrored by man's thinking mind. Merleau-Ponty's view of scientism has sometimes been attacked as if he condemns a naive realism which hardly anyone holds, so that his

---

[1] Merleau-Ponty discusses the relationship of science and philosophy mainly in two articles, "Le métaphysique dans l'homme," *Sens et non-sens,* pp. 165-196 (especially pp. 166-185), and "Le philosophe et la sociologie," *Signes,* pp. 123-142. He has lectured at the Sorbonne on this matter, and the text of these lectures has been made available by the Centre de Documentation Universitaire under the title, *Les sciences de l'homme et la phénoménologie.*

whole reaction against scientism is a battle against an illusion. This objection, however, is not to the point. Scientism may pervade also subjectivistic theories, which teach that the cognitive field of man is not an objective reality independent of man but exists as a whole of human impressions. For even in that case one may think that our cognitive field arises through necessary laws, e.g., through a necessary interaction between the senses and stimuli or through an association of impressions governed by necessary laws. According to Locke, for example, the so-called secondary sense qualities, such as colors, sounds and flavors, are subjective. Unlike, e.g., extension and motion, they do not belong to the real world, but are subjective impressions arising from a kind of causal interaction between the body and the world. For centuries psychologists have searched for the laws governing association, and in this search they assumed that the association of our impressions was ruled by necessary laws subject to scientific inquiry. When Merleau-Ponty speaks of scientism, it is irrelevant whether the scientist thinks as a naive realist or gives a subjectivistic interpretation of his field of inquiry. The decisive question is the attitude he assumes with respect to his field in his scientific reflection.

Two Modes of Experience. By its very nature science tends to objectify. One who pursues a science deliberately thinks *about* something, which cannot be done without placing oneself at a distance from the object of his thought. But the man who in his scientific reflection places himself at a distance from the world about which he thinks is one and the same individual who, before he pursued science, lived in this world, fused, as it were, with it and, in his ordinary existence when he is not actually busy with his science, continues to live and to be involved in this world. In other words, we are dealing with a twofold experience. As men of science, we place ourselves at a distance, we objectify; as living our everyday life, we are involved in the world and our life merges with it. To give an example, in our everyday life we live in "co-existence," as social beings existing together with our fellow men, and we participate in this co-existence; this co-existence is accessible to us by virtue of our personal participation in it. In scientific reflection, however, we begin to think about co-existence and are able to make even the way in which we personally co-exist with our fellow men an object of our reflection.

Scientific Experience as the Absolute Starting Point. Thus, the problem arises regarding the relationship existing between these two modes of experience. If so-called scientific experience is chosen as the absolute starting point, as the genuine road to truth and as the norm governing ordinary everyday experience, then we give preference to scientism.

It must be admitted that such a preference is not given without any inducement, for, when we assume the scientific attitude, we refine and interpret our ordinary experience. Science undoubtedly illuminates us. In the pursuit of science one is obliged to rise above all kinds of subjectivistic factors that play a role in ordinary experience. For instance, in everyday life we may experience a certain mood in the morning, and because of this mood we assume a clearly defined position with respect to intersubjective relationships. We, may be for instance, "impossible" until after breakfast. Obviously, such moods may not play any role in scientific inquiries, but they themselves may become the object of a scientific study in which we examine the character of such moods and the influence which they exercise. In science also we rise above all kinds of inaccuracies which play a role in ordinary experience. In everyday experience, for example, we estimate a distance, but in science we measure it as accurately as possible. In ordinary experience and its everyday expression we make an unhygienic use of words and sometimes indulge in dangerous ambiguities. When reality is discussed scientifically, we refine our terminology and speak in a rigorous and methodic fashion. Thus, scientific experience undoubtedly is a purification and correction of ordinary, prescientific experience.

The Attraction of Scientism. All this makes it easy to see that one may readily accept the illusion that reality comes to be "really" known only when it is considered scientifically, and that the scientific approach to reality is the only true and valid approach. Under this illusion one proceeds to approach and evaluate the field of ordinary existence from the standpoint of science. Science is asked to determine what is objective or not objective in our everyday field of experience. Science decides the truth value of all objects of experience. Whatever is scientifically unimportant, i.e., whatever lies outside the field of scientific inquiry, is unqualifiedly unimportant. An example may serve to illustrate the point. Science forms an idea of objective space in which everything is located. It rises above the ordinary, oriented space in which things are nearby or far-away, to my right or to my left; it rises above the space extending around me as a field which, through my body, is accessible to me. There is question of scientism as soon as one begins to think that this abstract and objective space is space in the strict and primary sense, and as soon as one proceeds to evaluate the concrete space in which we live from the standpoint of this objective space.

The scientistic approach contains also a theory of the subject. Just as we can make a distinction between the field of existence and the field of scientific inquiry, so also are we able to distinguish between the existing subject and the subject which makes the world a field of scientific study. The first subject is situated, but the second seems to have an absolute character, for its gaze dwells on the whole. Merleau-Ponty speaks of such an absolute subject as a "surveying glance" (*regard survolant*).

2. The Presence of Philosophy in Science

Manifestations of the Scientists' Implicit Philosophy. Scientism is the theory which considers the field of scientific inquiry as the field of knowledge *par excellence,* and makes it the norm evaluating the field of existence. It is the theory which evaluates the existing subject according to the scientific subject. We should be careful, however, in using the term "theory." For the above-formulated theses are rarely, if ever, posited explicitly by those who pursue the sciences. The theses in question do not even lend themselves to formulation in the technical language of science, for their content is philosophical. They reveal themselves only in the way in which science is pursued. They are an implicit philosophy that lies concealed in the scientific approach, in the way in which the scientist situates— or rather fails to situate—himself with respect to his field of inquiry.

Scientism reveals itself, for instance, in the way in which it understands the fact. The fact is supposed to be an absolute and indubitable starting point of science. It does not matter here whether the fact refers to a world that is independent of us or a field arising from a causal interaction between the senses and the world. It is irrelevant also whether the facts refer to an objective world, the human psyche, the social order, history or language. No matter what they refer to, the man of science, especially in the past, thought that he was able to establish objective facts, and in the name of these facts he expressed his lack of confidence in theories, as if facts could exist separately from any theory.

Scientism manifested itself also in the theory of induction. Everyone readily admitted that the fact was merely something particular, for it was an individual and contingent occurrence. Nevertheless, it was thought that by way of induction it would be possible to proceed from particular and contingent facts to universal laws—as if the mere observance of facts itself did not imply already a universality. In this way the particular situation in which the man of science lives becomes something of purely secondary importance or, rather, of no importance at all. The man of science is supposed to be guided by the objective light illuminating him from his field of inquiry.

"For this reason," says Merleau-Ponty, "the 'idealization' of the brute fact, which is the essential characteristic of scientific work, has to be concealed from the scientist. He has to close his eyes to the deciphering of the signification which guides his scientific work, to the construction of intellectual models of his object, without which sociology cannot exist now and without which the physics of Galileo could not have arisen in former times.[2] His eyes have to be covered with the "blinkers" of Bacon's or Mill's induction, even when his own research evidently escapes the canonical rules. He will pretend to approach the social fact as something that is foreign to him—as if his study does not owe anything to the experience of intersubjectivity which he has as a social subject. For, so they say, sociology is not yet given with our experience of life, but is the analysis, the unfolding, the objectification of our experience of life; it upsets our primitive consciousness of social relationships, so that ultimately the experienced social relationships appear to us as a very special variation of a social dynamism whose existence we had not at first suspected and with which we became acquainted only after the study

---

[2]In his last article, "L'oeil et l'esprit," *Les temps modernes,* vol. 17, nos. 184-5, pp. 193-227, Merleau-Ponty draws attention to the pragmatic attitude of contemporary science. It builds models and then proceeds to manipulate these models in many ways. This feature, he says, has given rise to a new philosophy of the sciences, which wants to make this "constructive procedure" autonomous. The entire body of scientific knowledge is now seen as a manipulation of the world. "Dire que le monde *est* par définition nominale l'objet X de nos opérations, c'est porter à l'absolu la situation de connaissance du savant, comme si tout ce qui fut ou est n'avait jamais été que pour entrer au laboratoire. La pensée 'opératoire' devient une sorte d'artificialisme absolu." *Op. cit.,* p. 194. In the United States there exists a kind of psychoanalysis and "culturalism" which views man himself solely as a manipulatable datum. This idea does not fully express what the sciences are and do, for the sciences are rooted ultimately in our situated experience, which is connected with our being-a-body. As soon as the sciences will recognize this, they will also make their pragmatic attitude relative and will discover their own philosophical scope. "Dans cette historicité primordiale, la pensée allègre et improvisatrice de la science apprendra à s'appesentir sur les choses mêmes et sur soi-même, redeviendra philosophie." *Op. cit.,* p. 195. Note that Merleau-Ponty again ascribes a philosophical scope to scientific thought itself.

of other cultural formations. In this way objectivism forgets that other evidence, which is that we can increase our experience of social relationships and form an idea of social relationships only by virtue of the analogy with, or opposition to the social relationships in which we have lived."[3]

Accordingly, scientism has forgotten that the scientific subject is rooted in the existing subject. It pays attention to everything that the existing subject acquires through the pursuit of science, to the correction of ordinary experience, to the entrance into a more objective world. But it forgets the dependence of the scientific subject on the existing subject. It forgets also that the scientific subject does not leave the situation in which this subject finds itself and will always continue to find itself as an existing subject. It forgets that science also always remains a view taken from a situation.

An Apparent Contradiction.   Scientism, as we have said, is an implicit philosophy, concealed in the way in which the sciences are pursued. Does it not follow, therefore, that Merleau-Ponty ultimately condemns the sciences themselves? True, one may distinguish between science as science and the same science as implicit philosophy. But if this implicit philosophy is hidden in the very pursuit of science, it follows that, concretely speaking, these two coincide, so that one cannot condemn scientism without condemning at the same time the sciences, at least, as they are concretely here and now. At most one could make the restriction that the condemnation applies only to the sciences of facts and not to the ideal sciences. As soon as the sciences are what, according to Merleau-Ponty, they are supposed to be, they escape the condemnation pronounced by him. In other words, is it not a contradiction to say, on the one hand, that one is not against the sciences but only against scientism and, on the other, to assert that scientism is interwoven with the very existence of the sciences?

Science Cannot be Separated from its Implicit Philosophy.   It must be admitted that the sciences cannot be divorced from the implicit philosophy living in them. It is not possible for the sciences to be in splendid health while the implicit philosophy contained in them is thoroughly sick. Unsurprisingly, therefore, we find that Merleau-Ponty in his discussion of certain topics sometimes criticizes a philosophical vision and sometimes agitates against a scentific interpretation of the facts. His footnotes show this clearly, for they contain

---

[3] *Signes,* p. 125.

the names of philosophers and of scientists. Let us illustrate the matter with an example.

The atomistic conception of the human psyche was at the same time a philosophical view and a scientific theory which led to the formation of all kinds of auxiliary scientific theories. It was thought that the most original form of man's cognitive life consisted of individual sensations produced by objective stimuli. Since, on the other hand, it was seen that our concrete perception constitutes a whole which in every direction goes beyond the individual sensations, the question arose as to how perception can originate and be built up from these building blocks of cognitive life. An appeal was made to association, viewed as a mechanical process.[4] Actual impressions, however, even when associated, do not sufficiently explain the wealth of perception. For this reason recourse was had to memory, which was supposed to supplement the actual impressions with remembered images.

Merleau-Ponty remarks very correctly that all these explanations presuppose precisely what they want to clarify—viz., perception itself.[5] Associations and their complementation through remembered images are meaningful only when and to the extent that they are motivated by what we actually observe, i.e., they are meaningful only through perception. Who is to blame for the mistake? The atomistic way of thinking, which undoubtedly is philosophical? Or the scientific theories which, on the one hand, are born from philosophical presuppositions and, on the other, seem to confirm the philosophical viewpoint? It is difficult to speak hereof an "either—or." It would be better to say "both—and."

Accordingly, scientism should not be conceived as a wrong self-interpretation of an otherwise healthy science. It does not mean merely that one misinterprets his relationship to his field of inquiry, but rather that one stands in a wrong relationship to this field. Scientism is not merely a wrong idea of one's scientific situation but also a wrong situation.

The Natural Unity of Life, Science, and Philosophy. All this is in harmony with what Merleau-Ponty calls the "convergent movement of history." It is one and the same human being who lives perceptively in his world, pursues the sciences, and makes life the

---

[4]Cf. Johan Linschoten, *"A Gentle Force", Beschouwingen over het associatiebegrip,* Groningen, 1957.

[5]"Au moment où l'évocation des souvenirs est rendue possible, elle devient superflue, puisque le travail qu'on en attend est déjà fait." *Phénoménologie de la perception,* p. 27.

theme of his philosophical reflection. One and the same man seeks light in three different ways. But in that case it is to be expected that the same good and evil traits will be present in all realms. In ordinary experience, in everyday life, we are exposed to the danger of the "natural attitude"—we are satisfied with the given meaning and pay no attention to the way in which this meaning is given to us; we disregard ourselves and fix our attention on the world which seems wholly natural to us. On the scientific level this attitude becomes scientism, and in the realm of philosophy it is known as empiricism or positivism. "The philosopher," says Merleau-Ponty, "is the man who wakes up and speaks, and man silently carries within his bosom the paradoxes of philosophy."[6] If a man has accepted a one-sided orientation of existence, the same one-sidedness will reveal itself in life, the sciences and philosophy, but if a man breaks away from this or that kind of one-sidedness and moves onward to a broader perspective, then this broadening wil extend to all three realms.

Scientism, says Merleau-Ponty, has ruptured the natural bond of life, science, and philosophy. It has substituted so-called "scientific experience" for the experience that is given in our existing in the world. Or rather, it has refined and interpreted our ordinary experience in a scientific way. It has detached the scientific gaze from the scientific field, which has led to the view that the scientific field of inquiry is a realm of facts through which induction is supposed to blaze a trail. It has made the bare facts the absolute starting point of the sciences and has relegated the concept and idea to the realm of the philosopher. In this way the sciences and philosophy have become estranged from each other. For the sciences are supposed to operate not with ideas or theories but with facts. An idea would have scientific value only if and to the extent that it is verified by the facts.

Because the facts were assigned to the realm of the sciences, philosophy was uprooted. "While all great philosophies," says Merleau-Ponty, "are characterized by their endeavor to reflect on both the mind *and its dependence*—e.g., on both ideas and their movement, the intellect and sensitivity—there is a myth about philosophy which represents it as the authoritative affirmation of the mind's absolute autonomy. Such a philosophy no longer asks

---

[6]*Eloge de la philosophie*, p. 86.

any questions. It becomes a doctrinal whole, planned to give a wholly *uprooted* mind delight in itself and its ideas. There is, moreover, a myth about the life of science, which from the simple observation of facts expects not only scientific knowledge concerning the things of the world but also the science about this scientific knowledge, as well as a sociology of knowledge, which itself is of course again conceived in an empiricist way. Thus, the universe of facts is locked in itself. It is made to include even the ideas which we invent to interpret the facts. In this way we get rid of ourselves. These myths are opposed to each other and nonetheless accomplices. The philosopher and the sociologist who oppose each other in this fashion agree at least in the demarcation of the boundaries which are to prevent them from encountering each other."[7]

Science and Philosophy are United by Mutual Implication. From all this it follows clearly that Merleau-Ponty rejects the divorce of philosophy and science. When he reacts against the sciences as pursued in a scientistic fashion, he attacks both the faulty philosophy implicitly contained in them and the sciences themselves as pursued in the wrong way. Here also Merleau-Ponty is a philosopher who pleads for unity—a unity which we may call "unity of reciprocal implication." According to him, this unity is found between subject and world, between spirit and body, between thinking and speaking, between the different components of the same event, and also between the sciences and philosophy. For this reason his philosophy is a "philosophy of ambiguity." As a rule, for him the "either—or" has to give way to the "both—and." Divorced from philosophy, Merleau-Ponty points out, the sciences do not know what they speak about.[8] The reason is that fact and idea cannot be separated from each other. We indicate facts in statements, judgments, and our judgments have not only a subject but also a predicate. This predicate is always a concept, a category, connected with concrete reality. We, therefore, know the facts also thanks to the concept. If we let the concept go, the facts also sink away in darkness.[9] The concept we use to indicate a fact is not isolated, but forms part and parcel of a coherent human

---

[7] *Signes,* p. 124.

[8] "Si l'objectivisme ou le scientisme réussissait jamais à priver la sociologie de tout recours aux significations, il ne la préserverait de la "philosophie" qu'en lui fermant l'intelligence de son objet." *Op. cit.,* p. 127.

[9] Cf. Remy C. Kwant, "The Ambiguity of the fact," *The Modern Schoolman,* vol. 37, pp. 287-300.

speech. As such, it always implies also a philosophical vision. Although this vision is not usually thematically considered, it is nonetheless implicitly present.

Note that Merleau-Ponty does not condemn the fact that scientism is an implicit philosophy, concealed in the life of science. For in his view it is absolutely inevitable that scientific knowledge contains a philosophical vision. What he condemns is scientistic philosophy because it is a wrong philosophy.

3. The Presence of Science in Philosophy

The Philosopher Needs the Sciences. In one way or in another the sciences are also always present in philosophy. For the philosopher wants to throw light on phenomena which have been or are being considered also in a scientific way. How, then, could philosophy remain uninterested in the light that the sciences throw on these phenomena? The fact that, according to Merleau-Ponty, philosophy needs the sciences manifests itself even in the external structure of his works. As we have mentioned, their footnotes quote both philosophers and men of science, and the scientists are certainly not quoted less frequently or only in less important matters.

"The divorce," to quote Merleau-Ponty, "which we combat is no less damaging to philosophy than it is to the development of the sciences. How could a conscientious philosopher seriously propose to forbid philosophy to enter the realm of science? For ultimately the philosopher always reflects on *something*, whether it be a square drawn in the sand, a donkey, horse, or mule, a cubic foot of extension, a certain kind of red, the Roman Empire or the hand thrust into iron filings. The philosopher reflects on his experience and his world. How, then, would anyone give him the right, save by order of the authorities, to forget what science says about this same experience and this same world? For, strictly speaking, the collective term 'science' covers nothing else than a systematic inquiry, a methodic pursuit of the same experience that begins with our first perception— even though the character of this knowing is now less and then more rigorous, now less and then more penetrating. What is involved is a whole of means to perceive, to imagine and, finally, to live, and all these means aim at the same truth which even our first experiences made us desire. It may be true that science pays for its exactness the price of a strict schematization. But if this is so, the cure is readily indicated. All we have to do is to confront science with integral experience, and not to oppose to it a philosophical knowledge of which no one is able to indicate the source."[10]

Merleau-Ponty's view is hardly surprising in a philosopher who identifies the transcendental field and the phenomenal field. The world in which we live and in which the sciences are pursued is also the world in which the philosopher reflects. The philosopher has no secret entry into a mysterious reality which would be accessible only to him. He does not penetrate into a realm of necessity supposedly concealed under contingent phenomena. Philosophy does not have an object that somehow would be its exclusive property. When we spoke about Merleau-Ponty's theory of reduction, we saw that he wants to reduce philosophy to the **chiaroscuro field of experience,** which he calls also "the lived world." But the sciences also are rooted in this same field. If, then, these two have the same object and the same roots, how could they be without any connection?

Science and Philosophy Remain Distinct. All this, of course, does not mean that Merleau-Ponty rejects every form of distinction between the sciences and philosophy. He knows very well that a science is not possible unless its proper field of inquiry is demarcated and that the assigned boundaries codetermine the nature of this science. He does not deny that a science comes into its own when it succeeds in determining its limits. Exactness, he says, in the above-quoted text, has to be paid for by strict schematization. But even if a science moves within certain limits, it attempts to understand something of the world in which we live and it forms concepts throwing light on this world. For this reason the experience of a particular science has to be understood within the broader framework of our integral experience. Thus, it follows that science is, in part, to be made intelligible from the standpoint of our original field of experience. While it is true that a science brings something of this field of experience to light, the reverse is equally true. This is precisely the meaning of the reduction.

"Philosophy," writes Merleau-Ponty, "is not a particular form of knowledge, but the vigilance which does not allow us to forget the source of all knowledge."[11] These words are very illuminating and help us better to understand his intention. First of all, philosophy

---

[10]*Signes*, pp. 127 f.
[11]*Op. cit.,* p. 138.

is not a particular form of knowledge. It does not have an object of its own, distinct from that of the sciences and of ordinary experience. The field of philosophy coincides with the field of our life. Secondly, however, the philosopher knows wherein all knowledge is rooted, viz., in the mystery of the birth of meaning, explained in the preceding chapters. All meaning grows in the dialog between man and world and, therefore, presupposes the fundamental fact of our existence as giver of meaning. Philosophy thinks from the standpoint of this fundamental fact, considers everything in its light, which is metaphysical consciousness. Yet not even this fundamental fact is the exclusive property of philosophy. For here lies also the source of all sciences. The sciences also think, or at least ought to think, starting from this source; otherwise they are forgetful of their own roots. However, because of their specialization, the sciences are exposed to the danger of disregarding their origin and purpose. Whence it is the function of philosophy to be vigilant and see to it that this danger is overcome. Once more, however, this philosophy, this vigilance often is at work also in the sciences themselves.

Science Inspires the Philosopher. Thus, it is very well possible that the philosopher will draw his inspiration from the development of the life of science. The reason is not only that the sciences force him to consider certain topics and provide him with new materials for his reflection, as is exemplified by the philosophy of science, by philosophy as the critique of the sciences. An added reason is that within the sciences themselves a light shows forth that has a genuinely philosophical character, and this light does not necessarily have to be of an inferior quality than the light discovered by the philosophers themselves. The life of science is a real source of inspiration for the philosopher, because in its innermost essence it is already philosophical and reveals that the source of all knowledge flows also in the sciences.

When he gives examples, Merleau-Ponty usually has recourse to the sciences which study human life, especially, psychology, sociology, linguistics, and history. He does so not as a matter of principle, for what he says applies also to the physical sciences. However, he does not borrow any examples from the sciences of nature because, so it seems, he has never made any special study of them. At least, he does not give the impression of being particularly competent in them. And when he happens to say something about the physical sciences, his statements are not exclusively valid for the physical sciences but apply also to the sciences of man. He says, for instance, that the facts of physical science are inseparably united with ideas, that induction alone does not suffice to justify a law, that no theory is ever definitively and irrevocably verified by a crucial experience, and that the various theses have to be understood within the whole of a scientific field. These and similar judgments are not exclusively proper to the field of inquiry called "physical science." Accordingly, one who wants to write a philosophy of the exact sciences will find only general norms in Merleau-Ponty but not any details.

4. THE SCIENTIFIC SUBJECT IS A SITUATED SUBJECT

Merleau-Ponty's most important thesis about the sciences, which likewise applies to all sciences, is that the scientific subject, the subject as pursuing science, is a stuated subject. Thinking man never becomes a "surveying glance." On this point also the sciences have not come to see this through an extraneous inspiration, but they themselves have discovered it or are on the way of discovering it.[12] The sociologist, for example, discovers that the social structures are accessible to him because he himself, as existing man, is involved in social life.[13] For this reason the way in which the sociologist takes part in social life is not at all irrelevant to the way in which he pursues sociology. From our very existence itself we have an "outlook" on social reality, although this term "outlook" is too intellectualistic. We experience society in a certain way, it reveals itself to us under a certain aspect. All this is still prior to our explicit judgments. However, these explicit judgments only then have roots when they are connected with our experience.

The same applies also to the sciences of history. We take part in history and we cannot conceive the past, that has prepared our present, divorced from the present in which we live. We are absolutely particular and absolutely universal. We are able to bring the entire

---

[12]The first part of the above-mentioned article "Le métaphysique dans l'homme," *Sens et non-sens,* pp. 166-185, is dedicated to this question.

[13]"Durkheim a traité le social comme une réalité extérieure à l'individu et l'a chargé d'expliquer tout ce qui se présente à l'individu comme devoir-être. Mais le social ne peut rendre ce service que s'il n'est pas lui-même comme une chose, s'il investit l'individu, s'il le sollicite et le menace à la fois, si chaque conscience à la fois se trouve et se perd dans son rapport avec d'autres consciences, enfin, si le social est non pas *conscience collective,* mais intersubjectivité, rapport vivant et tension entre des individus." *Sens et non-sens,* p. 179. Cf. *Signes,* p. 137: "Justement, l'inhérence de ma pensée à une certaine situation historique sienne et, à travers elle, à d'autres situations historiques qui l'intéressent,—puisqu'elle est originaire par rapport aux relations objectives dont la science nous entretient,—fait de la connaissance du social une connaissance de moi-même, appelle et autorise *vue de l'intersubjectivité comme mienne* que la science oublie tout en l'utilisant, et qui est le propre de la philosophie."

past back to life, but we can do so only from the standpoint of our particular situation, and the way in which man of the mid-twentieth century revives the past differs from that of a century ago. In both cases man considers the same past, but he does so from a different situation, and for this reason the past itself in its concrete form of appearance becomes different. For example, now that capitalism has given rise to Marxism, capitalism itself looks different to those who know Marxism.

An Apparent Contradiction. We have quoted here in this chapter a number of important texts, taken from an article published by Merleau-Ponty in *Signes*. In the preface of this book, which is probably one of the last texts written by Merleau-Ponty, he makes a remark concerning the relation of philosophy and the sciences which seems to contradict what we have said about him here. Speaking about the subject, he calls it a "from where," i.e., from the subject which we are we look out into the world without ever being able to make our own subjectivity really and fully visible. This subject is not a fullness of being but, on the other hand, it is also not a "nothingness." The thinking of philosophy originates in the subject as the source of meaning.

To quote Merleau-Ponty again, "Philosophy, which unveils this chiasm of visibility and invisibility, is the opposite of a surveying glance. It plunges into the perceptible, into time, into history, aiming at their central points. Philosophy transcends all this not through powers contained in its bosom, but goes beyond them only in the direction of the meaning which they themselves have. Someone recently recalled Montaigne's saying, 'Every motion reveals us,' and correctly concluded from it that man is only a being in motion. In the same way the world and Being have consistency only as something in motion. Only in this way is there connection between everything. Philosophy reminds us of this kind of being, with which science is not concerned. For science conceives the relationships between being and knowing like the relationships existing between the mathematician and his projections. Science forgets encompassing being, that which one could call the 'location of being.' The philosophy, however, which searches *below* science is not more profound than the passions, politics, or life. Nothing is more profound than the experience which breaks through the wall of being."[14]

---

[14]*Signes,* pp. 30-31. We have rendered this passage somewhat freely.

Merleau-Ponty seems to say here that philosophy is more profound than science, that it is concerned with what lies below science, and that it pays attention to a type of being which science neglects.

Thus, one could think that there is a contradiction between this passage from the preface of *Signes* and the above-quoted article contained in the same book. There seems to be likewise a contradiction between the text quoted above and the article "Le métaphysique dans l'homme," reprinted in *Sens et non-sens*. For in this article Merleau-Ponty says that *in* the sciences of man a mode of being reveals itself that is philosophically **very** important and consequently has to be thematized by philosophy.[15]

The contradiction, however, is merely apparent. For Merleau-Ponty does not at all say that the philosophical aspect, unveiling itself in the sciences, is thematized by the sciences themselves. And the above-quoted texts do not deny that the being thematized by philosophy does not reveal itself in the sciences. True, he says that the sciences are not concerned with "encompassing being," but this does not mean that they deny it in their concrete existence; on the contrary, they may affirm it existentially. The comparison, finally, between the relationship of knowing and being on the one hand, and that of the mathematician and his projections on the other, may be understood as a reference to the objectifying attitude that is typical of all science. Because of this attitude they lack a dimension of depth, which is present in the passions, politics, art and even life itself.

Concluding Remarks. From all this it should be clear that Merleau-Ponty does not ascribe a proper object to philosophy, that philosophy describes that which reveals itself in all aspects of life, science included, that the sciences do not know what they are speaking about if they keep aloof from all philosophy, that an implicit philosophy belongs to the essence of the sciences, and that philosophy has the right to enter into the realm of science, insofar at least as an implicit philosophy is contained in them. Philosophy, however, and it alone, thematizes that which reveals itself in everything. For in life we are too close to being to thematize it, and the sciences cannot thematize being because of their objectifying attitude and also because of the language which they use.

---

[15]"Dans les sciences mêmes elle [metaphysics] reparaît, non pas pour en limiter le champ ou pour leur opposer des barrières, mais comme l'inventaire délibéré d'un type d'être que le scientisme ignorait et que les sciences ont peu à peu appris à reconnaître." *Sens et non-sens,* p. 166.

It may be noted that Merleau-Ponty's view in this matter is not commonly accepted among other phenomenologists. Heidegger, for example, accepts that an abyss separates the philosophical attitude from that of science. According to Merleau-Ponty, Husserl was slowly moving in the direction of his standpoint without, however, ever fully arriving at it.[16] It cannot be denied that Merleau-Ponty's views contains certain valuable points about the relation of science and philosophy.

---

[16]"Nous ne prétendons pas que Husserl eût jamais consenti à quelque définition de ce genre, puisque, jusqu'à la fin, il a toujours considéré le retour à la parole et à l'histoire vivantes, le retour au *Lebenswelt* comme une démarche préparatoire, à laquelle devrait succéder la tâche proprement philosophique de constitution universelle." *Signes,* pp. 138 f. Merleau-Ponty concedes here that Husserl has always understood the function of philosophy differently from himself.

CHAPTER ELEVEN

MERLEAU-PONTY AND MARXISM

1. PRELIMINARY REMARKS

Bibliographical Data. Merleau-Ponty constantly confronts his thinking with Marxism. Quite frequently this confrontation is a kind of triangular affair, for, at the same time, he takes care to define his position with respect to Sartre's interpretation of Marxism. The reason is not far to seek. When after the war the magazine, *Les temps modernes,* was founded, Sartre and Merleau-Ponty became its two prominent philosophical contributors. Although, as we will see in the next chapter, there was even then a breach between these two, they were still considered kindred spirits. Many at that time still viewed Merleau-Ponty as a disciple of Sartre, an opinion that continues to be held by many in the United States. The orientation of *Les temps modernes* was rather leftist and displayed considerable sympathy for Marxism. Sartre was the leading spirit of the magazine, at least insofar as its philosophical direction was concerned, devoting much time and effort to the Marxist issue. Guided by his theory of freedom and his peculiar conception concerning human consciousness, Sartre gave to Marxism his own, highly personal interpretation. Thus, it came about that Merleau-Ponty in his intense concern with Marxism had to assume a position also with respect to Sartre's interpretation. However, this point more properly belongs to the next chapter, for it is a question of Merleau-Ponty versus Sartre rather than Merleau-Ponty versus Marxism.

Even in *Phénoménologie de la perception* there are long digressions about Marxism. In a footnote, covering several pages,[1] Merleau-Ponty takes issue with Marx' view that history is determined by the infrastructure, and in the chapter concerning freedom he dwells extensively on class and class-consciousness.[2] *Sens et non-sens* contains several articles about Marxism.[3] *Humanisme et terreur* is entirely devoted to the communist issue and raises especially the

---

[1] Pages 199-202.
[2] Pages 505-511.
[3] "Authour du Marxisme," pp. 197-251; "Marxisme et philosophie," pp. 253-277. Other articles in the same book likewise often speak about Marxism.

question whether and to what extent Marxist terrorism is justifiable. His *Eloge de la philosophie,* which was his inaugural address at the *Collège de France,* delineates his own philosophical standpoint in reference to the Christian and Marxist "explanations" of history.[4] *Les aventures de la dialectique* repeatedly considers the Marxist philosophy of history and the political action of Marxism.[5] Finally, the preface of *Signes* presents us with a valuable study of the relationship between philosophy and praxis, in which Merleau-Ponty takes issue with Marx' idea that these two form an absolute unity.[6] Thus, it is evident that Merleau-Ponty throughout his entire philosophical career never ceased to face Marxism. Following him in his dialog with Marxism will provide us with a better understanding of his own philosophical thought.

Why the Confrontation with Marxism? The fact that Merleau-Ponty constantly confronts himself with Marxism is not an historical coincidence but flows from the very nature of his philosophy. The era in which the lucid character of the mind was the object of much thought—it suffices to mention here Descartes' clear and distinct ideas, Kant's self-critique of the mind, and Hegel's spirit becoming aware of itself—has been followed by another era in which the emphasis is placed on the dark roots of human existence. In this era evolutionism teaches that man is the result of a material evolution. Freud draws attention to the all-pervading influence of the sexual instinct. Marx views human life from its economic infrastructure. Sociology discovers that our conscious life is largely dominated by social patterns of thought and evaluation which influence us but usually are not even known to us.

Merleau-Ponty's philosophy belongs to this second form of philosophical thought. He does not deny the light of the spirit, but he realizes that this light arises from darkness and remains internally permeated with this darkness. The light of the spirit cannot be opposed to the world but is itself permeated with worldliness. Because Marxism is the most striking philosophy which acknowledges the worldly character of the human spirit, it goes without saying that Merleau-Ponty has to define his position with respect to this philosophy.

---

[4]Marxism is considered in it on pp. 65-74.
[5]All chapters of this book speak about Marxism.
[6]*Signes,* pp. 10-20.

2. UNAUTHENTIC AND AUTHENTIC MARXISM

Merleau-Ponty's Aversion to Marxist Orthodoxy. Merleau-Ponty encountered Marxism in his own surroundings as an orthodoxy preached over the whole world under the direction of a powerful center. In principle it was impossible for him to agree with any orthodoxy, no matter what its character. For he views any orthodoxy as a conceptual fixation, a "city god," an absolutized way of thinking. A philosopher, says Merleau-Ponty, sees through all such absolutizing. Thus, he has always refused to accept Marxist orthodoxy.

It was not at all difficult for him to find in Marxist orthodoxy elements that are wholly irreconcilable with his own philosophy. First of all, Marxist orthodoxy thinks from the standpoint of matter as developing of necessity, even though this evolution is called "dialectic." For Marxism, man is the final result of a material process of evolution. Merleau-Ponty cannot accept this idea, for he rejects every explanation of man. Any explanation, he argues, has to begin with a starting point, and any starting point is already full of human meaning; consequently, it presupposes man. The attempt to explain man is absurd because it always assumes again what it is supposed to explain.

Secondly, orthodox Marxism points to a deterministic factor in human history. With Marxism, Merleau-Ponty admits that human history has many aspects and that the economic aspect exercises a very powerful influence on life. However, he refuses to accept that this single aspect determines all others. As we have pointed out, one of Merleau-Ponty's fundamental concepts is the unity of reciprocal implication. Everything refers to everything, and everything is influenced by everything, even in history. The very idea of a deterministic element in history goes counter to the heart of Merleau-Ponty's philosophy.

Thirdly, Marxism, at least in its orthodox form, believes in a goal, to be attained in the final stage of history. Merleau-Ponty admits that man attempts and will always attempt to make a coherent story of the confused course of history. However, the idea that he will ever succeed, so that history would no longer be a "day, separated by shreds of night,"[7] is, according to him, not a genuine idea but an illusion.

---

[7] *Sens et non-sens,* p. 9.

Moreover, Marxist orthodoxy generally uses a language that sounds scientistic to Merleau-Ponty. It speaks of determinism and necessity, of a strictly scientific explanation of history, of the mirror-like character of human knowledge, etc. Briefly, Marxist orthodoxy displays a spirit that is wholly irreconcilable with the very core of Merleau-Ponty's philosophy. Unsurprisingly, he has never extended his hand in friendship to this orthodoxy.

Marx and Marxist Orthodoxy. At first, however, Merleau-Ponty hoped that Marx himself could largely be exonerated from being responsible for this orthodoxy. In other words, he thought that the orthodoxy would be a faulty interpretation of Marx. Moreover, he hoped to discover, even in the Soviet Union, a "Marxism in motion" underneath the frozen face of orthodoxy, allowing him to consider the orthodoxy as a temporary concomitant phenomenon. In other words, he hoped to find in Marx, underneath many doubtful utterances, a core of philosophical insight that would be acceptable.[8] At the same time he hoped to discover that official Marxism was better than its own official doctrine.

In the name of Marx, writes Merleau-Ponty in an article published shortly after World War II,[9] it is claimed that man should be approached scientifically, that man and thing must not be put into opposition, and that the laws governing man's social existence have to be established. But all this is not at all in the spirit of Marx. For in his book, *Das Kapital,* Marx shows precisely that the so-called laws of nature, spoken of by capitalistic economists, are not at all entitled to this qualification, and this point belongs to the very essence of his book. In reality these "laws" are merely characteristics of

---

[8]"Le déclin de l'humanisme prolétarien n'est pas une expérience cruciale qui annule le marxisme entier. Comme critique de monde existant et des autres humanismes, il reste valable. A ce titre au moins, *il ne saurait pas être dépassé.* Même incapable de donner forme à l'histoire mondiale, il reste assez fort pour discréditer les autres solutions. Considéré de près, le marxisme n'est pas une hypothèse quelconque, remplaçable demain par une autre, c'est le simple énoncé des conditions sans lesquelles il n'y aura pas d'humanité au sens d'une relation réciproque entre les hommes, ni de rationalité dans l'histoire. En ce sens, ce n'est pas une philosophie de l'histoire, c'est la philosophie de l'histoire, et y renoncer, c'est faire une croix sur la Raison historique. Après quoi, il n'y a plus que rêveries ou aventures." *Humanisme et terreur,* p. 165. Judged by the norm of his own philosophy, Merleau-Ponty goes too far here. Despite certain restrictions, Marxism is offered here as *the* history of philosophy, and to give up Marxism is presented as abandoning the intelligibility of history. Merleau-Ponty himself creates here a "city god," while his entire philosophy protests against such an absolutizing procedure. We may add that his later works carefully abstain from making similar remarks.

[9]In the following pages we will closely follow this article, entitled "Marxisme et philosophie," *Sens et non-sens,* pp. 254-271.

capitalism's social structure and, therefore, they are just as contingent as this economic system itself. Marxism, Merleau-Ponty continues, is a structural idea *par excellence,* and for this reason a true Marxist can speak of laws only within the framework of historically existing social structures. Scientism, which absolutizes the scientific perspective, is not at all Marxist. For Marxism is essentially progressive, while scientism is conservative, for it gives an eternal value to what is merely temporal.

True, occasionally there are passages in Marx indicating that we should place our hope in the sciences, for they will reveal how nonsensical certain theories are. However, Merleau-Ponty goes on, these passages are very infrequent in Marx' works and they are, moreover, corrected by other more penetrating texts. For instance, Marx sometimes speaks about religion in a very critical way, as if religion would have no meaning at all. But elsewhere he indicates that religion is the heart of a heartless era, the spirit of a spiritless period. If communism really wants to be Marxism, Merleau-Ponty adds, then it will have to offer not less but more than is offered by religion. It has to fill the heart and mind of real life, so that religion becomes superfluous. The worship of the Church must not be replaced by that of the laboratory, and a registering cylinder is no substitute for the Holy Eucharist. It should be realized that religion manifests a human search for communication which real life has hitherto left unfulfilled. Marxism has to bring man into real communication with life, and in this way to eliminate the illusory communication of religion. Religion will disappear only when its core of truth has been integrated into human relationships.

Crude Communism and Its Foundation. There exists a false Marxism, says Merleau-Ponty, according to which everything is false and unauthentic, except the (communist) final phase of history. This Marxism is the ideal expression of rudimentary communism, born of envy and aiming at reducing absolutely everything to the same level. Marx himself had no esteem whatsoever for it. Authentic Marxism, however, wants to take up again all acquired values, but in a higher and better synthesis. It recognizes the value of everything and knows how to assign a place to everything. It has a feeling for history and an open eye for the meaning of everything. According to authentic Marxism, the meaning of history stands out in relief in estrangement, i.e., the man who has lost himself by adoring his idols regains awareness of his own truth in estrangement and proceeds to realize this truth. All these phenomena, Merleau-Ponty continues, do not reveal themselves in animals but only in man, and the reason is that man not merely "is," but also "exists."

How, then, are we to explain that there are texts in Marx which seem to offer support to a scientistic and positivistic interpretation of his thought? The reason, says Merleau-Ponty lies in the fact that Marx had to fight on two fronts—namely, against mechanistic materialism and against idealism. He had to struggle against Hegel's Spirit which, as a suprapersonal power, was supposed to dominate man against his will and to lead him to his goal. Against Hegel, Marx wanted to return to the earth and to real life. However, this turning to the real was not that of scientism or positivism. In Marx' philosophy man is not a blind exponent of earthly society's development, but he is conscious of his own being, and society is a real dimension of this real being. Society produces man, but man also produces society.

The bearer of history is neither Hegel's Spirit nor an earthly collectivity having man as its blind exponent. But the dialectic movement of history is borne by concrete man, who is involved in a certain way in the dialog with nature, in a certain economic constellation, in other words, situated man. The question has been asked, and very correctly so, says Merleau-Ponty, how Marx, who was a materialist, could defend a dialectic philosophy. How can matter play a role in a dialectic history? The reply is that Marx never thinks about matter as "brute matter," as an "in itself." He sees matter as taken up by man, as permeated with man's presence, as the place of human co-existence. Because of this way of viewing matter, consciousness is worldly, and the world is human. Because man is present in the world, a kind of logic reveals itself in the world. Marxism endeavors to understand this logic. Domestic animals are taken up into human existence without actively participating in it, without displaying any initiative. Man, however, actively takes up the situation in which he finds himself. He produces himself, he is self-realization. For this reason man is able to strive for a realm of freedom, for he feels that he can struggle and escape from his estrangement.

Marx' Practical Materialism. Marx, says Merleau-Ponty, often speaks about his materialism as "practical materialism." Matter plays a role in human life as the support and embodiment of praxis. In Marx there is no question of a brute, inhuman matter, through which man can be explained. As a dialog with matter, man co-determines matter. But human life has to be viewed within the framework of its bond with matter. For this reason society's ideological forms of existence are unbreakably united with man's material forms of existence, i.e., the interplay of man and matter. Economy and ideology, therefore, are internally connected. Just as the meaning of a painting or of a poem cannot be detached from the matter in which they exist, so likewise ideology cannot be separated from the economy. Even as the spirit of a work of art exists in its matter, so also does the spirit of a society exist in its economic constellation. For this reason Marx introduces the concept "human object," i.e., a material thing in which a human intention, a human attitude of mind, a human self-realization have found existence. The "human object" cannot be divorced from man, but man likewise cannot be separated from the "human objects."

These ideas, says Merleau-Ponty, would be deprived of their true value if one were to say that the economy alone is genuine reality and that the ideology is purely appearance or a mere concomitant phenomenon. The ideological factors of a society are just as real as the economy with which they are internally connected. Such factors acquire a haze of unreality only when they are overtaken, i.e., when a new economy, a new society begins to become visible. Once the new economy begins to postulate the socialistic way of life, the ideology of capitalism starts to exude the musty odor of the past. All this, however, does not take away from the fact that the ideology is a real factor in the giant drama of life.

Merleau-Ponty's Marx. This is the picture Merleau-Ponty draws of Marx. He is largely declared not guilty of all kinds of mistakes and one-sided ideas. We find here a Marx who fits in almost perfectly with the philosophy of Merleau-Ponty. Like Merleau-Ponty himself, Marx is supposed to struggle often against both idealism and positivistic realism. For Merleau-Ponty structure or Gestalt is one of the most important discoveries of philosophy, and the unity which we find everywhere is the unity of reciprocal implication. Marx likewise is supposed to have accepted a structural idea, and all laws are valid only within the structure. Merleau-Ponty rejects both the pure "in itself" and the worldless "for itself," and the same feature is claimed to characterize Marx' philosophy. Like Merleau-Ponty himself, Marx is supposed to have the tendency to place and understand everything in the historical development of meaning. Man and world permeate each other for Merleau-Ponty, and the same idea, he claims, is the core of the philosophy of Marx. Like Merleau-Ponty, Marx views everything within the unity of praxis.

In other words, Merleau-Ponty makes Marx speak his own philosophy. Undoubtedly, he idealizes Marx and, thus, takes away many of his one-sided ideas. It is rather striking that in the article summarized here Merleau-Ponty quotes mostly the earlier works of Marx. It is true that these early works lend themselves more easily to his interpretation than Marx' later writings. In this way Merleau-Ponty rejects Marxist orthodoxy and accepts authentic Marxism, demanding at the same time that orthodox Marxism amend itself by a return to the authentic Marx.

3. MERLEAU-PONTY AND SOVIET MARXISM

Philosophy Guided by Politics. What attitude did Merleau-Ponty assume with respect to Marxism as a ruling power, the Marxism of the Soviet Union? As we have already pointed out, he definitively rejects Marxism as a doctrinal orthodoxy, at least on certain points. This rejection is hardly surprising, for the philosophy of Merleau-Ponty and the doctrinal Marxism of the Soviet Union, especially under Stalin, are diametrically opposed on many points. However, Merleau-Ponty knows very well that philosophical view and political movement do not fully coincide, even though they are connected. What interests him most is the *communist praxis,* i.e., communism as movement, as political orientation. It is not excluded for him that communism as praxis is better than its philosophical theory.

The very idea of a philosophy guided by a political movement goes counter to Merleau-Ponty's view of philosophy. True, philosophy has to be in contact with praxis and, since politics plays a decisive role in praxis, it has to be in contact also with politics. This bond, however, consists in this that philosophy has to bring the praxis to light; the praxis is a source of inspiration for philosophy; philosophy gives expression to what goes on in praxis. The praxis gives birth to light and meaning, but there is a kind of light and meaning that is not clearly known to those who pursue the praxis. It is the philosopher's task to express this light and meaning. To be able to do this, he has to place himself at a distance, which implies freedom. Without freedom of thought, the philosopher is unable to fulfil his task.[10]

Compulsory "Philosophy." Those who guide the movement of praxis have, of course, the right to determine whether or not they

---

[10]We may recall here Merleau-Ponty's portrait of Socrates as the ideal (he says the "patron") of philosophers. *Éloge de la philosophie,* p. 48.

recognize themselves in a particular philosophy. For it is not at all excluded that a philosopher who from his distance brings the praxis to light, himself deviates from this praxis. The philosopher who voices true life will find an echo in the heart of his fellow men, while he who strays away from life will become isolated. Thus, one understands that those who guide the communist movement are not indifferent to philosophy, which claims to lay bare the fundamental lines of their movement.

Nevertheless, their concern may not exercise a compulsory power on philosophy, for otherwise philosophical thinking becomes a victim of the "city gods." The compelled philosopher is forced to abandon his distance, his freedom, so that he can no longer give voice to authentic philosophy.[11] For this reason Merleau-Ponty rejects the compulsion imposed by the Soviet Union on philosophical life. Unsurprisingly, therefore, he hardly ever enters into a discussion with the official philosophers of the U. S. S. R. He does not seem to take them seriously. On the other hand, he pays attention to Marxist thinkers who formulated their thoughts before the rise of Marxism as a political power, and he enters into discussion with Marxists who take some liberties with Marxism as an actual power, such as, e.g., Lucacs and some French Marxists.

Marxist Terrorism. We must now turn our attention to Marxism as a political movement, as an established system of power. This contains one aspect that causes Merleau-Ponty great uneasiness—namely, terrorism. Marxism, he knows, wants to bring man freedom, to liberate him from his estrangement. How, then, can a power which wants to bring freedom practice terrorism? Merleau-Ponty devotes a large part of his work, *Humanisme et terreur* to this question. He extensively analyzes the trials, held in Moscow under Stalin, of so-called "antirevolutionaries," and he endeavors to understand to some extent the terrorism displayed in these trials. He starts from the position that these trials, their climate, the self-accusations as well as the condemnations and their motives have to be understood from the

---

[11]"La position de Merleau-Ponty ne doit pas être mal comprise. Ce qu'il refuse, c'est un rêve de solution dialectique, un mythe qui se substitucrait à la dialectique réelle et nous empêcherait de comprendre notre histoire, ce que devient notre monde historique. L'a-communisme dont il parle a donc un sens précis, il signifie la distance nécessaire pour juger dans la réalité et dans son contexte mondial l'U. R. S. S., il permet de chasser les fantômes et de combattre aussi bien la croissade contre le communisme." Jean Hyppolite, "Existence et dialectique dans la philosophie de Merleau-Ponty," *Les temps modernes,* vol. 17, nos. 184-85, 1961, pp. 240-41.

standpoint of Marxism itself and not from without, from, for example, the viewpoint of a capitalistic ideology. While we cannot reproduce Merleau-Ponty's entire line of thinking, we will summarize a few of its essential parts.

First of all, Merleau-Ponty argues, one should realize that terrorism is found not only under the communistic regime but also in the capitalistic West.[12] For economic structures exist there which deprive many of the possibility of a reasonably decent life. These structures are sanctioned by law and protected by a political power. The West also knows a colonial system which deprives many of their human freedom. When those who oppose the existing regime resort to revolt and demand freedom to live a life worthy of man, the law and the established regime turn against them. This too is terrorism because a situation unworthy of man is kept in existence through force. This terrorism also acts against individual persons. Of course, it is true that the terrorism existing elsewhere does not justify communist terrorism. On the other hand, it should cause the accusers of the Soviet Union to be on guard and first to remove the serpent from their own bosom. The thoughtful philosopher should be careful not to see everything as either wholly black or purely white.

Terrorism Against Terrorism. Moreover, we should realize that terrorism is not always and in all conditions wrong.[13] As Hegel remarked, every conscious being strives to put to death the other conscious being. Even though we cannot accept this thesis in its

---

[12]"Toute critique du communisme ou de l'U.R.S.S., qui se sert de faits isolés, sans les situer dans leur contexte et par rapport aux problèmes de l'U.R.S.S.,—toute apologie des régimes démocratiques qui passe sous silence leur intervention violente dans le reste du monde, ou la porte par un jeu d'écritures à un compte spécial, toute politique en un mot qui ne cherche pas à 'comprendre' les sociétés rivales dans leur totalité ne peut servir qu'à masquer le problème du capitalisme, vise en réalité l'existence même du U.R.S.S. et doit être considérée comme un acte de guerre. En U.R.S.S., la violence et la ruse sont officielles, l'humanité est dans la vie quotidienne, dans les démocraties au contraire les principes sont humains, la ruse et la violence se trouvent dans la pratique. A partir de là, la propagande a beau jeu." *Humanisme et terreur,* pp. 196 f.

[13]"Quand on dit qu'il y a une histoire, on veut justement dire que chacun dans ce qu'il fait n'agit pas seulement en son nom, ne dispose pas seulement de soi, mais engage les autres et dispose d'eux, de sorte que, dès que nous vivons, nous perdons l'alibi des bonnes intentions, nous sommes ce que nous faisons aux autres, nous renonçons au droit d'être respectés comme belles âmes. Respecter celui qui ne respecte pas les autres, c'est finalement les mépriser, s'abstenir de violence envers les violents, c'est se faire leur complice. Nous n'avons pas le choix entre la pureté et la violence, mais entre différentes sortes de violence. La violence est notre lot en tant que nous sommes incarnés. . . . La violence est la situation de départ commune à tous les régimes." *Op. cit.,* pp. 117 f.

universality, it remains true that the self-affirmation of one man often is at the expense of the other. One who withdraws into a sphere of apparent interiority and spiritual purity may be able to conceal this ugly truth from his own gaze, but when he looks at the reality of existence, his eyes open themselves to the facts. Marxism sees the class struggle as an essential aspect of history. The bare fact alone that there are classes implies already that one group oppresses the other. This assertion remains true even if the class relations have become a supposedly lawful system. By its very structure, a society based on classes implies violence and terrorism, even when they are camouflaged under the guise of different names. But the only resistance to violence is violence. For this reason Marxism, which goes against oppression, violence and terrorism, can dispose only of one weapon to reach its goal—namely, itself also to make use of violence.

One could even say, Merleau-Ponty argues, that Marxist violence is more justified than capitalistic violence, for Marxist violence is a powerful attempt to banish violence from history.[14] If Marxism pursues a good purpose, its violence is justified, for the avoidance of violence leaves no other possibility than that of doing nothing and offering no opposition to the violence of the others. Let us not forget that all revolutions together have shed far less blood than the European kingdoms and empires have spilled to establish and maintain their power.

The Danger of Terrorism. However, Merleau-Ponty adds, it is dangerous to aim at a society-without-violence and at the same time to pursue this aim through violence as the necessary means of attaining it. For it may happen that the goal lies in a future that is far-away and not visible and that the entire present is dominated by violence, the means to this goal. In such a situation it easily comes to pass that the connection between goal and means remains perceptible only in the interiority of those who use violence, i.e., the real connection between the two is lost. In that case violence is no longer ruled by any norm and governs as unlimited terrorism.

---

[14]"La violence, la ruse, la terreur, le compromis, enfin la subjectivité des chefs et du parti qui riqueraient de transformer en objets les autres hommes trouvent leur limite et leur justification en ceci qu'ils sont au service d'une société humaine, celle des prolétaires, indivisiblement faisceau de volontés et fait économique, et, plus profond que tout cela, idée agissante de la vraie co-existence à laquelle il s'agit seulement de donner sa voix et son langage." *Op. cit.*, p. 120.

Here, too, Merleau-Ponty's philosophy emphasizes the unity of reciprocal implication. Aim and means must be interconnected, or
rather, they must, as it were, fuse. The goal has to appear clearly on
the road that is followed and may not be placed above it as an absolute
entity.[15] And in the means themselves a promise of meaning must
be discernible, which can be called the goal. In other words, the
meaning of violence must be unmistakably clear. The violence must
signify a liberation announcing itself here and now even as a real
possibility.

Self-Accusations. All this does not take away from the fact that
we live in a chiaroscuro, in which the meaning of social reality is
often concealed. Merleau-Ponty views the trials of Moscow from the
standpoint of this semidarkness. People in the West often express
surprise about the self-accusations of the accused. Didn't these party-
members, they wonder, act with a clear conscience? It often happens
that communists with the best of intentions commit acts which they
later decry as crimes. Is this not a sign of dishonesty, of hypocrisy?
Are such communists not forced to speak as their judges want?

In reply, Merleau-Ponty points out that such phenomena must be
viewed from the communist standpoint. Marxism admits the essential ambiguity of history. Thus, it may happen that one who acts
does not realize the meaning of his actions at the moment when he
performs them. At a given moment of history it is not clear whether
the party-approved line of conduct really serves the interest of the
proletarian revolution; for instance, whether Stalin's forced concentration on heavy industry was really the best course. In such
a case it may happen that some people think that they ought to resist
the leader and plan a revolt. Do they themselves know clearly and
distinctly what they are doing? Not at all. The same ambiguity pre-
vails here. It may be true that they take over the future of the
revolution, but it may also be true that they undermine this future.
The course of history itself only will show the meaning and, consequently, the morality of man's actions.

Bourgeois morality often speaks about internal intentions and
adheres to the idea that it depends on the intention whether an action

---

[15]"L'utile et le valable se confondent, non qu'on mesure le valable sur l'utile,
comme le fait le Commissaire, ou l'utile sur le valable, comme le fait le Yogi,
mais parce que l'utilité prolétarienne est le valable en acte dans l'histoire."
Op. cit., p. 137. "Fin et moyen peuvent échanger leur role parce que le moyen
n'est que la fin même,—le pouvoir du prolétariat,—dans sa figure momentanés."
Ibid., p. 138.

is good or evil. This is an illusion. Our true intentions do not lie in an illusory interiority. So-called inner intentions are self-interpretations of our real intentions, which lie in the sphere of the action itself, in the world. The real intention is an orientation to the future, and it is from this future that the character of our actions becomes clear to ourselves. For this reason it may happen that the accused in a Soviet trial later only recognize what they have really done. They made their decisions in semi-darkness, but later understood the true scope of these decisions. Thus, there is no hypocrisy in the fact that they gravely accuse themselves of actions whose false character they did not clearly perceive when they performed them. This is an inevitable consequence of the fact that man lives always in a situation. Being-situated is inseparably connected with the character of being-human and with the way in which we have to make our decisions.[16]

Dictatorship. In all this, moreover, says Merleau-Ponty, one should keep in mind the very special situation of the Soviet Union.[17] According to Marx, the revolution should have broken out in the technically most advanced countries. For in these countries the means of production were supposed to give rise, on the one hand, to a small and powerful bourgeoisie and, on the other, to an ever-growing proletarian population. In this way capitalism, by oppressing the overwhelming majority, would have shown its true character and at the same time would have revealed how untenable it really is. In such a country the situation would have been ripe for the seizure of power by the proletarians.

However, this is not the way things happened. The revolution broke out in a technologically backward country. True, there was oppression in Russia, but its character was feudal rather than capitalistic. Thus, the revolution was forced first to create its own objective conditions by the development of large-scale industrialization. The circumstances in which this had to be done were not at all favorable. For the "fatherland of the revolution" saw itself surrounded by hostile capitalistic powers, which could easily find agents within the Soviet Union itself. Therefore, the revolution had to protect itself, and its leaders, moreover, were compelled to ask great sacrifices of the population. This situation made dictatorial leadership inevitable. The leaders had to resort to violence to push their ideas through and

---

[16]"On peut donc avoir à répondre pour des actes de trahison sans en avoir voulu aucun." *Op. cit.*, p. 63.

[17]*Op. cit.*, pp. 196-98.

were not always able to make the masses see the reasons for this violence. In itself, however, in its most profound inspiration, Merleau-Ponty says, Marxism is not a dictatorial regime. It was merely forced to be so provisionally because of the conditions in which it became an historical reality.

Nevertheless, this situation contains a great danger—namely, that the provisional dictatorship, imposed by the circumstances, will become something permanent. It is not excluded that the dictatorship will fail to eliminate itself when the conditions allow it. In that case the existing regime makes itself a goal, and the terrorism and violence used by it lose their natural norm.

Merleau-Ponty's "Attitude of Waiting." How does all this apply concretely to the actually existing situation? When in 1947 Merleau-Ponty published his book, *Humanisme et terreur,* he did not yet dare to make any definitive judgment about this matter. On the one hand, for the above-mentioned reasons he could understand many aspects of the events occurring in the Soviet Union but, on the other, he did not fail to discern disturbing symptoms of degeneration. For he did not see any indication of a desire to do away with the dictatorship, and the dictatorial terrorism sometimes appeared meaningless to him. For this reason he expressed his grave concern with the way things were going in the Soviet Union.[18]

Outside the Soviet Union, however, says Merleau-Ponty, there are important groups really representing the proletarians. It is not impossible that these groups will aid the Soviet leaders to recover the revolutionary élan of Marxism.

Accordingly, Merleau-Ponty found the situation disturbing to such an extent, that he did not consider it justified unqualifiedly to declare his adherence to communism. Nevertheless, he continued to follow its fate with sympathy. In a later work he called this the "Marxist attitude of waiting" (*attentisme marxiste*).[19] While assuming this attitude, he manifested great sympathy with Marxism.

18"Il n'y a plus seulement, dans le cours du mouvement prolétarien, des détours inattendus, mais le mouvement prolétarien lui-même, en tant que mouvement conscient et spontané et comme dépassement de la sociologie éternelle, a cessé d'être le terme de référence de la pensée communiste." *Op. cit.,* p. 153.

19*Les aventures de la dialectique,* p. 307.

4. MERLEAU-PONTY'S CHANGE OF VIEWPOINT AFTER THE KOREAN WAR

Reasons for His Changed Political Standpoint. The fundamental change of Merleau-Ponty's viewpoint came about, he says, because his eyes were opened by the Korean war. Instead of renewing itself internally, as Merleau-Ponty had hoped, Marxism abandoned its defensive attitude and began to attack with the purpose of establishing elsewhere also "the regime of its own preference."[20] Thus, Marxism has resorted to conquest through violence. As a consequence, the "attitude of Marxist' waiting" assumes a different meaning.[21] When Marxism becomes a threat to the situation in which one lives, when it makes itself the enemy of one's own country, then the sympathetic attitude of waiting becomes a concealed declaration of agreement with an enemy. In such a case the "Marxist attitude of waiting" becomes communist action.[22]

The reason is that a situation of violence leaves no mean between communism and anticommunism. As long as people in one country favor a certain regime and people in another prefer a different system, one can say that he does not favor either one or the other, simply because he strives for an order which does not coincide with either of them. This was the attitude adopted by Merleau-Ponty. He was not in favor of capitalism but neither of the dictatorial regime of the Soviet Union. He wanted a social order in which the recognition of man by man would be realized as much as possible. In his view, this recognition was not attained in the capitalistic countries but likewise not in the Soviet Union. As long as opposite regimes co-exist peacefully, one can adopt an attitude of waiting and remain at a distance from both. When, however, the two regimes enter into conflict and declare war against each other, such an attitude becomes tantamount to treason. For it weakens the situation of one's own country and strengthens the enemy.

We see here how much Merleau-Ponty evaluates the significance of one's attitude in the light of the concrete circumstances. The attitude of waiting, which is good in a situation of peaceful co-existence, becomes evil when a conflict arises. Thus, when a movement, through

---

[20] *Op. cit.,* p. 308.

[21] In *Humanisme et terreur* Merleau-Ponty's attitude of waiting was based in part on the fact that the U. S. S. R. did not take the offensive.

[22] "L'attentisme marxiste devenait action communiste." *Les Aventures de la dialectique,* p. 308.

changed circumstances, reveals a different aspect, one is compelled to change also his own attitude. Merleau-Ponty himself has not hesitated to do so. There is no reason to be surprised by this when one keeps in mind that Marxism is not an abstract essence but a concrete historical phenomenon. As this phenomenon assumes a different form, one's attitude toward it has to be modified.

Reasons for His Changed Doctrinal Attitude.   Merleau-Ponty's change of attitude was not limited to the political scene but extended also to his doctrinal position. His work, *Les aventures de la dialectique,* clearly shows that he no longer considers tenable the benign interpretation given to Marx in *Humanisme et terreur* and *Sens et non-sens.*   The contradictions and ambiguities, he writes, encountered in communist politics were already present in the Russian revolution and ultimately even in the realism or objectivism of Marx himself.[23]   At first, Merleau-Ponty thought, Marx was battling on two fronts, viz., against both idealism and scientism, objectivism or positivism.   But in the second half of his life, after the middle of the nineteenth century, Marx fell for the temptation of "scientific socialism."[24]   He accepted the idea of a revolution that is already written, as it were, in the objective facts themselves, which are mirrored by consciousness.   "If the revolutionary function of the proletariat," Merleau-Ponty writes, "is written in the infrastructures of capital, then the political action which gives expression to this function is justified in the same way as the Inquisition is justified by an appeal to Providence."[25]

In other words, in such a case the human order is dominated and directed by an external force.   Absolute knowledge is now possible through knowledge of the objective facts.   One can now consider himself justified in imposing on his fellow men a direction demanded by brute facts that are hidden to them.   Dialectics is now sacrificed to the objectivism of science.   All this is already contained in Marx' works when he says that the revolution is present and operating before it is recognized as such by man.   Trotsky has taken over these ideas of Marx and drawn the ultimate consequences from them.

---

[23]"Oui, la pratique bolchevique et le trotskyisme sont dans la même ligne, et ce sont des conséquences légitimes de Marx. Si l'on remet en cause le bolchevisme, il faut remetter en cause aussi la philosophie objectiviste-subjectiviste de la praxis." *Op. cit.,* p. 119.

[24]*Op. Cit,* p. 116.

[25]*Ibid.*

It cannot be denied that Trotsky has developed ideas whose patterns were first outlined by Marx.

Marx entered the wrong track when he sought dialectics in objective things, when he substituted for the "human object" the objective thing itself, in other words, when he mixed his dialectic thought with realism.[26] For, by doing this, he partly withdrew the course of history from man, he opened the posibility that a group of men would claim to understand the objective demands of things and, thus, consider themselves justified in imposing their will on all. Marx' extreme objectivism has given birth to the extreme subjectivism of dictatorship.

Merleau-Ponty does not deny that Marx' thought contains many very valuable elements, that he thinks dialectically in many cases, shows usually great understanding of the true character of history, and, therefore, remains a source of inspiration. However, there is an undertone of objectivism in Marx, and it is this undertone which has led to all the degenerative aspects of the Soviet regime and communist politics.

Concluding Remarks. In the preface of his last book, *Signes,* Merleau-Ponty says that Marx is one of the classics,[27] one of the thinkers of great inspiration, whose words will always continue to stimulate mankind. However, classics are also thinkers whom no one repeats verbally. They continue to exercise influence, even on those who are against them. No one living after Marx is any longer able to study history as if Marx had not written his works. Yet Marx' fundamental inspiration has proved itself too rich, even for Marx himself. He has embodied his message in forms of thinking which demand revision. We may not stop with what Marx himself has said but must endeavor to express what he wanted to say, or rather ought to have said. Merleau-Ponty has never lost his admiration for Marx, but the weak points of Marxism have definitely not escaped him.

We do not think that Merleau-Ponty has modified his own philosophy by changing his position with respect to Marx. In his published works he is self-consistent. From the very beginning his philosophy could not be reconciled with certain ideas of Marx. What is true is that Merleau-Ponty did not immediately realize the distance separating

---

[26]*Op. cit.,* p. 122.

[27]*Signes,* pp. 16 f.

his thought from Marx. At first he made a mistake in his interpretation of Marx and this mistake accounts in part also for his too bene-
volent attitude toward communism. As soon, however, as he realized
that he was wrong, he was magnanimous enough to recognize his own
mistakes.[28]

---

[28]"Il est toujours malséant de se citer ou de se commenter. Mais, par
ailleurs, quiconque a publié ses opinions sur des problèmes vitaux est obligé,
s'il en change, de le dire et de dire pourquoi." *Les aventures de la dialectique,*
p. 306.

CHAPTER TWELVE

MERLEAU-PONTY AND SARTRE

1. INTRODUCTORY REMARKS

Personal Friendship and Concealed Differences. At the beginning
of the preceding chapter we have mentioned the bond which at first
united Merleau-Ponty and Sartre. Despite the various relationships
existing between the ideas of these two philosophers, it is very much
subject to doubt whether their original connection was primarily of a
doctrinal nature. For their divergence dates from as early as 1945,
when Merleau-Ponty published his *Phénoménologie de la perception.*
This book contains an entire chapter in which Merleau-Ponty attacks
one of Sartre's main ideas—namely, his concept of freedom.[1] True,
at first the thought of both thinkers seemed—this word is used here
intentionally—to move in a common fundamental sphere. But, on the
other hand, it is true also that the opposition of seemingly related
thinkers carries the greatest weight. There is no attack more painful
than that of a friend. Merleau-Ponty cannot have failed from the very
beginning to be aware of the great distance separating him from
Sartre and it is likewise inconceivable that a reader as intelligent as
Sartre would not at once have realized their divergence of views.

Thus, it is not surprising that Merleau-Ponty at first somewhat
concealed his disagreement with Sartre. His chapter about freedom
is wholly against Sartre's ideas, but Sartre himself is named only a
few times. Rather than naming him, Merleau-Ponty uses such expressions as "the doctrine which we are discussing here." He combats the doctrine but not at all the person who has formulated it.
When shortly after the war, Sartre's work was under attack, Merleau-
Ponty wrote an article, entitled, *Autour d'un auteur scandaleux,*[2] in
which he drew attention to what they had in common, but
made only vague references to their differences. The introduction to this article reveals to us something about the background of Merleau-Ponty's attitude: he and Sartre had been friends
since their early youth. Merleau-Ponty relates an episode of their
stay at the *Ecole Normale.* He and one of his fellow students had

[1]"La liberté," *Phénoménologie de la perception,* pp. 496-520.
[2]Reprinted in *Sens et non-sens,* pp. 83-96.

ridiculed traditional anthems, whereupon a large group advanced threateningly on them. Sartre courageously placed himself between the two and their pursuers, so that they could escape to safety without having to withdraw any of their criticisms.[3] Merleau-Ponty cites also many facts to show how good and kind Sartre is.[4] The two were friends and collaborators, and it cannot have been very agreeable to Merleau-Ponty when he had to attack Sartre's theories.

Open Critique. Some years later, however, in 1955, Merleau-Ponty published a critique which, without hiding anything, went straight against certain fundamental points of Sartre's philosophy.[5] Of course, Merleau-Ponty does not discuss the person of Sartre in it, but his doctrinal critique is sharp and occasionally even biting. Sartre himself did not react to this critique, but a reaction came from Simone de Beauvoir who, as is well-known, is on intimate terms with Sartre. In his latest work, *Critique de la raison dialectique,* Sartre names Merleau-Ponty once, but in a rather neutral context and without saying anything about their antagonism.[6]

In the preface to *Signes* Merleau-Ponty reacts to a self-criticism of Sartre, who turns against his own youth and accuses himself of having seriously lacked the spirit of rebellion. Merleau-Ponty uses some remarkable expressions here. He calls Sartre's essay a "nice commemoration of our youth,"[7] thereby recognizing their common past. He goes on to say that it "was not easy to be Sartre's friend,"[8] because the distance Sartre kept from his own facticity separated him at the same time also from what others had to go through.[9] He speaks of Sartre's "accursed lucidity,"[10] because he always views his own experiences from the standpoint of his so-called absolute freedom and, therefore, never allows himself to *be* something, i.e., to live really in sadness, anxiety and hope. He always remains at a distance and, by his very personality, demands the same of others.

These texts show that the original friendship between Sartre and Merleau-Ponty did not last and that Merleau-Ponty later, reflecting

---

[3]*Op. cit.,* p. 83.

[4]"Ce génie de la publicité prête des manuscrits encore inédits à des amis qui les perdent ou à d'obscure personnages qui les emportent à l'étranger. . . . 'L'enfer, c'est les autres' ne veut pas dire 'Le ciel, c'est moi'." *Op. cit.,* p. 84.

[5]"Sartre et l'ultra-bolchevisme," *Les aventures de la dialectique,* pp. 131-271.

[6]Vol. I, p. 55.

[7]*Signes,* p. 32.

[8]*Op. cit.,* p. 35.

[9]"La distance qu'il mettait entre lui-même et ses données le séparait aussi de ce que les autres ont à vivre." *Op. cit.,* p. 35.

[10]*Op. cit.,* p. 33.

on the development of his friendship, realized that it had never been genuine or could even have been genuine simply because Sartre did not fully "exist" in the situations in which he was involved. Placing himself on the standpoint of the lucidity of his reflection, Sartre remained too much aloof from the bonds in which he lived to gave himself fully to his social contacts. In this way the doctrinal opposition between Sartre and Merleau-Ponty was an obstacle also to their personal relationship.

We must now examine this doctrinal opposition somewhat more in detail, but we will limit ourselves to a few points of crucial importance.

2. ABSOLUTE OR SITUATED FREEDOM?

Sartre's Idea of Freedom. In the final chapter of *Phénoménologie de la perception,* Merleau-Ponty begins his study of freedom with a brief synthesis of Sartre's idea of freedom.[11] Consciousness, he says, is not a thing and, consequently, I, as a conscious being, cannot identify myself with my qualifications. Our qualifications are the toll we must pay for our being in the world; they are an obvious formality without any great importance. My qualifications cannot determine me, for, in order that something could determine me, I would have to be a thing. I cannot escape my consciousness, my freedom. If there is anything like freedom, it is absolute. It is inconceivable that I would be free in some actions but determined in others. For if freedom would disappear when it is not active, how could it ever be reborn? Once I am free, this freedom means that I am not a thing; and, therefore, I am never a thing. Likewise, freedom cannot be tempered because it is strongly influenced by motives. It is not possible to be a little free. If there is question of motives, we must make a choice; either these motives make me act, so that I am not free, or I am free and then I myself determine the force of these motives; I myself from the standpoint of my freedom make there motives influence me. If I recognize freedom, I should cease to speak of causes as well as of motives. Freedom, if it exists, has to be absolute. The so-called motive does not tip the balance to my decision, but my decision gives weight to the motive.

The same line of thought applies to interhuman relations. One may say that the other's gaze troubles me or moves me to something. However, I am free either to see the other as another human being

---

[11]These paragraphs are a brief summary of *Phénoménologie de la perception,* pp. 496-499.

who sees and judges me or simply to see him as an object. Thus, if the other's presence carries any weight for me, I myself again give it this weight from my freedom. We are often deceived in this matter because we confuse freedom with deliberation, in which we weigh the various motives against one another. But when we weigh motives, freedom has already been at work because it is freedom which confers on the motives their power.

Are there, then, we may ask, no limits to our freedom outside us, in nature? A rock, for instance, can show itself unscalable and thereby resist our free plan to climb it. Sartre's reply is as follows. There is no meaning in the world except for me and through me. It comes from my freedom that the rock is a height to be scaled; consequently, both scalability and unscalability ultimately are connected with the choice made by my freedom. Freedom lies at the foundation of all meaning, for it is the source of all giving of meaning.

Accordingly, nothing can limit my freedom, for all so-called limitations of freedom arise from freedom itself. No meaning can impose itself on my freedom because all meanings come forth from freedom itself. By assigning a cause or compelling motive to freedom, one destroys freedom. For this reason we are forced to choose either absolute unfreedom or absolute freedom.

Freedom in Sartre's Latest Work. We may add that Sartre maintains this idea of absolute freedom even in his latest work, *Critique de la raison dialectique.* True, there are certain modifications with respect to his previous works. To name a few examples, in his earlier works Sartre seemed to reject intersubjectivity as impossible, while in this book the formation of groups is the main topic, which implies that the author considers intersubjectivity really possible for man. In his earlier works the concept "in itself," thing-like massivity, played a crucial role, but in his latest work Sartre asserts that the "in itself" is absolutely unknowable and makes no or hardly any use of this concept.

However, with respect to the affirmation of absolute freedom, Sartre does not deviate from his former standpoint. He describes man as totalization of the world. The primary totalization of the world is found in the individual person, and in this person the totalization is free. Sartre speaks even of a sovereign and absolute freedom. While later he mentions obstacles to freedom, he asserts that these obstacles have to be explained from the standpoint of freedom. The absolutely free "practical organism"—his term to indicate individual human existence—is the "constituent reason" of everything, i.e., everything has to be understood from the standpoint of this free "practical organism," whether it be an obstacle to freedom or the formation of a group which overcomes this obstacle. True, Sartre describes the obstacles to freedom very impressively. He calls the totality of these obstacles "the practically-inert field," to indicate that, on the one hand, this field has arisen from the praxis while, on the other, it impedes praxis in its self-movement. However, he goes to considerable exertions to show that these obstacles really have arisen from freedom itself, even when they seem to be natural.

Merleau-Ponty's Critique of Absolute Freedom. Unsurprisingly, Merleau-Ponty is opposed to this absolute freedom. He begins his argument by making the remark that such an affirmation of freedom ultimately makes freedom impossible.[12] If freedom is always and everywhere present, then the distinction between freedom and unfreedom loses its meaning. For then the manacled slave is just as free as the one who revolts and breaks his chains. If freedom is present always and everywhere, then we are free when we control our situation as well as when we find ourselves utterly powerless. In such a case it is meaningless to draw attention to freedom by saying that here or there freedom manifests itself clearly. For such a remark is meaningful only against a background of unfreedom or diminished freedom. Freedom that is everywhere is nowhere, for it does not reveal itself anywhere in a particular fashion.

Moreover, such a freedom cannot embody itself in any forms of existence. As soon as freedom has realized something, we have to say at once that real freedom lies outside its so-called embodiments. Such a freedom is an interiority which can never come to exist in the world. Thus, we are with respect to things a non-being, and this non-being can never appear in the fullness of being, i.e., freedom, as not belonging to the material world, can never appear in this world. In this way we come close to the doctrine of inner intentions, so that the real action occurring in the world is threatened with becoming something of accidental importance.

Moreover, it is difficult to speak of choice with respect to such a freedom. For choice implies that the will sees value in something; but, how could there be question of seeing values from the standpoint

---

[12] *Op. cit.,* p. 499.

of a freedom which transcends all situations and maintains this transcendence even after taking a position? Such a freedom seems to be complete from the very beginning, for either it is or it is not, and if it is, it is fully.

Finally, Merleau-Ponty asks, in what sense can such an absolute freedom, which transcends all situations, be called *my* freedom? Our human selfhood is inseparably interwoven with a situation. There is a past which characterizes us in the present. If freedom is an absolute distance from all this, it would appear to be an anonymous nature distinct from us.

Merleau-Ponty concludes, therefore, that Sartre's thesis is indefensible and that freedom is essentially interwoven with a field of existence, that it is a mode of man's being in a situation. There is no other freedom than situated freedom. But in that case freedom is no longer absolute, for it is no longer an absolute beginning. It is not the absolute origin of all meaning because an existing field of meaning belongs to its very essence. Thus, our choice is never made from absolute zero, for there is always something which from the standpoint of our situation is the more obvious answer. Our situation, however, does not determine us fully, for otherwise our freedom would perish. For this reason we can never predict with absolute certainty what a man will do, even though it is true that, when we know someone very well, we know also what will seem his obvious choice.

Merleau-Ponty's Situated Freedom. The entire chapter about freedom in *Phénoménologie de la perception* is dominated by his dispute with Sartre concerning the situated or unsituated character of freedom. Merleau-Ponty tries to show that our freedom finds itself in a field of meaning and that this meaning is already a meaning, even for our freedom, in such a way that we, as free subjects, cannot escape from it.

"Outside myself," to quote him literally, "I do not find a limit to my freedom. But would I not find a limit in myself? A distinction has to be made between my explicit intentions, e.g., the plan I make today to climb these mountains, and general intentions which virtually fill my surroundings with meaning. Whether or not I decide to climb these mountains, they appear high to me, and even when I have just finished reading *Mikromegas* I cannot make them be low for me. Underneath me, therefore, as a thinking subject, underneath me insofar as I can arbitrarily situate myself on Sirius or on Earth, there is something like a natural 'I' which does not give up its earthly situation, and which constantly projects absolute valuations. Moreover, the plans which I as a thinking subject make are apparently based on these valuations. When, for instance, I decide to see things from the standpoint of Sirius, I am able to do so only by having recourse to my earthly experience and say, e.g., that the Alps appear to me as a mere molehill. Insofar as I have hands, feet, a body, a world, I am the bearer of intentions which do not depend on my freedom, and which my surroundings have provided with characteristics not chosen by me. These intentions are general in a twofold sense. First of all, they constitute a system in which all possible objects are encompassed at once. If, for example, the mountain appears high and steep to me, the tree appears small and slanting. Secondly, these intentions are not reversibly proper to me and come from a distance which lies beyond me. Hence it does not surprise me to find them in all psychophysical subjects having an organization similar to mine."[13]

Merleau-Ponty then proceeds to show in a more concrete fashion how in perception a meaning imposes itself that is not dependent on me, because I cannot structure the data in every arbitrary fashion.[14] While Sartre is right when he says that every structure, every meaning exists for me, the "I" for which it exists is not the free subject, at least not only, or in the first place, the free subject. The world which I as a free subject find has already a meaning and a structure. Moreover, certain dispositions, such as tiredness and sadness, are not under the control of my freedom but, as it were, impose themselves on it. For example, I am not tired when I will. Yet these dispositions carry weight in reference to the decisions of my freedom. The habits also which I have made my own are contributing factors. It is true, of course, that I may at any given moment choose to break with these habits, but it is very improbable that I will do so. Sartre does not want to have anything to do with the concept of probability. From the viewpoint of the absolute "yes" or "no," this concept, of course, hardly makes sense. But, says Merleau-Ponty, one cannot speak about real life without making use of it.[15] If, for example, somebody has lived for twenty years with an inferiority complex, he may be able to get rid of it, but it is not very likely that he will do so all at once.

Merleau-Ponty draws attention also to the weight of the historical situation.[16] A man is born, e.g., into the class of proletarian workers

[13] *Op. cit.*, p. 502.
[14] *Op. cit.*, pp. 502 f.
[15] *Op. cit.*, pp. 504 f.
[16] *Op. cit.*, pp. 505 f.

or into that of the bourgeoisie. He naturally breathes an atmosphere which permeates his entire thinking and doing. Of course, as Sartre point out, he can break away from his situation. Nevertheless, says Merleau-Ponty, a bourgeois who becomes active in the proletarian movement always remains a bourgeois who has broken with his class and the way in which he participates in the proletarian movement will be strongly influenced by his past. On the other hand, someone who has grown up in the proletarian situation undergoes its atmosphere as he undergoes the climate in which he lives. He does not choose this influence freely. "The view which we oppose," says Merleau-Ponty, "is wrong in that it pays attention only to our intellectual projects, and does not take into account the existential projects which polarize life toward a purpose in which being-determined and being-undetermined fuse, a purpose of which no man has any conception but which he recognizes only at the moment when he attains it."[17]

"We recognize, therefore," so Merleau-Ponty summarizes his view, "around our initiatives and the strictly individual project which we are, a zone of general existence and already-executed projects, of meanings which move between ourselves and things and which charactrize us as a human being, a bourgeois or a laborer. Their general character plays a role. Our presence to ourselves is mediated by it. We cease to be a pure consciousness from the moment when the natural and social constellation is not merely a meaningless givenness, but crystallizes into a situation and has a meaning—briefly, from the moment that we exist."[18] Man would be absolute freedom only if he did not find himself in a situation which has already a meaning.

Concluding Remarks. In this way we are back at Merleau-Ponty's fundamental viewpoint that man is a subject even on a level on which he is not yet conscious and free. The dialog with the world that man is begins at a level that lies deeper than consciousness and freedom. As a conscious and free existence, we take up a dialog that has already been going on; we continue a giving of meaning that was already being done. The philosophies of both Sartre and Merleau-Ponty are centered on the human subject, but they differ essentially in their idea of the human subject. Sartre's subject is a "for itself" which at once and essentially is at a distance from the world, which is a worldless consciousness and freedom. If this subject has any bonds with

---

[17] *Op. cit.,* p. 509.
[18] *Op. cit.,* pp. 513 f.

the world, these bonds have been chosen freely. While freedom is able to bind itself, it cannot be passively bound. Merleau-Ponty's subject, on the other hand, is a dialog with the world, but a dialog which initially has the character of an "I am able," which initially is pre-conscious and not yet free. The free subject is the taking-up of pre-conscious existence on a higher level.

It is to be regretted that Merleau-Ponty's chapter on freedom is written wholly as a dialog with Sartre. For, as a consequence of this, Merleau-Ponty places heavy emphasis on the situated character of freedom and does not raise the question of what freedom really is. The same must be said about the chapter dealing with the *Cogito,* in which he shows mainly that our thinking is rooted in pre-conscious existence. What is lacking in Merleau-Ponty's work is a description of the inner essence of the thinking and free subject. For we do not yet know what thinking and freedom are, when we know that they are rooted in pre-conscious existence. Because of the way in which he approaches thought and freedom, Merleau-Ponty does not ask whether they can be adequately understood as unfoldings of the pre-conscious dialog with the world. Yet there is undoubtedly a problem in the question of how a body-subject can rise to becoming conscious of itself and to determining its situation in freedom. While Merleau-Ponty shows that Sartre's position is not tenable, we can imagine that Sartre himself fails to be convinced by arguments which are not accompanied by a positive standpoint, presenting a philosophy of the subject different from his own. In this respect Merleau-Ponty's synthesis shows a serious deficiency.

3. The Fundamental Divergence of Merleau-Ponty and Sartre

A very long chapter of *Les aventures de la dialectique,* entitled, "Sartre et l'ultra-bolchevisme," contains the crucial confrontation of Merleau-Ponty and Sartre. It was written on the occasion of Sartre's dissertation on communism. Communism, says Merleau-Ponty, continues to speak in dialectic terms, but it has changed the innermost core of dialectics into a natural event.[19] A result of this is that dialectics no longer originates from man but is given with objective things and, as it were, read by man in nature. In this way, as Lucacs expresses it, dialectics becomes a technical process to be discussed by

---

[19]*Les aventures de la dialectique,* p. 131.

engineers only.[20] The meaning of history lies written in things and consequently is no longer a design resulting from human actions. We find here, in principle, the possibility of unrestricted terrorism, for the "engineers of the future," who understand objective things, have the right to impose their will on mankind even when the others do not at all understand the meaning of the imposed order.

Sartre, the Absolute Thinker. In this situation it was fortunate, says Merleau-Ponty, that a thinker freed himself of Marxist *a priori's* and tried to rethink communism.[21] In undertaking this task, Sartre endeavored to understand the communist policy and to justify it from the standpoint of his own philosophy, which differs basically from communist orthodoxy. True, Sartre is a Marxist but he argues from his own principles and not from those of Marxism. His principles, says Merleau-Ponty, are even radically opposed to those of communism.[22] Where communism places dialectics in an inhuman nature, Sartre deduces communist action from a dictate of free will, and locates so-called objective reality in an impenetrable darkness. According to Sartre, communist action arises from the categorical will to bring about what has never yet been.[23]

On reading Sartre's dissertation, which is heavily loaded with quotation of Marx, says Merleau-Ponty, one does not know what distinction Sartre makes between the teachings of Marx, the official teachings of Soviet philosophy, and his own view. The reason is that Sartre, as a "brave" philosopher, absorbs the whole of this world of thought into his own thinking. Sartre disregards true history and knows only the history conceived by him, in which Marx, Lenin, Stalin and Duclos can no longer be distinguished from one another or even from Sartre himself. Sartre is the absolute thinker, for whom everything becomes an object and who, therefore, is able neatly to gather everything in a coherent and clear synthesis.[24]

Sartre's Rejection of History. Sartre's dissertation, Merleau-Ponty adds, is permeated with a strange ambiguity. On the one hand, he constantly appeals to facts, which he analyzes in his writings. On

---

[20]*Ibid.*
[21]*Op. cit.,* p. 132.
[22]*Op. cit.,* p. 133.
[23]"Sartre fonde justement l'action communiste en refusant toute productivité à l'histoire, en faisant d'elle, pour ce qu'elle a de connaissable, le résultat immédiat de nos volontés, et pour le reste une opacité impénétrable." *Op. cit.,* p. 134.
[24]*Op. cit.,* p. 137.

the other hand, the facts derive their meaning from Sartre's absolute philosophy. For this reason these facts assume an absolute character. Communism *is* truth, the party *is* the embodiment of the future, the proletariat *is* the bearer of history. But this meaning of the facts does not arise from a patient analysis but is, as it were, imposed on them from the standpoint of a philosophy. In this way the fact itself becomes a part of a theory. This view harmonizes with Sartre's opinion that nothing can function as cause or motive of our conscious acts. For Sartre, history either is born from man's will or does not exist. For Sartre, the communist party is the reply of free consciousness to the facts, and this reply is all the more categorical the less the bare facts themselves have an inner meaning.

All this, says Merleau-Ponty is very strange. Sartre 's work is a curious paradox.[25] He has become famous for his powerful descriptions of a field lying midway between consciousness and thing, a field that has the heaviness of things and nonetheless is really human. He has given wonderful descriptions of the human situation and his descriptions sharply indicate the ambiguity of this situation. At the same time, however, his philosophical thought always revolts against this ambiguity, in which meanings are merely probable. His philosophical thinking conceives the situation as an invitation to transcend it, to undertake the reconstruction of the world of meaning from the "nothingness" of freedom. Sartre's descriptions show that he knows the field of ambiguous meanings, the field of Merleau-Ponty's philosophical inquiry. But through his absolute thought and absolute freedom he immediately rises again above this field. He knows the historical field, but it is not in this field that his meaning arises. His meaning is born from freedom's absolute choice, and he does not want to have anything to do with what he calls "organicism,"[26] i.e., he rejects the idea that individual existences together constitute a mysterious kind of supra-organism. However, says Merleau-Ponty, what he rejects in this way is history itself as the field of ambiguous meanings, which are realized in the individual and at the same time transcend the realms of individual life. Thus, the only thing that remains as source of meaning is freedom.

Following Sartre in his description of facts, Merleau-Ponty shows through many examples how the meaning which Sartre ascribes to the facts does not originate in these facts themselves but in Sartre's

---

[25]*Op. cit.*, p. 185.
[26]*Op. cit.*, p. 191.

philosophy. It is clear, therefore, that Merleau-Ponty's standpoint differs fundamentally from that of Sartre, not because he has in view different facts, but because he gives a different interpretation to the same facts. Merleau-Ponty prefers the patient analysis of the facts themselves to Sartre's *a priori.* In this way, he goes on, the disagreement becomes even greater, for it is rooted in the method followed by Sartre in the use of the facts, in the reply he gives to the facts. In other words, the disagreement is of a philosophical character. Merleau-Ponty then indicates three basic philosophical concepts which Sartre and he himself describe in radically different ways.

Divergence Concerning the Idea of "Involvement." First of all, Merleau-Ponty and Sartre differ in their description of the concept "involvement" (*engagement*). Although Sartre's philosophical work shows certain developments, he has remained self-consistent in the evolution of this concept.[27] At first, he described involvement as the resolve to show oneself externally as one is within. What he meant was that one's external position should be fully in harmony with freedom's resolve, that one should seek an absolute reply to the whole of the situation in which one is. For this reason the editors of *Les temps modernes* demanded that their collaborators did not belong to any party or church. For, one who is bound to a certain group is no longer able to reflect on everything. All particular involvements had to be given up in order to plan a new involvement which would encompass the situation in its totality.

While this program sounded rather positive, says Merleau-Ponty, it contained one suspect angle—namely, the way in which Sartre described the relationship between freedom and action. One is free, so Sartre said, to bind oneself, but one has to bind oneself in order to manifest the reality of freedom. This means that freedom has to become involved, not in order to exist but in order to show its reality. Nevertheless, Merleau-Ponty argues, this involvement does not modify the character of Sartre's freedom. For the involvement is merely a self-affirmation of a freedom which maintains its position above the involvement. A choice is made, not because of the value of that which is chosen but to testify to one's freedom. Freedom, then, makes a plan as a kind of testimony of itself but without becoming involved.

Later Sartre himself became involved by pronouncing himself in favor of the U. S. S. R. However, if we consider this involvement

---

[27] *Op. cit.,* pp. 255-263.

carefully, it appears not to be a genuine joining of an historical group. For Sartre accepts the abstract aim of communism, the changing of the world, but not its concrete program. So far as the concrete program is concerned, he reserves the right to agree to certain points and to reject others.

Thus, Sartre always remains the inscrutable. First he wants to withdraw from all present involvements to plan a new involvement in harmony with his idea of absolute freedom. Then he becomes involved with a certain group, but his so-called adherence appears to be merely the acceptance of an abstract aim and not that of a concrete plan of action.

Sartre, Merleau-Ponty adds, cannot really become involved because in his innermost depth he is absolute freedom. For this reason it is possible for him to modify his external attitude without being, in his own opinion, disloyal to himself. Whatever continuity there is in Sartre lies not in the external but in the internal. His unity of life is abstractly philosophical and not concrete and existential. Thus, he remains inscrutable to others.

Merleau-Ponty is unable to accept this concept of involvement because, for him, such an involvement is unreal and, therefore, not an involvement.[28] Real action, real involvement, he says, demands more and at the same time is less massive. It demands more because freedom which becomes involved does not exist above the involvement, but exists precisely in it. Involvement is not an external sign of an internal freedom but the existence of freedom in the world. Freedom itself is affected by the involvement. A person's freedom is compromised by his involvement. At the same time, however, involvement is less massive according to Merleau-Ponty. For it is born of the laborious interpretation of the facts, in which others also, and even the whole of history, play a role. Involvement is not born of a choice of freedom without causes and without motives, but of the interpretation of a datum on which we fix our gaze but which at the same time transcends our gaze. Genuine involvement, therefore, is subject to the critique of others. When we become genuinely involved, we accept more than we know, and our responsibility transcends the lucidity of our thinking. But Sartre's involvement leaves freedom absolute. The character of involvement, says Merleau-Ponty, reveals the ambiguity of freedom. Sartre's involvement bears wit-

---

[28]*Op. cit.*, pp. 263 f.

ness to a freedom which remains un-involved in its innermost depth, while Merleau-Ponty's involvement compromises the freedom which becomes involved.

Divergence of the Description of Freedom. As the second fundamental difference between his own philosophy and that of Sartre, Merleau-Ponty names the concept of freedom, thereby taking up again a discussion that had already been started in *Phénoménologie de la perception.*

Sartre's freedom, he says,[29] is the pure power to act or not to act spoken of by Descartes. Because this power to act remains itself during the whole course of the action, this action dissolves into a plurality of successive phases that are not innerly united, but connected merely because they flow from the same freedom. This freedom always continues to act creatively and to posit forever new self-manifestations. But such a freedom never identifies itself with its action and consequently never becomes *doing.* Its action is a kind of a magic *"fiat."* This freedom never comes down into the world and does not attach itself to any facticity. It is the freedom to judge, which remains proper even to the manacled slave. The "yes" and "no" of this freedom are inviolable and refer only to known things, not to reality.

For Merleau-Ponty it is evident that such freedom is nothing but an illusion.[30] Between me and what I experience, he says, there is no distance which has to be constantly bridged through a free-will decision. I exist in my field of meaning. My thoughts, the meaning which I give to life, are present within a whole of meanings and I myself am situated in this whole. For this reason I am related in a particular way to my fellow men and to our common history, and no dictate of freedom can withdraw me from this relationship. True, the relationships which I have do not determine me, for I am able to take them up and transform them. However, in doing so, I have to start from the situation in which I find myself. The term "choice" is often almost meaningless, not because my future is fully fixed, but because it is fully obvious what it will be. My situation is not a practice field for an absolute freedom but an existential situation in which my freedom must find its way. The meaning of my future does not arise from a dictate of my freedom, but outlines itself within

---

[29] *Op. cit.,* pp. 264 f.
[30] *Op. cit.,* pp. 265 f.

my existential field. As a rule, I am not able to indicate exactly when I began to will something and when I stopped willing it. The continuity of my life is to be understood from the standpoint of my field of existence and not from an illusory absolute freedom.

Divergence Concerning the Idea of Consciousness. The third difference, says Merleau-Ponty, lies in the conception of consciousness. According to Sartre, consciousness is a power to give meaning to that which lies outside consciousness.[31] Consciousness, therefore, is centrifugal, for it projects its meanings outside itself and does not become embodied in the density of the world. The action done in the world remains subject to the understanding of consciousness and to the dictate of freedom. But, asks Merleau-Ponty, are not the understanding of consciousness and the dictate of freedom action in the strict sense? Does not Sartre's position lead to a closed consciousness, despite the fact that he denies this closed consciousness so emphatically in his phenomenological analyses? Thus, no darkness whatsoever remains in consciousness itself. Since the meanings flow wholly from consciousness itself, they are complete and closed. Whence Sartre's "accursed lucidity."

In reality, so Merleau-Ponty objects,[32] all meanings existing for us are incomplete and open to the future. This implies that our consciousness is not a pure and unmixed presence with itself. We do not find completed meanings in perception. For every thing which we perceive is a certain condensation of the bonds involving us in the fields of the senses and in the world. It is as if the world contracts into the perceived thing. For this reason the perceived always refers to an horizon within which it appears, and this horizon is a chiaroscuro. There is likewise no closed meaning in the domain of our thoughts. For an idea arises in us by virtue of the words that are at our disposal; these words, as it were, arrange themselves in an orderly fashion and indicate a ray of light which never becomes fully light because it is born of darkness.

Thus, consciousness cannot be described as a reality whose whole essence consists of clear self-knowledge. My self-presence is conditioned by my existential field, which is never wholly a field of light. Thinking also is orientation to the world. My tasks outline themselves against this world. They are not aims set by me in a sovereign free-

[31]*Op. cit.,* p. 267.
[32]*Op. cit.,* pp. 267-69.

dom, but they appear to me from the field of my praxis. I do not set any task for myself, but I have to decipher laboriously what my tasks are. Living in such a field, I find myself also in contact with other human beings; hence my freedom is likewise not the absolute origin of my contact with them.

Ultimately, says Merleau-Ponty, everything amounts to this. According to Sartre, there are human beings and things, and everything has to be understood from the standpoint of these two poles. The thing functions only as material for the concept. Thus, we find ourselves in a dichotomy.[33] Man is condemned to an almost unbearable tension, for each human being is an absolute center of meaning. According to Merleau-Ponty, all of us together are in an historical field. We all come to life from this field and take it up in such a way that our being is at once a being-together. Thus, our plurality as well as our mutual bond are an original datum.

Concluding Remarks. From the preceding pages it should be evident how much the philosophy of Merleau-Ponty differs from that of Sartre. There always was opposition between these two philosophies, but the depth of their divergence revealed itself only slowly. It was Merleau-Ponty who gave expression to the distance separating him from Sartre.

Merleau-Ponty's death prevented him from reacting to Sartre's latest work, *Critique de la raison dialectique,* but its appearance was a confirmation of Merleau-Ponty's understanding of Sartre's philosophy. This whole book is permeated with the "accursed lucidity" of which Merleau-Ponty complained. Sartre the phenomenologist has disappeared entirely in it, to be replaced by Sartre the rationalist, viewing history in the light of "constituent reason," i.e., of individual existence, of absolute freedom. Sartre's latest work is wholly dominated by absolute categories, no matter how many pages he needs to describe them, for these descriptions themselves are made from the viewpoint of the absolute idea. It is as if Sartre is blinded by the light of his own concepts, so that he is no longer able to see the many-sidedness of reality. Reading his book, one's surprise becomes increasingly painful and leads to the question of how it is possible for a thinker to be blinded to such an extent by his own thoughts. Yet throughout the book, Sartre remains the ingenious dialectician who knows how to connect the facts with his ideas.

---

[33]"Si l'on se tient à la dichotomie, les hommes, lieu de tout ce qui peut avoir sens, sont condamnés à une incroyable tension." *Op. cit.,* p. 269.

Merleau-Ponty's dialog with Sartre has undoubtedly been fruitful for his own philosophy, because it made him more forcefully aware of the character proper to his thinking. The confrontation with Sartre made him understand much better to what extent his own thought is a "philosophy of ambiguity."

4. Appendix—Sartre About Merleau-Ponty

The manuscript of this book was already finished when *Les temps modernes* published a special issue dedicated to the memory of Merleau-Ponty. This issue contains a long article of Sartre, entitled, "Merleau-Ponty vivant" (pp. 304-376). Sartre's study does not offer us any reason to modify anything in what we have said, but only to add an appendix to this chapter For, after hearing what Merleau-Ponty had to say in critique of Sartre, the reader may be interested in finding out what Sartre has to say about Merleau-Ponty.

The General Tone of Sartre's Article. In no respect is Sartre's contribution to this issue a reply to Merleau-Ponty. Such a "reply" would have been meaningless anyhow in a commemorative issue. Sartre does not even defend himself against the reproaches addressed to him by Merleau-Ponty. His article hardly tells us anything concerning the relationship between his own philosophical thinking and that of Merleau-Ponty. When Merleau-Ponty speaks of Sartre, he is concerned with his philosophy and personal questions are mentioned only in an incidental way. Sartre's article, however, is almost entirely personal and hardly touches their philosophical differences.

Sartre describes the history of their mutual person-to-person relations. It is the story of a friendship that has largely failed. Sartre offers us also an analysis of Merleau-Ponty's life, and sometimes tries to make the development of his philosophical thought intelligible in the light of his life story. On reading Sartre's article, one has the impression that their philosophical divergence was merely incidental and that their differences of opinion were mainly concerned with the magazine, *Les temps modernes,* and the political realm. We doubt very much that Merleau-Ponty would agree with him on this point.

Sartre relates an interesting confidence made to him by Merleau-Ponty in 1947—namely, that he was never "cured" of an incomparably happy childhood and youth.[34] This confidence becomes the

---

[34]"Merleau-Ponty vivant," *Les temps modernes,* vol. 17, 1961, nos. 184-185, p. 305.

Leitmotiv of his article. What else, Sartre asks, was Merleau-Ponty than Paradise lost? Our possibility to lead a happy life, he says, depends largely on a certain equilibrium between what our youth has offered us and what it has refused us. It was Merleau-Ponty's fate to have received too much too soon; thus he continued forever to seek the lost happiness of life, the golden period which would never be able to return.

Nevertheless, Sartre goes on, Merleau-Ponty had to live his life, and this meant that he had to take his life into his own hands until the very end, a life, however, whose fundamental lines were fixed by the above-mentioned facticity. For this reason he showed a preference for the traditions which recall the way of life of the child and for the "spontaneity" which is proper to the guarded freedom of childhood. For this reason also, says Sartre, Merleau-Ponty exhibited an "archaic naïveness," which approached the meaning of the present from the past and made up the balance of today. Merleau-Ponty always looked with an astonished gaze at the world in which he lived, for he could never find back in it the obvious world of his childhood.

Sartre sees here also the reason for Merleau-Ponty's attention to contingency and his aversion to become definitively involved in anything. From Marxism he borrowed the living idea, but he refused to accept its dogmatic system. He reproached Marxism for neglecting contingency. The contingency of everyone and of all, the contingency of the common adventure of mankind, the contingency also of the Marxist venture—such was Merleau-Ponty's fundamental experience, which Sartre conceives in the light of Merleau-Ponty's personal history of life. Merleau-Ponty was a Christian also, but he sought in Christianity a security that it could not offer. For the same reason he was unable to feel at home in the communist party. He was a seeker for the kind of security which he had lost forever when his childhood ended.

Three Phases of Merleau-Ponty's Thought. In the light of this personal analysis Sartre distinguishes three periods in the philosophical thought of Merleau-Ponty. The first, he says, lasted until he had finished his two academic dissertations. In this period "this youthful Oedipus" sought the "rational irrationality" from which he had risen, i.e., the pre-rational roots of existence. In the subsequent years, from 1943 to about 1950, says Sartre, Merleau-Ponty extended his research to the roots of common history: he became aware of political life. During this period he wrote his political articles in *Les temps modernes.* The third period began in 1950, but assumed a definite form only in 1953 when his mother died. It is characterized especially by Merleau-Ponty's penetration into the mystery of the human "I." He reflected mainly on the person as the mysterious interlocking of particularity and universality. Merleau-Ponty's mother occupied a very large place in his life. She was, so to speak, the symbol of his security, the embodiment of his happy past. He could not accept that this past was definitely gone. During the last years of his life, Sartre says, he refused to call himself an atheist, not because he believed in the truth of Christianity but because he wanted to give a chance to the deceased.

Merleau-Ponty, Sartre continues, was a thinker concerned with origins. At first, he sought the pre-conscious basis of individual existence, then he searched for the origin of common history, and finally he devoted his attention to the origin and meaning of personal existence. He was a philosopher who gradually became more profound. Coming forth from his original security, he had a sharp eye for the contrasts, the ambiguities of life. In dialectics he avidly accepted thesis and antithesis, but rejected the synthesis as a playing with constructions that was not in keeping with the real seriousness of life. Because of this rejection, Sartre calls his dialectics "decapitated."

Personal Relations. From these perspectives Sartre interprets his relationship with Merleau-Ponty. They knew each other from childhood, he says, without ever becoming intensely friendly. During the war they met again as members of the circle, "Socialism and Freedom." This circle did not have any definitive future, but served to bring Merleau-Ponty and Sartre together again because of their common interest in Husserl and in the post-war future. Yet their exchange of ideas was always full of reserves. Merleau-Ponty reproached Sartre for giving in too easily in these colloquies and then later presenting his own opinion as that of both, thus manifesting his pride and disregard for others. Sartre rejects this reproach, pointing out that Merleau-Ponty was endeavoring to render his own thinking more profound and that discussions proved more of an obstacle than an aid in this endeavor. It was my fault, Sartre adds, to neglect unimportant things for the sake of the common truth.

"Les Temps Modernes." Their meeting led to the initiative to found the magazine, *Les Temps Modernes.* Its responsible editor

was Sartre, but Merleau-Ponty served as its political editor. Sartre repeatedly asked Merleau-Ponty to put his name alongside his own on the masthead of the magazine, but Merleau-Ponty never wanted to agree to this. Why he refused, says Sartres, has always remained a mystery to me. The entire political orientation of the magazine was taken care of by Merleau-Ponty, for Sartre vigorously stresses that he was personally not competent in this matter. He suspects that Merleau-Ponty did not trust him, and did not want to accept the role of a responsible editor in order to be able to withdraw at any moment without any public scandal.

With respect to the political orientation of the magazine, there was a peculiar situation at the time in France. The communist party had joined the bourgeois parties to govern the country and therefore had become unfaithful to the ideal of the revolution. Both Merleau-Ponty and Sartre were very much in sympathy with Marx and his ideals. They desired a leftist government and the rise of the proletariat. For this reason they could not adhere to the governing coalition. On the other hand, they could not adhere either to the communist party, for, firstly, this party had become unfaithful to the proletariat; secondly, they did not wish to accept communist dogmatism; and thirdly, they were convinced revolutionaries. For this reason the magazine launched an ideal and then began to indulge in speculations about this ideal without declaring its adherence to anything. Merleau-Ponty, says Sartre, was the leader in this and he followed him. Even then the two had disagreements, e.g., concerning a text of Sartre or about Albert Camus.

Gradually they became more and more estranged. Merleau-Ponty learned about the true situation in Russia, e.g., about the existence of enormous concentration camps. As a man seeking security for all, he could not resign himself to this situation. He began to write against the Soviet Union without, however, declaring himself for the United States. Sartre, on the other hand, felt constantly more strongly that it was not possible to profess an ideal without adhering to the political group which pursues this ideal. Being unable to keep silent any longer, he says, he declared himself in agreement with the communist party. Merleau-Ponty then resigned by telephone as political editor of *Les temps modernes.* Later he wrote the article against Sartre in *Les aventures de la dialectique,* about which we have spoken above. Surprisingly, Sartre remains silent concerning the content of this article.

Thus, he continues, the magazine that had brought them together also led to their separation. Sartre's tone in relating this story is rather fatalist. It is as if everything went as it had to happen.

After Merleau-Ponty's resignation he still met Sartre on several occasions. They still felt much for each other, says Sartre, but did not succeed in re-establishing an effective contact, because they no longer pursued a common enterprise. A shadow has always continued to cloud their last encounter. Hitherto it had always been Sartre who sought contact and the initiative had never come from Merleau-Ponty. The last time they met, however, it was Merleau-Ponty who came to listen to a lecture of Sartre. Suffering as he was from an attack of influenza, Sartre says, he could not really give himself in their conversation, and Merleau-Ponty felt insulted. Thus, their last contact ended in a misunderstanding, caused by a fortuitous accident. Sartre sees the way this last meeting went as a paradigm of their entire relationship.

Conclusion. This brief summary of Sartre's article shows that he does not at all pay attention to the doctrinal opposition between himself and Merleau-Ponty. He writes as if this opposition had been something of secondary importance to him. He speaks admiringly about Merleau-Ponty and readily even recognizes that his former friend was superior to him in many realms. So far, however, as the philosophy of Merleau-Ponty is concerned, he assumes a peculiar attitude and limits himself to a kind of psychoanalytic explanation.

We must confess that we do not relish this approach. It is true, of course, that there is a connection between the way in which a man lives and the way in which he sees reality as a philosopher. Nevertheless, a philosophical vision remains a vision. Merleau-Ponty turned against Sartre for the sake of truth and always kept the personal element out of his difference. Sartre, on the other hand, speaks mainly about the person and views Merleau-Ponty's philosophy in the light of his personality. This is disconcerting. The discussion is transferred to a level on which it becomes impossible. Sartre "understands" Merleau-Ponty, but he understands him from a distance. He understands him and publicly expresses this understanding in a way in which many people do not wish to be understood. Doesn't Sartre's attitude, we may ask, reveal here again, though on a different level and in a different way, the rationalism which Merleau-Ponty opposed so strongly?

CHAPTER THIRTEEN

CRITICAL CONSIDERATIONS

1. INTRODUCTORY REMARKS

Internal Versus External Critique. If it is not easy to present a survey of Merleau-Ponty's philosophy, it is even more difficult to form a critical view of his thought. For one who has a philosophical conviction of his own, it would be no trouble, of course, to indicate in which respects Merleau-Ponty deviates from his own view, and then to declare where he agrees or disagrees with Merleau-Ponty. Such a procedure, however, is not a critique and, moreover, of little or no interest to the reader.

The procedure in question is not a critique in the strict sense of the term, for critique comes from *krinein,* to separate, to distinguish what is judged to be valuable and valueless, meaningful and meaningless. It implies the use of a norm, and genuine critique demands that a human achievement be evaluated by means of the norm by which it is internally governed. Anyone who produces something, who writes or presents a philosophical synthesis realizes that he is subject to a norm. For he is critical of himself and constantly checks his own actions to see whether he has proceeded correctly. In other words, he makes use of a norm. A human accomplishment, therefore, should be evaluated through the norm to which it is intrinsically subject. Evaluating a philosophy according to what one thinks personally is judging it by means of an extrinsic norm. Such an extrinsic evaluation is not very interesting, at least in a book such as this. For the average reader will not care whether or not the described philosophy agrees or disagrees with the viewpoint of the describer. What we have to do, therefore, is to ask ourselves whether Merleau-Ponty has succeeded in reaching the goal which he pursued.

Undoubtedly, Merleau-Ponty was an original thinker. This implies that he has seen something which no one else had seen before. He writes as one who "sees," as appears from the groping character of his descriptions. He constantly complements his own expressions and corrects their one-sidedness. It is as if he feels that he has not yet clearly expressed what he sees and wants to say. One who wants to criticize Merleau-Ponty should really try to correct Merleau-Ponty through Merleau-Ponty. He should show that Merleau-Ponty puts forward valuable ideas but himself is not wholly faithful to his own ideas. It goes without saying that such a task is extraordinarily difficult. It could be done only by someone who more or less ranks equal with Merleau-Ponty as a philosopher. If a philosopher of lesser rank attempts to criticize someone of Merleau-Ponty's caliber, he more or less resembles a High School student who with praiseworthy courage but painfully visible lack of depth and competence dares to attack the leading minds of the time.

This final chapter does not claim to be an adequate critique of Merleau-Ponty. It is merely a hesitant attempt to make a few critical remarks concerning the work of this great thinker.

2. CONSCIOUS SUBJECTIVITY

Merleau-Ponty's philosophy is a philosophy of human subjectivity. What he is concerned with is the human subject and his situation. In the spirit of his philosophy, we may even say that he speaks of *nothing else,* for, so he says, there is no other being than being-for-us. This statement does not mean that we are locked up in a world of subjective phenomena and, therefore, isolated from reality itself. For the human subject unveils, it makes reality appear and brings it to light. However, we are not able to step outside ourselves to see how things are independently of us. If we try the impossible and think ourselves away as givers of meaning, we make at the same time disappear also everything else that appears to us, no matter how.

Merleau-Ponty's Insufficient Analysis of Thinking. Merleau-Ponty speaks about man and his situation as a philosopher. It is striking, however, that his analysis of the act of philosophical thinking and even of the act of thinking in general gives the impression of being most incomplete. We do not mean to say that he does not write about thinking in general and philosophizing in particular, but that his philosophy is rather one-sided on this point. He constantly emphasizes that the act of philosophizing has the character of a reflection, that philosophical thinking is rooted in a pre-conscious existence. With respect to thinking in general, he points out that it is an expression of a previously "lived experience" of the world. Thought is an expression of the *"irréfléchi,"* i.e., of a contact with reality which has not yet arrived at reflection on itself. He constantly analyzes the roots of thinking, that which precedes thought, is presupposed by it, and gives rise to it. Man raises himself from a not-yet-thinking existence to a thinking existence, from semi-darkness to light. In Merleau-Ponty the emphasis is constantly placed on the fact that rational, conceptual knowledge is not our original mode of existence.

On the other hand, Merleau-Ponty clearly recognizes that thinking is not merely the expression of something pre-existing, for otherwise the rational, conceptual expression would be meaningless. Man is a self-transcending movement, and man's self-elevation to thinking implies his entrance in a new dimension. This point is made already in Merleau-Ponty's first work, *La structure du comportement,* in which he describes the relationship of body and soul. The body is that which is already acquired. But the acquired becomes a substratum, used by man for a new form of giving of meaning. And with the term "soul" Merleau-Ponty indicates the new meaning that is realized. Thus, when man raises himself to the level of rational thinking, he uses the previously acquired meaning as a body and establishes a new meaning, which may be called a "soul." Rational thinking, therefore, has two aspects. First, it is rooted in a previous giving of meaning and, secondly, it itself is a new mode of giving meaning.

For this reason we should expect two chapters concerning thinking, one about its roots, and another about its own inner character. By saying "inner character," we do not refer to a kind of interiority, as if thinking were localized within our skull, within our consciousness. Thinking cannot be localized in the way we localize, e.g., our process of digestion. With Merleau-Ponty and Sartre, we reject such an "illusion of immanence." What we mean is that the "sense" of thinking is a sense *sui generis,* that thinking has a character that is wholly its own. The act of thinking contains something that is not yet present in perception. However, Merleau-Ponty has written only the first of these chapters and not the second. He himself was aware of this, for he promised us a work that would describe the transition from "perceptive faith" to the idea, the concept.

No one, of course, can blame a philosopher simply for failing to write a particular chapter of philosophy. However, the situation changes when this philosopher gives descriptions and draws conclusions which presuppose this unwritten chapter. This is the case with Merleau-Ponty. Let us demonstrate it by means of a few examples.

Insufficient Analysis of "Evidence." Merleau-Ponty discusses the scope of evidence and considers it justified to say that evidence is never absolute, that light is always permeated with darkness. If we ask about his arguments, he appeals to the roots of evidence, to the bodily means used to formulate evidences. He discerns, and justly so, much darkness in these roots and especially in the words in which we given existence to them. He says that Descartes has neglected all this and that, therefore, his assertions are far from solid.

However, Merleau-Ponty provides us with no analysis concerning the inner character of rational evidence. Yet he himself admits that this inner character cannot be fully understood from the roots of evidence, for the light of evidence results from man's self-revelation. This light is a soul, and as such is more than the body in which and through which it comes into existence. It would appear to us that Descartes could admit everything stated by Merleau-Ponty, that evidence arises from a dark soil, and that we make use of obscure words to give it existence. At the same time, however, he could continue largely to maintain his own positions on the ground that he is concerned with the inner character of the light in question. Merleau-Ponty has not given any description of the innermost character of this light, but he draws his conclusions as if he has presented such a description. For the reader of Merleau-Ponty who is aware of this deficiency the texts in question lose their convincing power.

Deficiency in Merleau-Ponty's Theory of Truth. The same defect appears in Merleau-Ponty's teaching concerning truth. His philosophy throws light on the origin of truth but not on its inner character. In this respect Heidegger offers us a wealth of insights that are lacking in Merleau-Ponty. Yet Merleau-Ponty speaks as if he has given a description of truth, for he determines its possibilities and limits. He adopts a very decided attitude in telling us where we do not and cannot have true knowledge.

He says, for instance, that the universality of truth is the result of the dialog, of the successful, common giving of meaning. Truth, he says, is not *"a priori"* universal. While refusing to consider this statement from a standpoint different from that of Merleau-Ponty, we ask ourselves whether he is entitled to draw such conclusions without first analyzing the proper inner character of rational truth. Those who affirm the intrinsic universality of truth and claim that this universality transcends the actual convergence of human opinions, appeal precisely to the inner character of rational truth, in other words, to the chapter which Merleau-Ponty has failed to write.

No Analysis of Freedom and of Consciousness. As we have seen in the preceding chapter, a similar line of thought applies also to freedom. Merleau-Ponty shows that human freedom is bound up with a situation, that it cannot be divorced from a field of existence, and that, consequently, it cannot be the absolute origin of all meanings presenting themselves to us. But he fails to investigate what freedom itself is. It may be true that our freedom takes up a pathway on which we are already travelling, but this free taking-up, precisely as free, has a character of its own, and it is this character that Merleau-Ponty fails to analyze.

His philosophy likewise contains no analysis of consciousness. True, he often speaks of it and describes it as "a presence of man to himself." He shows also that, contrary to Descartes' claim, man is not pure consciousness in his innermost being. Nowhere, not even in the core of our mental life, are we perfectly present to ourselves. If we call our self-presence a light, Merleau-Ponty has shown that even this light always remains permeated with darkness in us. All this may be true, but it does not take away from the fact that the mode of being called "consciousness" has a character of its own. Again, Merleau-Ponty fails to pay attention to this character.

These various points may be conveniently summarized in the following way. Merleau-Ponty himself makes a distinction between two levels of subjectivity—namely, the pre-conscious body-subject and conscious, free subjectivity. He has neglected to analyze the inner nature of this second kind of subjectivity.

3. Is There Room for an Analysis of Conscious Subjectivity in the Philosophy of Merleau-Ponty?

Left Wing and Right Wing Existentialism. The question whether there would be room for such an analysis within the framework of Merleau-Ponty's philosophy is undoubtedly a meaningful question. Sartre, to whom Merleau-Ponty, in spite of all differences, remains somewhat related, offers a reply that is to some extent negative. He distinguishes between right wing and left wing existentialism. Left wing existentialism conceives man as freedom involved in the world, and studies man's bond with the world. This bond is primarily individual, for only the individual person is free. In other words, left wing existentialism is concerned with individual existence as freedom involved in the world. It examines how man projects himself in the world toward his future. Right wing existentialism, on the other hand, investigates so-called human interiority. It analyzes man's inner experiences and feelings and shows a preference for tragic categories. It is concerned with illusions and fictions.

Sartre's explanation of the distinction sounds rather Marxist. The bourgeoisie, he says, no longer makes history. Its time is past and the initiative is now in the hands of Marxism. However, the bourgeoisie refuses to adhere to the movement which really makes history and rejects communism. Thus, it is condemned to meditating on its own failures. In this situation it is rather obvious that its thinking will make use of tragic categories. It speaks of despair, anxiety, failure, "being thrown into existence," loneliness and abandonment. It sees all this as man's essential situation, and finds support in Christian pessimism. However, it is abundantly clear, says Sartre, that it raises its own failure to a general human situation, that the rejection of history sees itself as a picture of man possessing universal validity for all men. Briefly, right wing existentialism chooses as its object the inner emptiness of the bourgeois meditating on his own failures. In other words, Sartre denies that right wing existentialism is of any value for the understanding of reality.

Merleau-Ponty's Position. The question, we asked, was: Would Merleau-Ponty be in principle opposed to a philosophy of subjectivity, in the sense of right wing existentialism, as a meaningless, objectless pursuit? Is there room within the framework of his thought for an analysis of the subject in the above-indicated sense? Commenting on Descartes: "I think, therefore, I am," Merleau-Ponty says: "Descartes' word is the gesture which indicates in each one of us the 'thinking thought' that is to be discovered, the 'Open Sesame' of thought which pushes on to its own ground. Thought is no longer supported here by a material substratum. There is no ground here in the sense that we could establish ourselves here, could dwell here. Thought is bottomless here; it touches, so to speak, an abyss. This means that on this level thought is never with itself, that we discover thought from the things thought about, that thought is openness. Thought is the other, invisible extreme of the bond connecting us with things and ideas. Are we to say that this extreme is *nothingness?* If it were nothingness, the difference between far-away and nearby would disappear; being appearing to us would lose its relief. Dimensionality and openness would no longer be meaningful."[1] In this passage Merleau-Ponty touches the human subject in its deepest

---

[1]*Signes,* pp. 29 f.

dimensions. Descartes also has pointed to them. It is unquestionably true that we are here in the presence of the ground giving rise to philosophical meaning. However, Merleau-Ponty continues, we cannot establish ourselves here, i.e., we cannot thematize this subjectivity, we cannot fix our attention on it, gaze at it and speak about what our gaze encounters. This subjectivity is the "from where" of our entire existence, and we cannot make an intentional correlate of it.

Two conclusions follow from all this. First of all, Merleau-Ponty does not deny the subjectivity of which we are speaking here. Thought realizes that it springs from a ground which is not nothingness. Secondly, this ground resists reflection, so that a philosophy about subjectivity in this sense is not possible.

However, it seems to us that this second conclusion is somewhat too hasty. True, this subjectivity cannot be made the object of direct contemplation; it cannot become the object of our philosophical gaze. But what about an indirect approach? If this subjectivity, as Merleau-Ponty says, is the "from where" of our life, the source of meaning, can it not be approached indirectly by way of the meaning springing from it? Is it not possible to argue in this way: the meaning springing from human subjectivity has such and such a character; therefore, the subject itself has to be of this or that character? In this way we would get to know something about human subjectivity, even though this knowledge would remain very imperfect.

The Two Levels of Subjectivity. As we have indicated, Merleau-Ponty distinguishes two levels of human subjectivity—viz., the preconscious and the conscious level. What, we may ask, is the nature of this distinction? Two replies present themselves for consideration. In the first place, these two levels could be given from the very beginning as two dimensions constituting together the one human being without, however, being reducible to each other. Secondly, the two levels could be development phases of one and the same subjectivity, so that pre-conscious subjectivity would elevate itself to consciousness. It seems to us that Merleau-Ponty's thinking tends to the second reply, that his philosophy is a monistic conception of man.

The following points may be mentioned in support of this view. First of all, Merleau-Ponty constantly opposes his thinking to Cartesian dualism. This would be meaningless if he did not try to come to a monistic view of man. Secondly, the monistic view lies contained in his description of the relationship between body and soul. There are several "layers" of giving of meaning. The previously constituted layer of meaning is called the "body," and serves as the starting point for a higher giving of meaning, which he calls the "soul." This idea implies that the "soul" not only presupposes the "body" but also arises from the body. Man is a being which constantly "works himself up," places himself on a higher level. Whence also Merleau-Ponty calls man a "self-transcending movement." A third indication is contained in the fact that Merleau-Ponty systematically endeavors to find the body's darkness in the light of the soul. All this gives rise to the suspicion that Merleau-Ponty's philosophy is borne by the fundamental view which makes the whole man an unfolding of the "body-subject." We must now examine this fundamental *a priori* somewhat more in detail.

4. MERLEAU-PONTY'S FUNDAMENTAL A PRIORI AND ITS CONSEQUENCES

Man, the Unfolding of the "Body-Subject." The supposition that man remains a body-subject even in the highest achievements of his spirit throws light on the above-quoted text. Our subjectivity, as we have seen, in its innermost depth is a "from where" that is not accessible to our gaze. This statement is undoubtedly true if human subjectivity is ultimately a body-subject. For in that case we are in our innermost depth a preconscious source of meaning, and the root from which we draw existence and give meaning is *in principle* inaccessible to our gaze.

No matter, however, how strong the indications are that Merleau-Ponty has thought from this standpoint, he does not formulate it explicitly. Although this may appear rather surprising, it fits in with the climate of his philosophical thought. Merleau-Ponty is not a man to propose fundamental theses in a categorical fashion. He prefers to move from all kinds of indications toward a depth that is merely pointed out rather than thematically discussed.

Nevertheless, so it seems to us, we are dealing here with one of the basic ideas which orientate Merleau-Ponty's philosophy. Yet it would not do to speak about it as the starting point of a kind of deductive process. In general, Merleau-Ponty does not think deductively. He lays bare a situation and is, of course, most interested in the fundamental situation of man. On the other hand, he himself says that the description of facts is guided by the light of an idea.

This statement should not be understood as if the idea hovers above the facts as an absolute datum. On the contrary, the idea outlines itself in the facts. At the same time, however, the idea is a light helping us to understand and interpret the facts. Between fact and idea there is a unity of reciprocal implication, a circular casuality. In this sense we may say that the idea of man as a body-subject which, as a "movement of transcendence," rises from one level to another is an orientating idea of Merleau-Ponty's philosophy.

This idea explains also why he tries to find aspects of darkness in the light of the spirit. It is hard to escape from the impression that a certain "*a priori*" is active in Merleau-Ponty's thinking. The direction of his philosophical thinking may be formulated as follows. Because man is a body-subject, truth cannot be absolute; truth cannot be in principle universal; evidence cannot be absolute. Because Merleau-Ponty approaches the reality of man in the light of a certain idea, he sees certain aspects very clearly but is unable to see others. For this reason there is no room for a conscious existence that would not be reducible to the body-subject. For this reason also he endeavors to stress in our conscious existence those aspects which point to its roots in the body-subject.

There are many pages in his works which create the impression that Merleau-Ponty interprets man's life of the spirit in the light of his philosophical vision, rather than that he listens carefully to what this life has to say. Husserl formulated the idea of returning to "the things themselves" (*die Sachen selbst*). What he meant was that we should approach the phenomena, that we should speak from what appears itself, and should not let ourselves be guided by previously acquired ideas. We should impose silence on all preconceived theories and let the phenomenal itself speak. It is very much to be doubted that Merleau-Ponty has followed this rule in his description of man's life of the spirit. It is to be doubted even whether he wholly agrees with Husserl's ideal, as is evidenced by his affirmation of circular causality between idea and fact.

We have raised the problem of why Merleau-Ponty does not offer us any patient analysis of man's spirit, why he constantly insists on bringing forward the dark patches in the light of the spirit, and in general why he does not place any stress on the typically proper character of the phenomenon "the human spirit." Our conclusion was that there is question of a certain "*a priori*" in his thinking. Merleau-Ponty is guided by a fundamental idea which, on the one hand, is certainly based on the facts but, on the other, also makes him interpret these facts in a certain way.

The Unintelligibility of Reality. As a result, certain aspects of experience fail to receive due consideration in his philosophy. For instance, in man we observe a desire to encompass the whole of everything in a synthesis. It is not necessary to postpone the rise of this desire to the time when philosophy originated. For the desire reveals itself even in any mythology and in every religious doctrine. A distinction has to be made between, on the one hand, man's desire to explain reality and, on the other, the explanation that is actually offered. Any actual explanation either is entirely primitive or contains at least some primitive elements. Yet man's desire to explain reality seems to be indestructible. Any new form of knowledge raises his hope again that reality will find an explanation. The physical sciences, for instance, are relatively new, yet an appeal has been made to them also to explain the whole of reality.

According to Merleau-Ponty, however, the reality appearing to us is ultimately and in principle unintelligible. For in any explanation we always appeal to a human meaning, thereby presupposing man. But the presence of the existence which gives meaning and which we call "man," is something pertaining to the order of facts and in principle cannot be explained, because it is presupposed by every explanation. Thus, according to Merleau-Ponty, man's eternal inclination to explain the whole of reality must be a sign of degeneration. In his view metaphysical consciousness consists in this, that one abandons this inclination by recognizing that man's factual presence is the ultimate root of all meaning. However, we may ask: which is stronger, the line of thought presented by Merleau-Ponty or the human desire to find an ultimate explanation of everything? Is it correct to consider this desire as a kind of disease? In that case all religions and almost all forms of philosophy are born from a disease or at least afflicted with a disease. It seems to us that Merleau-Ponty is claiming too much here for his philosophy. However, let us examine his arguments.

Are Merleau-Ponty's Arguments Convincing? Let us begin by pointing out that Merleau-Ponty's entire synthesis is, so to speak, suspended in mid-air; everything in it depends on a single fact. The entire rise of meaning, the whole of history, all meaning exist thanks to the presence of man and this presence is a contingent fact. Thus, everything is permeated with contingency. The past was convinced that being is intelligible, but in Merleau-Ponty's philosophy this truth is stricken at last.

Nevertheless, Merleau-Ponty, so it seems, undertakes again what he wants to exclude, for he also constantly proceeds to offer explanations. For instance, to understand religion, he says, is not the same as to adhere to it but almost exactly the opposite. To understand religion would seem to be the same as to explain it, for Merleau-Ponty understands the true source of religion and thereby explains it. Likewise, the philosopher Socrates—whose portrait is that of Merleau-Ponty himself—understands the state and its true values better than do his judges and he understands also the projects and illusions of his judges. Merleau-Ponty does not believe in the absolute universality of truth and values, for he understands this universality better than those who believe in it, because in the light of his philosophy of language he is able to understand and explain the belief in this universality. He rejects a humanism which wants to explain everything from the standpoint of man because, he says, nothing can be explained in the light of man, that "hole in being." Yet he himself explains many phenomena through his view of man. His fundamental fact, the presence of an existence as giver of meaning, makes the origin of human meaning intelligible, and makes it clear even why it can be intelligible only in the way described by Merleau-Ponty.

Although Merleau-Ponty raises contingency, which is the fundamental sphere of everything, above all explanations because any explanation would destroy this contingency, his own philosophy is in many ways an explanatory philosophy. We may even say that it explains all being, for it explains being-for-us and there is no other being. Thus, one could say that Merleau-Ponty himself falls victim to the disease infecting mankind of trying to explain the phenomenal.

The Ultimate Ground of Intelligibility. Is it conceivable that the entire lucidity of the spirit has its ultimate ground in a fact, in the factual presence of an existence as giver of meaning in the world? This thesis, too, is hard to maintain. For, according to Merleau-Ponty himself, meaning does not flow solely from our existence as giver of meaning but also from the world with which this existence enters into a dialog. But in that case one has to admit that such a dialog is possible. We do not mean that the actual dialog can be deduced from its possibility, but only that the possibility of dialog is manifest from the fact that it occurs. Man and world, then, have to be attuned to each other. Since, according to Merleau-Ponty, our existence is universal, i.e., extends to everything, everything has to be attuned to the dialog with man, everything has to be able to assume a human meaning. Everything can be brought to light by the human word. Strange as it may seem, this light is not foreign, not external to the things. We mean that intelligibility is not given ready-made, independently of us, but that this intelligible light is not attached to things as an external appendage. It is the things themselves which, in their own structure, in their own mode of being, shine for us, thanks to the word that brings them to light.

The Dialog of Subject and World. Merleau-Ponty sometimes make use of the expression, "a body that is sensitive to the world." This expression indicates a connection between openness to the world and the body-subject. Undoubtedly it is true that even in the perceptive order, in the sphere which Merleau-Ponty calls "anonymous existence," we are already openness to the world. He is right when he says that the birth of meaning takes place on the pre-rational level. However, we have to add the remark that the closer we are to anonymous bodily existence, the more this openness to the world and the birth of meaning seem to be of a merely particular character. Merleau-Ponty himself noticed this, for he speaks about the senses as "consciousness limited to a certain field." Our sense of sight attains the visual, hearing the audible, etc. On this level we cannot yet say that we are a universal openness, a possibility of a dialog with anything whatsoever. According as human subjectivity rises higher toward the level of consciousness, it seems to become also more universal. And it is precisely in the order of the word, as bringing to light, that universality manifests itself *par excellence*.

According to Merleau-Ponty, as we have seen, "I am absolutely particular and I am absolutely universal." He has, however, not paid any attention to the fact that particularity and universality seem to be connected with different dimensions of our being. This connection could be expressed in the following way. The more we pay attention to pre-conscious subjectivity, the closer we approach to the particular, and the more we pay attention to conscious subjectivity, the closer we come into contact with the universal. We do not want to say that particularity pertains solely to pre-conscious subjectivity and universality solely to conscious subjectivity, but only that particularity lies more in the foreground in one dimension and universality in the other. It is for this reason that through our intellect we realize the limited sphere of certain sense perceptions and that we make efforts to remedy this condition. For instance, we know that things of this world are invisible to the eye if they do not have a certain minimal size, but we have devised means to extend the realm of the visible and, if something cannot at all be made visible, we manage to make it indirectly betray its presence to our eye by means of certain visible signs.

Everything lends itself to a dialog with man; everything lets itself be given a human meaning. From the preceding considerations it appears that this thesis has to be expressed more qualifiedly. Not on all levels of our existence as giver of meaning are we a dialog with everything that is. The more, however, we enter into the sphere of conscious existence, the truer this statement becomes. The universality of our existence is found *par excellence* in the act of thinking, in the sphere of the spirit, which is precisely the dimension whose proper character has been insufficiently analyzed by Merleau-Ponty. Universality reveals itself eminently where there is question of our understanding, explaining and bringing to light through speech.

"Formed" and "Unformed" Perception. In certain passages Merleau-Ponty seems to want to ascribe too much to perception and to view intellectual expression as the expression and unfolding of what is already present in perception. On this point there is a peculiar ambiguity in Merleau-Ponty's philosophy. The term "perception," so it seems, can be used in more than one sense. For instance, we may speak of perception with respect to a situation which we, precisely as human beings, observe. The office superintendent, for example, lets his gaze wander over the personnel at work. The traffic policeman watches the traffic at an intersection. One who looks for a certain book checks his library. The painter stares attentively at the canvas on which he is working to discover any omissions or mistakes. While we may use the term "perception" in these contexts, we should not forget that almost all human faculties play a role here in the single act of seeing. What we have learned in the past, our entire education takes part in our act of perceiving. Even our scientific training has its influence. Only a well-formed individual can "perceive" in this fashion. When a traffic expert of international repute walks around in a city for a few days and absorbs the situation, he learns more about it than the ordinary city dweller who has been there for years.

We are willing to grant Merleau-Ponty that very much has to be ascribed to *this* kind of perception. On this level it is really true that conceptual expression is born from perception. The traffic expert, mentioned above, after looking around for a few days, will write a report guided by what he has seen. But, it should be evident that in this kind of perception the intellect is already fully at work. Is this the kind of perception which Merleau-Ponty has in mind when he speaks about perception in his book, *Phénoménologie de la perception?* There are many signs that this is not the case. For he often calls perception pre-conscious while the above-mentioned perception is highly conscious. He calls perception pre-personal, anonymous, but the perception mentioned above is very personal and not at all anonymous, for only the famous traffic expert can look at a city in this fashion.

Accordingly, Merleau-Ponty seems to speak about perception in a different sense. What he means is, it seems, a perception that is already present on a level where man is a body-subject and not yet conscious existence, a perception that precedes intellectual explicitation and does not presuppose a formed personality. His perception seems to be a more original act than "formed perception," an act in which not yet all aspects of man's development play a role. Thus, it is not easy to determine what exactly Merleau-Ponty means by "perception." It is not something that can be determined through reflection, but has to be uncovered through a reduction.

However, we may ask: if Merleau-Ponty understands perception in this way, may he ascribe to it as much as he does? May he say that our entire cognitive life is an unfolding of this perception? Is *this* perception already universal openness? Is this perception already an act virtually containing our entire dialog with the world? Merleau-Ponty has written a phenomenology of perception, but his concept of perception appears to be ambiguous and, we may add, even annoyingly vague.

Thus, man's universal openness, the possibility to enter into a dialog with anything whatsoever, nonetheless seems to pertain to our existence insofar as it understands, explains and brings to light through speech, briefly, insofar as it is *consciousness* of the world. We are not universal where our perception is "tied to a field," in the sphere of the senses, but in the intellectual sphere, i.e., precisely in the realm which Merleau-Ponty has hardly analyzed.

If all this is true, then the question becomes all the more pressing whether Merleau-Ponty is justified in describing the possibilities of our knowledge and of philosophy as he has actually done. For he has not presented us with an analysis of precisely that dimension whose possibilities appear to be largest. Thus, it becomes constantly more evident that the chapter of philosophy which he has not written is of crucial importance even for the philosophical issues that he has discussed.

5. MERLEAU-PONTY AND DUALISM

The Monistic View of Man. To summarize and explain more closely the preceding considerations, we may say that Merleau-Ponty wanted to overcome dualism but that his attempt has led him to neglect certain aspects of the problem which the dualism of former times endeavored to solve.

That Merleau-Ponty wanted to overcome dualism is evident from his own repeated explicit statements. Moreover, he interprets the modern evolution of thought in this way, and sees the victory over the opposition between body and spirit as the most striking characteristic of philosophical thought in our century. In the spirit of this evolution of thinking he wanted to deliver the death blow to dualism. Dualism consisted in this that the body was described as a thing among things, a factor in a reciprocal causal process, while the spirit or soul was considered the origin of everything we call knowledge or openness. The great credit of Merleau-Ponty's philosophy is that he has shown that bodily being is already existence, openness to and dialog with the world. The body understands its world, it is permeated with intentions and thereby gives meaning to its surroundings. The world of meaning in which we live manifests everywhere the structure of our bodily existence, as is manifested by the sensitive fields of meaning, sexual meaning, oriented space.

Nevertheless, the dualistic idea of the past was not entirely without a foundation. It was based especially on the fact that we experience ourselves as universal openness, as the possibility to bring everything to light, the fact that we are able to know unselfishly everything that is, that also in the order of willing and striving we are able to transcend our own interest and are capable, e.g., of unselfish love. Our existence, as bodily, is limited by boundaries on all sides but, nevertheless, we are aware of these limits, which means that our vision transcends them. Merleau-Ponty has made the radical victory over dualism easy for himself by closing his eyes to these aspects of our existence. He does not mention that universality increases according as we rise above bodily being and move more on the level of the spirit, that we enter into a dialog with everything that is precisely on the level of the spirit, that it is on the level of the spirit that we become conscious of the limits imposed on our bodily existence, and that it is on the level of the spirit that we gaze at reality with an unselfish regard. He does not pay sufficient attention to those aspects of our existence from which in the past the dualistic conception was born, and for this reason we say that he has made his victory over dualism too easy.

Unity of Thought and Word. The same remarks can be made with respect to Merleau-Ponty's philosophy of language, which, as we have seen, is the main argument for his monistic view. He has recourse to many reasons that plead for the unity of thought and speech. On reading his arguments, one realizes increasingly that the word is not merely an external expression of a thought which itself does not need the word. Thought indeed comes to be in speech, and we cannot divorce from each other the meaning of thought and the meaning of speech. However, later the reader notices that Merleau-Ponty does not speak of other facts which seem to point to a distinction between thought and speech. It happens, for example, rather often that we really see something in our mind without being able to embody it in speech. We often feel how inadequate words render what we have in mind. It is as if thought has depths which resist verbal expression.

Moreover, speech is not born only from Merleau-Ponty's "silent cogito." Anyone who in any realm endeavors to think in a creative fashion sees sometimes a perspective in which many lines of thought suddenly converge into an harmonious pattern. A focus arises before the mind's eye, allowing us to throw a bundle of light on a diversity of problems. Such an experience is a vision in which an entire book is virtually contained. However, this vision is not yet expressed in words, albeit waiting for it. It also needs to be put into words. For, when one has, or thinks himself to have, such a vision, it is not yet clear whether or not this vision is really valuable. Its value becomes apparent only when it is expressed in words. Such a vision, however, which precedes verbal expression is more than Merleau-Ponty's "silent cogito." The seeing has, as it were, a density which verbally expressed thinking can never have. Verbal expression displays, separates into many parts, a vision which contains these many parts as a unit.

These and other aspects of thinking indicate that thinking rises also above language, that thinking transcends its embodiment in language, that our mind sees more than we express, and that verbal expression implies also a certain impoverishment of our vision.

"Thinking Thought" and "Thought Thought." Merleau-Ponty does not sufficiently account for the genuine universality of man's intellectual "vision." In this respect there is a disharmony between what he himself calls "thinking thought" and "thought thought." By "thinking thought" we mean here Merleau-Ponty's philosophical attitude as it presents itself in his works, as it "exists" in his philosophizing. By "thought thought" we mean the conceptual determination which he gives of the philosophical attitude of mind. As we have seen, Merleau-Ponty denies that philosophical thinking attains absoluteness; he makes it enter into the growth of the meaning of history, and points out that we may not presuppose its intersubjectivity but have to establish its truth within the dialog, etc.

However, his own "thinking thought" does not agree with this description. His thinking aims at unqualified truths, such as that the human body is a subject, that it is radically worldly, that perception is ultimately anonymous, and many other similar theses. Moreover, his "thinking thought" interprets and situates the philosophers of the past; it determines on which points they have put forward truths and on which they have deviated from the truth. This "thinking thought" presents itself as a synthesis of the philosophical past, a synthesis from which it is possible to make a genuine critique of the past. His "thinking thought" offers itself as unqualifiedly true and does not have to wait for the dialog to become conscious of its truth content. It presents itself, therefore, also as unqualified truth for others and it is, so to speak, *a priori* certain that the reader, if he adopts the proper perspective, will have to accept it. Maritain and de Lubac are wrong, says Merleau-Ponty, and he indicates why this is so in his view. He also pinpoints rather exactly where Hegel and Marx have deviated from the right road and he tells us what Freud should have said to do justice to his valuable insights.

All this shows that Merleau-Ponty's description of philosophy does not harmonize with the philosophical attitude of mind manifesting itself in his works. His writings are animated by the search for a kind of truth which Merleau-Ponty himself rejects as impossible. This search reveals itself, e.g., in his dissatisfaction with his own formulas, in his constant attempts to correct and supplement his own expressions. The reason why Merleau-Ponty's "thinking thought" does not adequately render his "thought thought" is rather obvious. He is dealing with a topic which he has not, or at least only very superficially, investigated.

Consequence for the Philosophy of History. Accordingly, Merleau-Ponty's work is dominated by the search for unqualified truth, and this explains the restlessness manifesting itself so clearly in his writings. For how could intellectual restlessness be explained, if not through the ceaseless search for unqualified truth? In the light of these thoughts a serious deficiency reveals itself also in his philosophy of history. Man, he says, is a self-transcending movement. Yet, can this description of man be explained by considering man as a body-subject? The animal also is a body-subject, nevertheless, animal existence is not a "historizing" existence, an existence which projects a history. Why is it that precisely man is a "historizing" existence? Merleau-Ponty's reply is that man places himself at a distance from himself. From this distance he is no longer able to cling with an unqualified "yes" to his own self-realizations, his facticity, and therefore he is bored by that which is already constituted. However, is this distance alone sufficient to explain why man discovers a "no" in every "yes," why he can nihilate his facticity? The reply is in the negative. Something has to be added to this distance—namely, that man aims at more than he has *de facto* attained. Just as intellectual restlessness results from the search for unqualified truth, so the restlessness from which history is born arises from the search for unqualified values. A spirit of quest animates man, in the light of which that which *de facto* has been acquired or achieved can be nihilated. Merleau-Ponty, however, does not speak of this aspect of man because it lies in that dimension of existence which he has not investigated.

6. Conclusion

Two Principal Deficiencies. Our critical analysis has led us to draw special attention to two main deficiencies in Merleau-Ponty's work.

First of all, he has neglected to investigate that which in common parlance is called the "life of the spirit." His efforts have been concentrated on understanding the spirit in the light of the body-subject and for this reason he has not paid sufficient attention to the proper character of the human spirit.

Secondly, he has not asked the question why it is that everything lends itself to a dialog with man. He has failed to note that things are more attuned to such a dialog the more we approach the life of the spirit. Not everything can be made visible to the senses, but everything can be brought to light through our speech. From the actual occurrence of this dialog with everything its possibility is manifest. Man, therefore, is *found* as a possibility to enter into a dialog with everything. The reality of this world is *found* as something that lends itself to a human meaning. It is intentionally that we use here the term "found," for man's dialog, as giver of meaning, does not create its own possibility. Man, then, *is* enlightening existence and the reality of the world *is* a potential light. We know this, of course, only from our *de facto* dialog with the world, but given this fact, we have to affirm that man and the world *are* such that this dialog is possible. Accordingly, in the dialog itself a mode of being becomes manifest that is not dependent on the dialog.

Merleau-Ponty resists the attempt, and rightly so, to deduce what *de facto* is from the conditions making it possible. However, he cannot forbid either himself or us to see the condition of possibility in what *de facto* is. This possibility, known in what *de facto* is, precedes the birth of meaning or history. The birth of meaning shows that man and the world are attuned to each other, that man is a possibility to reflect on everything, that everything lends itself to being brought to light.

Merleau-Ponty wants to force our thinking to stay within the dialog that is actually taking place, within the growth of meaning that *de facto* occurs. However, man is ultimately unable to do so. He is forced to enter again the realm whose access is forbidden by Merleau-Ponty. Merleau-Ponty wants to limit our gaze to meaning, to being-for-us. Yet he cannot deny that *in* being-for-us we become aware of the possibility of being to begin to be for us and that this possibility is given with being itself.

Merleau-Ponty calls the birth of meaning a mystery, and claims that it is the most original of all mysteries. This claim is not entirely true. In this mystery itself a new question arises—namely, of how this mystery itself is possible. How is it that man encompasses everything? How is it that everything lends itself to being taken up into the dimension of human meaning? No matter how much Merleau-Ponty forbids us to ask for an explanation, the question imposes itself irresistibly. And strange as it may seem, this question lies wholly within the line of Merleau-Ponty's perspective. His philosophical perspective contains more possibilities than he himself is willing to recognize. He has stopped where he should have gone on.

From these considerations it follows that Merleau-Ponty's denial of God is not justified. For the starting point of the affirmation of God lies in a dimension which he has not investigated. His philosophical thinking has not penetrated the realm in which a justified denial of God would have to take its starting point.

Value of Merleau-Ponty's Work. As we have pointed out several times, it is not our intention to oppose here another philosophy to that of Merleau-Ponty. Our aim is merely to indicate the strong points and the weak points of his philosophical perspective. We have discovered many deficiencies, some of which are serious. All this, however, does not take away from the fact that Merleau-Ponty's philosophy contains a very valuable vision. Especially his philosophy of the body is extremely important, for it shows how much our life of the spirit is rooted in the body-subject. It would be irresponsible for any contemporary to write a philosophical anthropology without making a thorough study of Merleau-Ponty.

In the last years of his life, says Paul Ricoeur, his friend, Merleau-Ponty became aware of the gaps in his philosophical synthesis and undertook a radical revision of his perspective. It is unfortunate that the results of his final investigations have not become known. According to his own judgment, then, his writings are incomplete. Yet, in spite of all the unasked questions, all deficiencies and gaps, his work has great value.

The reading of this book about Merleau-Ponty's philosophical perspective cannot be a substitute for the study of his own works. Those, however, who do not have the time or the opportunity to read his books may find here an indication of the wealth contained in them. Others, we hope, will be induced to become personally acquainted with his thinking. No matter in what form the encounter with Merleau-Ponty takes place, it always enriches anyone who attempts to understand the world and life.

BIBLIOGRAPHY

Publications of Merleau-Ponty

La structure du comportement, Paris, 1942. New edition "précédé de *Une philosophie de l'ambiguité* par Alphonse de Waehlens," Paris, 1949. Spanish edition, *La estructura del comportamiento,* tr. by Enrique Alonso. Precedido de *Una filosofía de la ambigüedad* de Alphonse de Waehlens, Buenos Aires, 1957.

"La quérelle de l'existentialisme," *Les Temps Modernes,* 1945-46, pp. 344-355.[1]

"L'existentialisme chez Hegel," *ibid.,* 1945-46, pp. 1311-1319.

Phénoménologie de la perception, Paris, 1945. English ed. to appear shortly. Preface, tr. by John F. Bannan, in *Cross Currents,* 1956, pp. 59-70.

"Le roman et la métaphysique," *Cahiers du Sud,* 1945, no. 270, pp. 194-207.[1]

"La guerre a eu lieu," *Les Temps Modernes,* 1945, pp. 48-66.[1]

"Le doute de Cézanne," *Fontaine,* 1945, pp. 80-100.[1] Abridged tr., "Cézanne's Doubt," *Partisan Review,* 1946, pp. 464-478.

"Foi et bonne foi," *Les Temps Modernes,* 1946, pp. 769-782.[1]

"Le Yogi et le prolétaire," *ibid.,* 1946, pp. 1-29, 253-287; 1947, pp. 676-711.[2]

"Pour la vérité," *ibid.,* 1946, pp. 577-600.[1]

"Autour du marxisme," *Fontaine,* 1946, pp. 309-331.[1]

"Crise de conscience européenne," *La Nef,* Nov. 1946, pp. 66-73. Discussion with Marcel Raymond and others at the *Rencontres internationales de Genève,* Sept. 1946.

"Deux philosophies de l'Europe (Marxisme-Existentialisme)," *ibid.,* Nov. 1946, pp. 87-98. Discussion with Karl Jaspars and others at the *Rencontres.*

"Pour les rencontres internationales," *Les Temps Modernes,* 1947, pp. 1340-1344.

---

[1]Incorporated in *Sens et non-sens.*
[2]Revised text in *Humanisme et terreur.*

"Apprendre à lire," *ibid.*, 1947, pp. 1-27.

"Marxisme et philosophie," *Revue internationale*, 1947.[1] Abridged tr., "Marxism and Philosophy," *Politics*, 1947, pp. 173-175.

"Les cahiers de la pléiade, avril 1947. Gallimard, éditeur," *Les Temps Modernes*, 1947, pp. 1151-1152.

"Jean-Paul Sartre ou autour d'un auteur scandaleux," *Le Figaro Litteraire*, 3 Jan. 1948.[1]

"Le 'Manifeste communiste' a cent ans," *ibid.*, 3 apr. 1948.

"Communisme-anticommunisme," *Les Temps Modernes*, 1948, pp. 175-188.

"Le primat de la perception et ses conséquences philosophiques," *Bulletin de la Société française de philosophie*, 1947, no. 4, pp. 119-153.

"Lecture de Montaigne," *Les Temps Modernes*, 1947, pp. 1044-1060.[4]

"Le cinéma et la nouvelle psychologie," *ibid.*, 1947, 26, pp. 930-943.[1]

"Le métaphysique dans l'homme," *Revue de métaphysique et de morale*, 1947, pp. 290-307.[1]

Sens et non-sens, Paris, (1948).

Humanisme et terreur, Paris, 1948.

"Note sur Machiavel," *Les Temps Modernes*, 1949, pp. 577-593.[4]

"Le philosophe et la sociologie," *Cahiers internationaux de sociologie*, 1951, pp. 500-569.[4]

"Machiavélisme et modernité," *Umanesimo e scienza politica*, ed. by Enrico Castelli, Milan, 1951, pp. 297-308.

"L'homme et l'adversité," *Rencontres internationales de Genève, 1951*, Neuchâtel, 1952, pp. 51-75.[4]

"Sur la phénoménologie du langage," *Problèmes actuels de la phénoménologie*, ed. by Herman L. Van Breda, Paris, 1952, pp. 89-109.[4]

"Le langage indirect et les voix du silence," *Les Temps Modernes*, 1952 (7), pp. 2113-44 and 1952 (8), pp. 70-94.[4]

"Der Mensch und die Widerstandigkeit des Daseins," *Merkur*, 1952, pp. 801-821.

---

[1]Incorporated in *Sens et non-sens.*
[4]Incorporated in *Signes.*

Les science de l'homme et la phénoménologie. Introduction et 1re partie: le problème des sciences de l'homme selon Husserl. (Les cours de Sorbonne), Paris, 1953.

Les relations avec autrui chez l'enfant. 1re partie (Les cours de Sorbonne), Paris, 1953.

Eloge de la philosophie, Paris, 1953. Italian ed., *Elogio della filosofia,* tr. by Enzo Paci. Torino, 1958.

Les aventures de la dialectique, Paris, 1953.

(ed.) *Les philosophes celèbres,* Paris, 1956. In which of Merleau-Ponty himself:

"Christianisme et philosophie," pp. 104-109.[4]

"Le grand rationalisme," pp. 134-137.[4]

"Le découverte de l'histoire," pp. 250-251.

"La découverte de la subjectivité," pp. 186-187.[4]

"L'existence et la dialectique," pp. 288-291.[4]

"L'Orient et la philosophie," pp. 13-18.[4]

"La psychoanalyse et son enseignement," *Bulletin de la Société française de philosophie,* 1957, No. 2, pp. 65-104 (Merleau-Ponty in discussion with others).

"Le philosophe et son ombre," *Edmund Husserl 1859-1959,* The Hague, 1959, pp. 195-220.[4]

"Bergson se faisant," *Bulletin de la Société française de philosophie,* 1960, vol. 54, no. 1, Paris, 1960.[4]

Signes, Paris, 1960.

"La volonté dans la philosophie de Malebranche," *Bulletin de la Société française de philosophie,* 1960, vol. 54, no. 3. Contains Merleau-Ponty's contribution to a discussion.

"Cinq notes sur Claude Simon," *Médiations,* 1961, no. 4, pp. 5-10.

"L'oeil et l'esprit," *Art de France,* 1961, 1961, no. 1. Also in *Les Temps Modernes,* 1961, nos. 184-185, pp. 193-227.

Publications About Merleau-Ponty

Anonymous, "Merleau-Ponty, fenomenologo existencialista," *Filosofia,* 1958, pp. 291-293.

---

[4]Incorporated in *Signes.*

F. Alquié, "Une philosophie de l'ambiguité: L'existentialisme de Maurice Merleau-Ponty," *Fontaine,* no. 59 (1947), pp. 47-70.

Didier Anzieu, "Thèses et diplômes d'études superiéures de philosophie," *Essais et études universitaires,* 1946, pp. 151-121. (à propos de *Phénoménologie de la perception*).

Reinout Bakker, "De leer van 'de ander' in de fenomenologie van Merleau-Ponty," *Handelingen v.h. 25e nederl. filologencongres, 1958,* Groningen, 1958, pp. 86-88.

"Der andere Mensch in der Phänomenologie Merleau-Pontys," *Evangelische Ethik,* Heft 1, 1960, pp. 10-26.

Graziella Ballanti, "L'esistenzialismo di Maurice Merleau-Ponty," *Rivista di filosofia neo-scolastica,* 1952, pp. 458-461.

Edward G. Ballard, "The Philosophy of Merleau-Ponty," *Tulane Studies in Philosophy,* 1960.

"On Cognition of the Precognitive—Merleau-Ponty," *Philosophical Quarterly,* 1961, pp. 238-244.

John F. Bannan, "Philosophical Reflection and the Phenomenology of Merleau-Ponty," *Review of Metaphysics,* 1955, pp. 418-442.

Raymond Bayer, "Merleau-Ponty et l'existentialisme," *Revue philosophique de la France et de l'étranger,* 1962, pp. 107-117.

   "Merleau-Ponty's Existentialism," *The University of Buffalo Studies,* 1953, pp. 95-104.

Etienne Borne "Les aventures de la dialectique de Maurice Merleau-Ponty," *La vie intellectuelle,* 1955, no. 7, pp. 6-19.

Michel M. Bouet, "Le problème de l'intériorité objective dans la psychologie phénoménologique de M. Merleau-Ponty," *Etudes philosophiques,* 1948, pp. 297-312.

B. Brus, "De taal by Merleau-Ponty," *Ned. Tijdschrift v. Psychologie,* 1958, pp. 26-80.

Roland Caillois, "Note sur l'analyse réflexive et la réflexion phénoménologique. A propos de la *Phénoménologie de la perception* de Maurice Merleau-Ponty," *Deucalion,* 1946, pp. 125-139.

"De la perception à l'histoire. La philosophie de M. Merleau-Ponty," *ibid.,* 1946, pp. 59-85.

Roland P. Caillois, "Destin de l'humanisme marxiste," *Critique,* 1948, no. 22, pp. 243-251. (à propos de *Humanisme et terreur*).

Ettore Centineo, *Una fenomenologia della storia. L'esistenzialismo di M. Merleau-Ponty,* Palermo, 1959.

Simone de Beauvoir, *"La phénoménologie de la perception"* de Maurice Merleau-Ponty, *Les Temps Modernes,* 1945-46 (1), pp. 363-367.

> *Privileges. Faut-il bruler Sade? La pensee de droite, aujourd'hui. Merleau-Ponty et le pseudo-sartrisme,* Paris, 1955.

> "Merleau-Ponty et le pseudo-sartrisme," *Les Temps Modernes,* 1955, pp. 2072-2122.

Maurice de Gandillac, "Maurice Merleau-Ponty," *Revue philosophique de la France et de l'étranger,* 1962, pp. 103-106.

B. Delfgaauw, "De inaugurale rede van Maurice Merleau-Ponty," *Studia catholica,* 1953, pp. 137-139.

Georges de Plinval, "Quand la vérité passe à travers M. Merleau-Ponty," *Ecrits de Paris,* févr. 1953, pp. 37-44.

Alphonse de Waehlens *Une philosophie de l'ambiguité. L'existentialisme de Maurice Merleau-Ponty,* Louvain, 1951.

> "Over de betekenis van het oeuvre van Maurice Merleau-Ponty," *Tijdschrift v. philosophie,* 1950, pp. 477ff.

> "De taalphilosophie volgens M. Merleau-Ponty," *Tijdschrift v. philosophie,* 1954, pp. 402-408.

> "In memoriam Maurice Merleau-Ponty," *ibid.,* 1961, pp. 340-347.

> "Situation de Merleau-Ponty," *Les Temps Modernes,* 1961, nos. 184-185, pp. 377-398.

Albert Dondeyne, *Foi chrétienne et pensée contemporaine,* Louvain 1952. Revised English tr. *Contemporary European Thought and Christian Faith,* Pittsburgh, 1958.

Jean Ecole, "Rentrée au College de France avec M. Merleau-Ponty," *Revue thomiste,* 1953, pp. 193-196.

Pierre Fontan, "Le primat de l'acte sur l'énoncé. A propos de *La phénoménologie de la perception," Revue philosophique de Louvain,* 1955, pp. 40-53.

R. Garaudy e.a., *Mésaventures de l'antimarxisme. Les malheurs de M. Merleau-Ponty,* Paris, 1956.

Andre Hayen, "La phénoménologie de M. Merleau-Ponty et la métaphysique," *Revue philosophique de Louvain,* 1952, pp. 102-123.

Jean Hippolyte, "Existence et dialectique dans la philosophie de Merleau-Ponty," *Les Temps Modernes,* 1961, nos. 184-185, pp. 228-244.

R. Jolivet, "Le problème de l'absolu dans la philosophie de M. Merleau-Ponty," *Tijdschrift v. Philosophie,* 1957, pp. 53-100.

Joseph A. Kockelmans, "Ruimtewaarneming en ruimte volgens Merleau-Ponty," *Tijdschrift v. Philosophie,* 1957, pp. 372-427.

Helmut Kuhn, "Existentialismus und Marxismus. Zu Merleau-Pontys Philosophie der Zweideutigkeit," *Philosophisches Jahrbuch,* 1953, pp. 327-346.

Remy C. Kwant, "Transcendeert Merleau-Ponty het realisme?" *Tijdschrift v. Philosophie,* 1954, pp. 236-264 (summary in English).

"Menselijke existentie en geschiedenis volgens het wijsgerig denken van Maurice Merleau-Ponty," *Alg. Nederl. Tijdschrift v. Wijsbegeerte en Psychologie,* 1954, pp. 230-247 (summary in French).

"De historie en het absolute. Kritische analyse van de opvatting van Merleau-Ponty," *Tydschrift v. Philosophie,* 1955, pp. 255-304 (summary in French).

"De zingedachte van Maurice Merleau-Ponty," *Bijdragen der phil. en theol. fac. N. en Z. Ned. Jez.,* 1955, pp. 1-31 (summary in French).

"De harmonische uitgroei van een wijsbegeerte. Naar aanleiding van de laatste publicatie van Maurice Merleau-Ponty [*Les adventures de la dialectique*]," *Studia catholica,* 1955, pp. 203-219.

"Maurice Merleau-Ponty: de hoop in de wereld," *Kultuurleven,* 1956, pp. 137-145.

"De geslotenheid van Merleau-Ponty's wijsbegeerte," *Tijdschrift v. Philosophie,* 1957, pp. 217-271 (summary in French).

"Merleau-Ponty's zienswijze omtrent de waarheid," *Handelingen v.h. XXIIe Vlaams Filologencongres,* 1957, pp. 74-78.

"De verhouding tussen wijsbegeerte en psychologie in het denken van Maurice Merleau-Ponty." *Annalen v.h. Thijmgenootschap,* vol. 45, no. 2, 1957, pp. 164-81.

Wijsbegeerte van de ontmoeting, Utrecht, 1959. English ed., *Encounter,* Pittsburgh, 1960.

"In memoriam M. Merleau-Ponty," *Streven,* 1960-1961, pp. 946-960.

"De wijsbegeerte van Merleau-Ponty," *Alg. Ned. Tijdschrift v. Wijsb. en Psychologie,* 1961-62, pp. 1-21.

"Levensechte wijsbegeerte. Naar aanleiding van de dood van Maurice Merleau-Ponty," *Gawein, Tijdschrift v. Psychologie,* vol. 10, 1961, pp. 71-81.

Jacques Lacan, "Maurice Merleau-Ponty," *Les Temps Modernes,* 1961, nos. 184-185, pp. 245-254.

Claude Lefort, "L'idée d' 'être brut' et d' 'esprit sauvage'," *Les Temps Modernes,* 1961, nos. 184-185, pp. 255-286.

Jean-Marie Le Blond, "Le sens de l'histoire et l'action politique," *Etudes,* 1955, pp. 209-219.

Henri Lefebvre, "M. Merleau-Ponty et la philosophie de l'ambiguité," *Pensée,* 1956, no. 68, pp. 44-58; 1957 no. 73, pp. 37-52;

W. Luijpen, *Existentiële Fenomenologie,* Utrecht, 1959. English ed., *Existential Phenomenology,* Pittsburgh, 1960.

Diamantino Martins, "O communismo existencialista de M. Merleau-Ponty," *Revista portuguesa di filosofia,* 1953, pp. 225-250.

Rudolf W. Meyer, "Maurice Merleau-Ponty und das Schicksal des französischen Existentialismus," *Philosophische Rundschau,* 1955, pp. 129-165.

Joseph Moreau, *L'horizon des esprits. Essai critique sur "La phenomenologie de la perception,"* Paris, 1960.

Fulvio Papi, "Libertà e marxismo in Merleau-Ponty," *Atti del* XII *Congresso intern. di Filosofia, 1958,* vol. 12, Firenze 1961, pp. 361-368.

J. B. Pontalis, "Note sur le problème de l'inconscient chez Merleau-Ponty," *Les Temps Modernes,* 1961, nos. 184-185, pp. 287-303.

G. Puente Ojea, "Fenomenología y marxismo en el pensamiento de M. Merleau-Ponty," *Cuadernos Hispanoamericanos,* 1956, vol. 26, pp. 295-326 and 1956, vol. 29, pp. 221-256.

"Existencialismo y Marxismo en el pensamiento de Merleau-Ponty," *loc. cit.,* 1957, vol. 30, pp. 41-88.

Jean Paul Sartre, "Merleau-Ponty vivant," *Les Temps Modernes,* 1961, nos. 184-185, pp. 304-376.

Ben-Ami Scharstein, "Bergson and Merleau-Ponty," *Journal of Philosophy,* 1955, pp. 380-386.

Alfred Schuetz, "Language, Language Disturbances, and the Texture of Consciousness," *Social Research,* 1950, pp. 380-382.

Giuseppina Scotti, "Originarietà e relazione in Merleau-Ponty," *Aut aut,* 1957, no. 39, pp. 295-309; no. 38, pp. 172-184.

"Originalità e relazione nella *Phénoménologie de la perception,*" *ibid.,* 1957, no. 41, pp. 436-442.

"Sulla percezione in Merleau-Ponty," *ibid.,* 1957, no. 42, pp. 512-523.

Giuseppe Semerari, "Critica e projetto dell'uomo nella fenomenologia di Maurice Merleau-Ponty," *Pensiero,* 1960, pp. 329-359.

"Esistenzialismo e marxismo nella fenomenologia della percezione," *Rivista di filosofia,* 1961, pp. 167-191; 330-353.

Herbert Spiegelberg, *The Phenomenological Movement,* The Hague, 1960, vol. 2, pp. 516-562: "The Phenomenological Philosophy of Maurice Merleau-Ponty."

"French Existentialism: Its Social Philosophies," *Kenyon Review,* 1954, pp. 454-462.

Pierre Thévenaz, "Qu'est-ce que la phénoménologie?" *Revue de théologie et de philosophie,* 1952, 3e sér., pp. 294-316.

Xavier Tilliette, "Merleau-Ponty ou la mesure de l'homme," *Archives de philosophie,* 1961, pp. 399-413.

Eliseo Touron del Pie, *El hombre, el mundo en la fenomenología de Merleau-Ponty,* Madrid, 1961.

Jean Ullmo, "Une étape de la pensée politique. [A propos de *Les adventures de la dialectique*]," *Critique,* 1955, pp. 625-643.

E. Uranga, "Maurice Merleau-Ponty: Fenomenología y existencialismo," *Filosofía y Letras,* 1948, no. 30, pp. 219-242.

Henri Van Lier, "A propos des 'Aventures de la dialectique,' Philosophie et politique," *La revue nouvelle,* 1955, pp. 222-232.

Carlo Viano, "Esistenzialismo ed umanesimo in Maurice Merleau-Ponty," *Rivista di filosofia,* 1953, pp. 39-60.

Manuel Virasoro, "Merleau-Ponty y el mundo al nivel de la percepcion," *Ciencia y Fe,* 1957, pp. 147-155.

Jean Wahl, "A propos d'une conférence de Maurice Merleau-Ponty sur les aspects politiques et sociaux de l'existentialisme," *Renaissances,* 1946, no. 51, pp. 678-679.

"Cette pensée . . .," *Les Temps Modernes,* 1961, nos. 184-185, pp. 399-436.

L. Zani, "Fenomenologia dell'essere in Maurice Merleau-Ponty," *Rivista di filosofia neo-scolastica,* 1957, pp. 542-549.

S. U. Zuidema, "Een confrontatie tussen Barths theologische theologie en Merleau-Ponty's filosofische filosofie," *Philosophia reformata,* 1959, pp. 90-96.

INDEX OF NAMES

INDEX OF SUBJECT MATTER